Housing and Politics in Urban India

Providing adequate housing in an increasingly urbanized world is a major challenge in current times. *Housing and Politics in Urban India* puts together a compelling story based on fine-grained analysis of housing processes, as lived by slum-dwellers and their voice-bearers. It situates the lived experience of claiming adequate housing within informal transactions and negotiations of patronage networks vis-à-vis the formal institutional opportunities and closures of Indian democracy. In doing so, it extends an innovative array of conceptual and methodological tools to grasp the context in which housing claims succeed and fail. This book contributes by responding to critical areas of social movement scholarship and by displaying community engagements and tactical strategies to bring about transformative change to claim adequate housing and resist co-opting forces for socially sustainable housing futures.

The book attempts to map India's political opportunities and closures for claim making in general and housing grievances in particular. It offers a comprehensive insight into community processes and the imbricated worlds of formal policy prescription, implementation, and informal practices of negotiation and political loyalties that affect housing provisions for the urban poor.

Swetha Rao Dhananka is Associate Professor at the University of Applied Sciences and Arts Western Switzerland (HES-SO), School of Social Work Fribourg. Her research focuses on formal and informal institutional frameworks of urban governance and meso-level organizing of communities. Her interests articulate around communities and space, governance practices, information networks, commons and green social work.

Housing and Politics in Urban India
Opportunities and Contention

Swetha Rao Dhananka

CAMBRIDGE
UNIVERSITY PRESS

CAMBRIDGE
UNIVERSITY PRESS

University Printing House, Cambridge CB2 8BS, United Kingdom

One Liberty Plaza, 20th Floor, New York, NY 10006, USA

477 Williamstown Road, Port Melbourne, VIC 3207, Australia

314–321, 3rd Floor, Plot 3, Splendor Forum, Jasola District Centre, New Delhi–110025, India

79 Anson Road, #06–04/06, Singapore 079906

Cambridge University Press is part of the University of Cambridge.

It furthers the University's mission by disseminating knowledge in the pursuit of education, learning and research at the highest international levels of excellence.

www.cambridge.org
Information on this title: www.cambridge.org/9781108484268

First published 2020

Printed in India by Nutech Print Services, New Delhi 110020

A catalogue record for this publication is available from the British Library

ISBN 978-1-108-48426-8 Hardback

To my family,
my house and my home

Contents

List of Figures   ix

List of Tables and Box   x

Acknowledgements   xi

List of Abbreviations   xv

1. Claiming Adequate Housing in Urban India: An Introduction   1

2. Indian Democracy: Normative Prescriptions and Everyday Practices   28

3. Governmentality of Housing and the Politics of Access   69

4. Mobilization on Behalf of the Urban Poor   96

5. Mobilizations by the Urban Poor   128

6. Claiming Housing despite Indian Politics and Governance   154

Epilogue   184

Bibliography   199

Index   220

Figures

1.1 Theoretical framework   16
1.2 Research design   24
4.1 CIVIC Episode 'The quest for transit housing' (2009)   101
4.2 AVAS Episode 'About community and its leaders', upcoming ground-floor + 1 houses.   113
5.1 SJKV Episode 'The value of our lives' – the state of the community's residence at the time of fieldwork   132
5.2 SJKV Episode 'The value of our lives' – a community member vividly narrating how they faced government officials   133
5.3 SJKV Episode 'The value of our lives' – future dwelling of the community under BSUP   133
5.4 Episode 'Blackmailing through housing' – clearing the ground for construction   144
5.5 Episode 'Blackmailing through housing' – arrangements for transit accommodation for one-third of the residents   145
5.6 Episode 'Blackmailing through housing' – status of construction site   145
6.1 Electoral cycle and closure of opportunities   167

Tables and Box

Tables

2.1 Constitutional List   37
2.2 Report Card on India's Political Opportunities   63

Box

2.1 Legal Instruments as Tactical Choice for Civil Society Organizations   56

Acknowledgements

It was within the fury of honking cars and rickshaws on the jammed roads of Bangalore that I spotted a woman crouching on the first floor of a facade-less building that was to be demolished for the widening of the road it stood on. A home had to make way for cars. The look on her face was empty. Did she have a shelter over her head for the night? Where would she go? In a transforming city of multiple metro tracks, glorious malls, and world-class ambitions, where is the place for these urban dwellers that service the city? Through which means do they assure that they can make a dignified home in the city? They are so many of them, what if they all mobilized and paralysed the city – would they get heard? How would their interests manifest in the city? What are the factors possibly inhibiting such a political process? These are some of the simple questions that I asked myself during my numerous visits to Bangalore, which by now I also call home. What does it take to think, create, and enable an inclusive city in a post-colonial country as diverse as India? My theoretical reasoning and my encounters in the field described in this book attempt to give some answers to these questions.

My fieldwork took me through neat meandering alleys of slum settlements, onto ongoing construction sites and their neighbouring transit housing arrangements, into the homes of humble slum-dwellers, activists, and well-established intellectuals, but also into the offices of civil society organizations and government staff. My gratitude belongs to all them for having shared their experiences and given me so much of their time, their insights and reflections, and the opportunity to learn from them.

They are and will remain my professors. I found these professors through the support and the guidance of various friends and informants in Bangalore, who helped me identify interview partners, illuminated me about the sociopolitical forces in Bangalore, and contributed to brush up my Kannada. I am particularly grateful to the assistance brought by Usha B. N., Kshithij Urs, and Varsha Iyengar.

This research enormously benefitted from the able eyes and ears of both my supervisors. Professor Florence Passy (University of Lausanne) was a guiding star intellectually and methodologically, who engrained academic rigour in me, skilfully being exigent but also encouraging and empathetic. Professor Isabelle Milbert (Graduate Institute Geneva), thank you for your kindness, support, and continuous encouragement for this research.

I was indeed blessed with a fabulous cohort of fellow doctoral candidates. Thank you for reading, challenging, inspiring, comforting, and sharing this adventure: Manuela Honegger, Gian-Andrea Monsch, Jan Rosset, Jakob Eberhard, Atanasio Bugliari Gioggia. Sharing common interests and fieldwork with Kaveri Thara, was a boon – I am grateful for our exchanges, conversations, and bonding over research, food, and our families. The encouragement given by my supervisors and Professors René Véron (University of Lausanne), David Giauque (University of Lausanne), Shalini Randeria (Graduate Institute Geneva), David. S. Meyer (UCLA USA), and also by Doug McAdam (Stanford University) and Solomon Benjamin (IIT Chennai) during the final leap of the research process gave me the required confidence to even imagine publishing this research as a book.

This research has inhabited me for long. Several institutions supported this journey. First and foremost, the faculty of social and political sciences at the University of Lausanne, Switzerland, who trusted my application as a methods teacher with an 'exotic' interest in Indian urbanism. They gave me impeccable institutional support and infrastructure and also appreciated my work to the extent of awarding me (and others) with the faculty prize for doctoral thesis! The leap after the doctorate was facilitated by René Véron. Thanks for the multiple opportunities that you created for me, all the supporting letters that you wrote, and thanks for the wonderful ongoing collaborations!

Many lessons post the PhD research period have earned their place in this book. It was during the post-doc fellowship period generously granted by the Swiss National Foundation that I had the opportunity to indulge in the vivid academic vibes of London and in particular of the Development Planning Unit (DPU) at the Bartlett Faculty of Built Environment at University College London. What a beautiful and vibrant group of researchers and teachers I encountered at the DPU – inspirations from you all are still enduring! I would like to thank in particular Adriana Allen and Julio Davila. Thank you, Jérôme Chénal, for putting DPU on my radar and brokering the connections! The seeds of this book germinated in DPU offices, where I developed the book proposal. The grant further allowed my family and me to make Bangalore home for a while. I met a vibrant and diverse community of city thinkers, shapers, writers, and administrators at the Indian Institute for Human Settlements (Bangalore). Thanks for hosting me, the wonderful memories, and the many learnings! Arpita Das, thanks for the hints on publishing. The Bangalore adventure continued for several more months and my learning curve got steeper when working with the NGO Environment Support Group. Thanks, Leo Saldanha and K. R. Mallesh, for sharing your rich knowledge and experience. This book sees the light of day, after a short tenure at the University of Applied Sciences and Arts Western Switzerland (HES-SO), at the School of Social Work Fribourg. I thank the school for welcoming and protecting my time to finish this book project, inherited from previous commitments.

The research's journey has benefitted from comments of various audiences at conferences worldwide and the peers that reviewed the manuscript. Thanks for the effort! I am so grateful that it has found a home in the able hands of the editors of Cambridge University Press. The group of editors –Aniruddha De, Sohini Ghosh, Qudsiya Ahmed, and Anwesha Roy – have been patient and understanding with me, and equally rigorous, exigent, and meticulous with the manuscript. Your eye for detail, your endurance with the proofs, and your handholding to navigate the publishing industry have made this journey smooth and encouraging. Thanks to the CUP team for believing in the contribution that this book can make!

Bountiful of gratitude goes to both sets of parents, Girija and Sathya Rao and Indira Seshadri and M. R. Seshadri, my sister, Divya, and brother-in-law, Vasu, and little Ari who supported me all through with their love and affection. We lost a dear family member along the way, I fondly remember him. His hard work and ambition to strive despite his struggles will always remain a source of inspiration to me. My beautiful children, bright treasure Tejal and luminous star Roshan, whom I took along this adventure of doing, writing, and rewriting this research. Thanks for simply accepting that 'Mama is writing her book' every now and then. I feel most grateful towards my beloved companion, Pavan Dhananka, who unconditionally supported me all the way with his love and patience and protected my time for writing. This book's journey is only a small part of the journey we are leading together that feels larger than life! Thank you!

Last but not least, I owe my gratitude and deep respect to all those activists and social workers finding the courage to fight and give meaning to rights. During fieldwork the slum-dwellers did ask me, what my business was to come to them and ask all these questions. While I was explaining to them my endeavours in lengthy phrases, one of the slum-dweller lead-activist said: 'For centuries our stories have been written by the dominant castes, she will write our stories of our daily hardships and struggles, the way we are.' This research indeed intends to give those communities more visibility, not only by telling about their struggles, but also about their remarkable courage and their visions of a more just city.

Abbreviations

AVAS	Association for Voluntary Action and Service
BBMP	Greater Bangalore Municipal Corporation
BDA	Bangalore Development Authority
BSUP	Basic Services to the Urban Poor
CBO	community-based organization
CDP	city development plan
CIVIC	Citizens Voluntary Initiative for the City
CPF	community participation fund
CTAG	city-level technical advisory group
CUPP	critical urban public pedagogy
CVTC	city volunteer technical committee
DBM	Dalit Bahujan Movement
DPI	Dalit Panthers of India
DPR	detailed project report
FCRA	Foreign Contribution (Regulation) Act
GOI	Government of India
IHSDP	Integrated Housing and Slum Development Programme
IRMA	independent review and monitoring agency
JNNURM	Jawaharlal Nehru National Urban Renewal Mission
KHB	Karnataka Housing Board
KSDB	Karnataka Slum Development Board
KUIDFC	Karnataka Urban Infrastructure Development and Finance Corporation
MHUPA	Ministry of Housing and Urban Poverty Alleviation
MLA	member of legislative assembly
MoUD	Ministry of Urban Development
MP	member of parliament
MPLAD	Members of Parliament Local Area Development Scheme
NGO	non-governmental organization
OBC	Other Backward Classes

PEARL	Peer Experience and Reflective Learning Programme
PO	political opportunities
SC/ST	Scheduled Caste/Scheduled Tribe
SJKV	Slum Janaara Kriya Vedike
SJSRY	Swarna Jayanati Shahari Rojgar Yojana
SMO	social movement organization
TAG	technical advisory group
UIG	Urban Infrastructure and Governance
ULB	urban local body
VAMBAY	Valminiki Ambedkar Awas Yojana

Claiming adequate housing in urban India

An introduction

Mahesh[1] got a call. A 40-year-old slum[2] in the heart of the south Indian city of Bangalore (officially known as Bengaluru) was to be demolished the next day to make way for the upcoming metro tracks. Mahesh – a slum-dweller himself – and his fellow activists hurried to the site. It was a race against time to gain the trust of 48 families and to convince them to resist taking the compensation of $1,100 and not to vacate the land. Within three days, the mobilizers got the documentation ready and sent it out to the Legal Board, the Governor, the Chief Minister, and the Human Rights Commission. They demanded that the Metro Corporation explain how they could displace these families without notice, when the rich were getting compensated for every inch of land. The justification of the Corporation was that these families were occupying that land illegally. Calling upon their humanity, the activists managed to buy 15 days' time. Within this grace period, the mobilizers along with the community managed to get a preliminary slum declaration sealed. This meant that the state had recognized that their 'dwelling was unfit for human habitation' and that their situation was to be improved. The Metro Corporation offered to double the compensation amount if they vacated immediately. The activists brought to their attention that the metro implementation guidelines demanded housing for the displaced communities be ready before vacating the land. So, the community remained there for the next one and a half years until they were rehoused in a mass social housing unit complex at the periphery of the city, for which competing urban poor communities were squatting in front of the complex to claim units for themselves.

I asked Mahesh if he was satisfied with the trajectory of the mobilization against the Metro Corporation. He answered that it had just contributed to reproducing the same patterns that were upheld since centuries in India, namely to keep the poor and lower caste communities out! While community members at first were fascinated by the brick and mortar unit and urban services, they were soon to realize the cost of rebuilding their lives at the margin of the city of never-ending IT codes, metro-tracks, and glorious temples of consumerism for the 1 per cent club. Now they were supposed to service the city from the margins.

This episode reveals the multiple rationales of diverse state agencies and their aspirations at work that are shaping up this city aiming to be 'world-class' (Roy and Ong 2011). It also depicts the mechanics of claiming social justice in the city. In this case, the mobilizers and the community had learnt to navigate the opaque fabric of legal, bureaucratic, and policy constraints and opportunities to skilfully assert a chance at adequate housing in a city of rocketing real estate value. This was rather a rare case though.

In the metropolitan city of Bangalore, according to the official statistics from the Karnataka Slum Development Board (KSDB), there were 597 slums in 2013 and 16.45 per cent of the city's population of roughly 9 million lived in them. Activists pegged the percentage rather between 25 and 35 per cent. Sixty-eight million of the 400 million Indians living in urban areas (*Census of India, 2011*: see Government of India 2011) live in slums and have missed out on the promise of urbanization and are rather bearing the brunt of it. India's political economy of land and housing has produced a situation in which there is place for vacant flats to accommodate the investments of the rich but not to house the poor. Around 12 million completed flats are lying vacant across urban India and despite this there is a huge shortage of housing; 95.6 per cent of this shortage affects economically weaker sections (Kaul 2015) for whom 'affordable housing is inadequate, adequate housing is unaffordable' (Revi, Jana, and Malladi 2015). The politicians representing the poor and iterations of social housing policy had failed them.

What if the 2 million slum-dwellers of the city flooded the streets of Bangalore to demand adequate housing? What if these slum-dwellers brought to notice the failures of housing policy, the negligence experienced, and claimed their rightful place in the city? What if? What prevents the voice from the 'urban underbelly' in a democracy that endows each citizen with a voice (Aiyar 2013)? When democracies present opportunities for the poor to vote leaders of their choice into power, why have these representatives failed to address poverty (Laxman 2011, 38)? If they all came out on the streets, they would paralyse the city they service! But would they get heard? Would the public and state care? Would they get a response? A sustained movement bringing out the mighty number of dwellers affected by the shortage of adequate and affordable housing has not emerged in the recent past of Bangalore, whereas diverse movements on a wide variety of issues have seen the light of day. What is peculiar about housing that potentially silences the voices?

The Indian architect-activist P. K. Das, cited in the English-language Indian newspaper *The Hindu* (31 March 2009), claimed, 'Social movement sought to ensure housing for urban poor.' In a second instance he questioned, 'How do we tackle urban planning?' (*The Hindu* 19 July 2013). In the former, the activist appealed for an engagement with 'social movements and struggle as that alone would help in establishing the basic right of housing for the economically weaker section'. In the latter article he claimed that Indian cities were not necessarily 'urban', due to the exclusionary access to the benefits of development and the shrinking democratic rights and public spaces despite the expansion of cities. The special issue on 'Housing Policy Innovation in the Global South' (2018) published by the *International Journal of Housing Policy* states at a global level that housing policy innovation ought to focus less on housing subsidies and design financing schemes and rather on social movements, legal systems, and planning policies, confirming P. K. Das' argument that a movement is the sole way to assert housing for the 68 million (Government of India 2011) slum-dwellers across India's cities to lead dignified lives.

What this book sets out to do is to reveal to what extent the existing socio-political conditions are favourable or unfavourable for the emergence of a social movement on the issue of adequate housing for the urban poor in the metropolitan city of Bangalore. For this endeavour, social movement theory makes available a conceptual toolbox to examine conditions for the emergence of social movements. The central concept is called political opportunities, which specifies the interaction between the macro-level political context that represents certain opportunities or threats and the meso-level agency in the form of tactics deployed by social movement organizations (SMOs) in response to them. Political opportunities hence refer to those more structural aspects of the (formal) political system that affects the possibility that challenger groups or social movement organizations have to mobilize effectively (Giugni 2011, 271). One major shortcoming is that the US and European case studies that have informed this concept have mainly focused on formal political opportunities, as found in the blueprint of liberal democracies. I argue that for the purpose of analysing social movement emergence on housing in post-colonial India, the investigation of political opportunities must go beyond the contextual blueprints of legal and policy prescriptions and examine the everyday reality for mobilizing opportunities and constraints in a context rife with contradictory vagaries of informality including corruption, volatile political networks, and power asymmetries.

With this task ahead, this book will strongly anchor itself not only in social movement theory but also in studies that illuminate colonial continuities, sociology of law, global urbanism and planning, corruption, and governance practices. Evaluation of the housing policy and outcomes, evictions, and urban politics will be discussed in light of how they shape up conditions for mobilizing. I will be juxtaposing legal and policy prescription analysed through formal and informal dimensions of political opportunities with everyday practices at the different levels. This will allow the decryption of the specific on-the-ground modalities by which policy is implemented to demonstrate the ruptures with formal prescriptions, and also shed light on why deplorable housing conditions persist, are perpetuated, and conditions for mobilizing on the issue are demobilizing or at the most scattered.

In order to examine in a deeply situated manner the conditions for the emergence of a social movement on adequate housing in Bangalore, in this chapter I will, in a first step, discuss the pressures of rapid urbanization that shape conditions for mobilizing. Second, I will discuss the way Indian democracy operates and carve out peculiarities that contrast certain conceptual assumptions underlying the concept of political opportunities elaborated on the basis of European and American liberal democracies in the aim to offer a more adapted conceptual toolbox. This will lead to the third section, in which I review the central concept, develop the conceptual framework, and argue that focusing on a post-colonial city such as Bangalore has the potential to expand social movement scholarship beyond its self-referential confines. Fourth, I elaborate briefly on methodology and the data-sets used to explain social movement emergence in this particular context and, lastly, I present to the reader the structure of argument for the remainder of the book.

The introduction gives the reader in broad strokes an overview of the issues relevant to the enquiry and depicts how they relate to one another in order to contextualize and build the theoretical argument with pertinent literature and secondary data. As will be presented in the structure of the argument, I will elaborate on certain reflections and explicate in detail relevant concepts and methods when and where necessary within the particular chapters.

Pressures of rapid urbanization that shape conditions for mobilizing

Rapid urbanization and rural–urban migration leading to higher and volatile population densities shape conditions for movement emergence in the sense that these pressures create higher competition and demand for land and housing. In 1951, only 15 per cent of India's population lived in urban areas, whereas by 2011 more than a third had become urban citizens. The UN World Urbanization Prospects (revised 2014) report projects that by 2050 India's urban areas will grow to accommodate 404 million people and will be the largest contributor to the global increase in urban population. In regard to housing shortage, the Ministry of Housing and Poverty Alleviation noted in 2012 that 80 per cent of India's housing shortage was in the form of existing but inadequate housing, as they are either physically inadequate, in hazardous locations, or lack security of tenure. Bangalore's population growth due to the booming service industry has been remarkable. According to the UN World Urbanization Prospects, Bangalore's 2018 population was estimated at 11,171,000. In 1950, the population of Bangalore was merely 746,000. In 2011, there were 4,378 people per square kilometre, up from 2,985 10 years before – which represents an increase in density of 47 per cent (Government of India 2011)!

Estimating that a minimum of 20 per cent of Bangalore's 9.6 million population (Government of India 2011) lives in slums, this would amount to around 1.9 million people lacking adequate housing. Even with a modest assumption that four dwellers occupy one dwelling, 480,000 will still be lacking.

Bangalore's recent history of how it has handled its slums is rather gloomy. In the 1960s slums were seen as a transitory phenomenon, due to disappear with economic growth, but by the 1980s there grew the realization that they were here to stay. The government launched the radical approach of forced eviction and demolition in view of the persistence of the squatter settlements that came in the way of the vision of beautification (Schenk 2001). Issues of legalizing slums or land entitlements for its dwellers, compensation, and the upgradation of housing have been at the mercy of each election at any level, forcing the habitants to wait for years for any electoral promise to be fulfilled. Like in other cities, major slum redevelopment programmes have been carried out. Urban renewal programmes have driven underprivileged residents from the centre to the periphery of Bangalore, which now forms 'the dumping ground for those urban residents whose labour is wanted in the urban economy, but whose visual presence should be reduced as much as possible' (Davis 2006, 172).

The shortage of adequate housing compels urban planning and politics to negotiate pro-poor approaches. But 'India can't plan its cities', Ananya Roy (2009) points out, as India's planning regime itself is in a constant state of deregulation, ambiguity, and exception. The governance systems operate by an 'unmapping' of cities through a territorialized flexibility to alter land use and resources. I argue that this territorial flexibility is imperative to accommodate interests of capital for mega-projects that is resulting in an evolving political economy of land development, reflected in the sheer rate of urban growth and rise in land value (Goldman 2017). Bangalore being situated on a plateau with an almost never-ending periphery embodies regional primacy that is felt throughout Karnataka, imposing connecting infrastructure and land economy and thereby gulping up every village in its way. To accommodate industrial interests and capital landing (Halbert and Rouanet 2013), the city is transforming its institutional set-up, governance, and regulation practices. This state of affairs has led to anarchic growth coupled with infrastructure pressures.

Access to land for the purpose of housing the urban poor is the prerequisite for any housing intervention. Land is largely regulated by the state, hence political will to realize housing for the urban poor is the crux. In India under the federal system of government, the constitutional list allocates urban development, housing, and land into the functional domain of the state governments (Banarjee 2002).

Today, urban-planning trends are pushing densification and redevelopment strategies (in contrast to upgradation of existing settlements). Bangalore's Draft Masterplan 2031, presented to the public in November 2017, stated that 'no separate land provisions have been made for the existing backlog in the housing stock' and recognized slums as 'contributors to affordable housing stock' (BDA 2017, 84). The document further stated with great confidence that it could be safely said that 'Bengaluru's share of slum population is between 8–14% of the total population and considered at an average of 10% for the purpose of assessment' (ibid., 82). According to the survey run by the 2013–2014 iteration of housing policy, there were 576 slums in Bangalore. The plan foresees that 'the major share of slum population (75%) can be provided the housing through redevelopment of the existing land to cover up for the existing slum population and the balance of about 25% of the total slum' (ibid., 84). Civil society organizations and activists were gearing up to counter the conservative number of the city's slum inhabitants, the pejorative language used to describe low-income communities, and to assert their claim to a fair share of land from a plan that did note envision mixed and inclusive neighbourhoods but rather ghettoized stacking of dwelling units for the poor.

Against this background all efforts in directing and shaping the political will, which is starkly influenced by corporate consultancy firms and interests, are necessary to claim access to land and housing for the urban poor. The challenge that public housing policy ought to address is: How can housing that meets families' needs be provided at large scale and quickly, while considering livelihoods, evolving family compositions, and opportunities for increased social cohesion? The state being the one articulating, planning, financing, and implementing (increasingly with private sector partnership) housing policy, it remains the primary target to address housing claims, as delivery of housing by the development aid or civil society sector can only be very limited due to a lack of funds and expertise (Sen 1998).

The socio-economic, legal, and political context, democratic polity, and governance practice intrinsically shape how housing claims are articulated and addressed to the target.

Welfare between governance and negotiations

Representative democracy presents opportunities to vote for a political leader who would articulate the interest of the constituency. The habitants of low-income settlements represent an important electoral base, so why have political representatives failed to bring their housing needs on the political agenda to uplift them from shelter poverty? At the core, political representation of the interest of the poor is a double-edged sword. While there is a rise in identity-based politics based on caste and religion that is provoking high political aspirations, it has also hijacked the political process through vested interests (Himanshu 2018; Chandhoke 2005). Even cash transfers and vote-bank politics through patronage networks have not produced the desired outcomes (Björkman 2014a). Hence, when political representation is not promoting the poor's interest, is then mobilization really the likely option?

Housing is a domain that is starkly regulated and delivered by the state; it becomes, hence, pivotal and necessary not only to know the duties and organization of public Indian institutions, but also to understand their workings and how they translate into everyday interactions. The search for answers for the absence of movements leads me to investigate the conditions for mobilizing in democratic India, interrogating the socio-political and institutional set-up and to understand in what type of everyday transactions and practices the aforementioned set-up translates and how it shapes mobilization efforts.

W. H. Morris-Jones described the political system of the largest democracy in the world as a 'mediating framework for a dialogue between the two inherited traditions of governance and movement' (Morris-Jones 1964, 126 quoted in Mitra 2006, 50), having inherited a large colonial administrative apparatus to govern the populations of the territory and an independence movement which had developed its unique and powerful action repertoire that had held the world in its thrall. Could it not be expected that addressing the basic human need for adequate shelter would be claimed and made possible?

Following Independence in 1947, India walked the path of nation building, having to bridge ethnic and religious diversity as well as economic disparity, overcome a societal system crippled by casteism, raise an economic system from exploitation, and emancipate an administration.

There have been numerous appraisals of India's institutional performance. I outline three perspectives. Some scholars (Mitra 2006; Vora and Palshikar 2004; Drèze and Sen 2002; Lijphart 1996) regard the Indian democratic experiment to be a success story due to its sheer survival in a society as diverse and complex as India and to have established a working procedural democracy. Others commend its 'surprising' resilience due to the internal institutional complexities of the state (Kapur and Mehta 2005, 12).

Drèze and Sen (2002) argue that the main particularities of Indian democracy relates more to democratic practice, which in India has often been deeply compromised by a variety of social limitations inherited from the past (ibid., 12). One such social limitation in India is the still rigid stratification of society through caste. In an effort to redress inequalities structured by caste, India was among the first countries to include legislation aimed at affirmative action to combat the lasting influence of caste. The 'reservations' and other priorities for Scheduled Castes (formerly, the 'untouchables') and Scheduled Tribes expanded the horizon of legal support for social equity through constitutional provisions (ibid., 7). These reservation policies aim to identify subjects that are eligible to become targets of reservation or welfare benefits. This implies that there is a link from the constitution of the subject to the rationalities of the state, which is grasped by the Foucauldian concept called governmentality, which differentiates between those dominated and those holding powers to govern these subjects (Lemke 2000).

Anthropological studies on the Indian state that focus on practice, perceptions, and the everyday embodiments of such systems of governmentality paint a picture of an Indian bureaucracy that is unique. Gupta (2012, 38) states that a focus on the practices of governmentality allows us to uncover that the state is not the only organization in pursuit of welfare of the populations, but that there are other agencies that either compete with the state in the provision of services or complement it by performing functions that it is incapable of doing. Gupta (2012, 23) argues that the Indian state probably outdoes any other poor nation-state in the number and range of its benevolent interventions, as 'it would be difficult to imagine a more extensive set of development interventions in the fields of nutrition, health, education, housing, employment, sanitation, and so forth than those found in India'. When rhetorically benevolent intentions are cyclically proclaimed loud and clear, why is it that welfare programmes fail and when they succeed, why do they so erratically (ibid., 24)? In other words, why are outcomes of such programmes systematically arbitrary? Numbers speak it out.

According to Pande (2003), the vast majority of the poor stem from the lower castes and classes. Three hundred and fifty million Indians (Rangarajan Report 2014) are surviving without their basic human needs adequately met and turn to the state for welfare benefits. According to Census 2011, there were 44,226,917 Scheduled Caste households, out of which 3,564,292 lived in dilapidated houses and 21,649,238 dwelled in just liveable housing conditions.[3] A number this high that could potentially avail welfare benefits from systems of governmentality; could the Indian state deliver? At least rhetorically it seems to want to, but the equation is skewed: the demand is much larger than the supply. Hence, a welfare entitlement (housing or others) becomes political currency. Politics embodies the competition over a scarce resource. So, the allocation/delivery of a welfare entitlement is politicized, competed over, demanded because of political loyalties – to influence arbitration. Chatterjee (2004) calls populations ascribed as targets of welfare policies 'political society'. He describes political society as a site of constant negotiation and contestation opened up by the allocation of welfare entitlements by governmental agencies. They hence have an inherently political relationship with the state. The competition over these few entitlements opens up paralegal and informal modalities of claim-making. Chatterjee (2004, 74) describes them as 'tenuously' right-bearing citizens in the manner that they have to negotiate for entitlements, rather than rights (ibid., 38). This is in contrast to the smaller section of 'civil society', who are given equal rights and freedom, as they are not dependent on the state and are not ascribed policy targets (ibid., 38). In this study, Chatterjee's 'civil society' will be referred to as elite society for the sake of clarity. In this book, I will use the term 'civil society' as comprising both political and elite society. In essence,

Chatterjee's (2004) treatise suggests that civil society in post-colonial society is deeply segmented with respective public spheres, in which distinct forms of political cultures may be observed.

Welfare benefits in exchange for votes, political loyalty, or a bribe extends the formal Weberian welfare model into the fray zone of the informal transactions that are enmeshed in everyday lives. Some call it corruption, others call it a substitution for absent services. Seen through the former perspective, corruption then disenfranchises the poor by making essential goods and services more expensive. The latter perspective suggests that the poor are not only victims of corruption but use the levels of the state and the networks around it to obtain some leverage and direct arbitrariness in their favour, hence giving them agency (ibid., 34; Björkman 2014a; Witsoe 2011; de Wit and Berner 2009).

The power to influence arbitrariness is equally influenced by an institutional context that is perceived to be flexible and informal. Laguerre (1994) argues that informality must be understood as being not separate from formality but rather shaped by it. Informality transcends livelihood and habitation to forge an 'informal way of life' (Bayat 2010). This way of life represents natural and logical ways in which the disenfranchised survive hardships and improve their lives (Bayat 1997). In this sense, the informal way of life brings about continuities between everyday life, routine politics, contentious action (Auyero 2004), and what I call informal repression against claimants engaged in mobilizing. Repression is generally within the monopoly of the state to ensure law, order, and security within its jurisdiction. The locales from which informal repression also sprouts are where actors engrossed in violence secretly meet and enmesh rationales of political aspirations. There is almost complete silence in the literature of possible participation of authorities in 'unofficial' violent acts as Auyero (2011) suggests.

Democracy provides the framework and the modalities for these negotiations, interaction, contestation, and its extension into the informal grey zone provided by arbitrary power that facilitate unpredictable outcomes. These in turn condition these modalities of citizen–state interaction and hence shape the status and practice of citizenship. *Housing and Politics in Urban India* tackles these interactions to decipher the surprising outcomes despite formal, democratic, and predictable modalities of interaction.

In the following section, I develop a conceptual framework that articulates a bridging mechanism between the macro level of formal state institutions and informal institutions and the meso-level agency of two types of social movement organization. At the macro level, institutions are entrenched through a historical, socio-economic trajectory, which embodies the political opportunities for the sampled and differently resourced movement organizations: political society and elite society social movement organizations, as characterized by Chatterjee (2004). The bridging mechanism between the analytical levels is of particular interest to understand how political opportunities actually translate into action repertoires.

The quest for appropriate conceptual tools

Embarking on the journey to investigate conditions for social movement emergence on the right to adequate housing within the Indian way of democracy and governance leads me to seek the appropriate conceptual tools to make sense of how a certain politico-institutional context shapes claim-making. Pondering on this relation, the first and obvious place to look was social movement theory, as the name of the scholarship itself suggests. The field is now more than 40 years old and has become an established sub-discipline. Two scholars of urban politics, M. Lipsky and P. Eisinger, were the first to set out and seek to understand movements in a dynamic relationship with the systems of institutionalized political power the movements sought to challenge (McAdam and Schaffer-Boudet 2012, 13). Lipsky believed that a given political system was more or less open to specific groups at different times and at different places and hence emphasized that opportunities for challengers to engage in successful collective action varied (ibid., 14). These two urban scholars taught us that protest was no more just an anomalous symptomatic sign from society (Smelser 1962 in ibid.), but that it could be seen as 'a sign that the opportunity structure is flexible and vulnerable to the political assaults of excluded groups' (Eisinger in ibid., 14). The interaction between challenger groups and the state authority was further elaborated by the works of Gamson and Tilly and it remained for McAdam to formally explicate a political process model of social movement. McAdam argued that 'structural potential for a movement was defined by favourable political opportunities and access to mobilising structures (established groups or networks) independent of elite control' and that subjective meanings they attached to their situation mediated between opportunities and action (ibid., 15). In the formulation of the political process model the key concepts hence were the opportunities represented by the political context, the perceptions of them, and the action repertoire they legitimized by social movement organization. The interaction outlined through these concepts was clearly between the macro-level political context that represent certain political opportunities or threats and the meso-level agency in the form of tactics deployed by SMOs in response to them.

The consolidation of this political process model was based on the 'narrow U.S.-based sociological account' (McAdam and Schaffer-Boudet 2012, 13) that later got extended through western European empirical studies. This transatlantic bias characterizes the field of social movement scholarship until today (Thompson and Tapscott 2010).

What does this bias imply concretely for the purpose of this investigation? It is important to recall what type of political systems the United States and western European countries are and how they contrast with the Indian case. These transatlantic regions both have undergone political reform triggered from within their respective societies that led to the type of democracy they developed. Even on economic terms, periods of industrialization, urbanization, and the settling in of capitalist systems were paralleled with political reforms. India's path to democracy is quite different. After Independence it embraced a journey to strive towards a recovery from colonial exploitation and rapid economic development, rather than the ability to realize liberal and equal citizenship from the moment of the ratification of the progressive Constitution. India's heritage from the past is characterized by its colonial impositions, primordial caste structures, and the predominantly primary sector of economy at the time of Independence. Given these different trajectories, what does it mean for the conceptualization of social movement emergence and its scope to analyse movements occurring in non-transatlantic geographies, particularly in post-colonial contexts? Cities of the post-colony occupy a very different, marginalized, socio-spatial positionality compared to Euro-American cities. Development trajectories of post-colonial cities were substantially abridged and held back by exploitative global geo-economic and geopolitical forces, creating marginalized positions up to the present day (Sheppard and Leitner 2015). Post-colonial here does not only mean the temporal reference for the period after colonialism; rather, the term 'post-colonial' will relate to the notion of the 'colonial present' (Gregory 2004 in Sharp 2009), recognizing the existing continuities of colonial modalities and imagined geographies. While states might be physically decolonized, it is important to consider the cultural products of colonialism that remain and have integrated into the fabric of contemporary societies.

While many researchers do state that there is a need to situate these concepts better, the conceptual toolbox offered by American and European scholars is widely used beyond these geographies (Inclan 2018; Shigetomi and Makino

2009) with no critical effort to adapt them. Two volumes published in 2011 and edited by Oomennn (2010a, 2010b) take stock of social movements in twentieth-century India. The reviewer of these volumes (Thakur 2011, 347) notes that Indian scholars have hardly contributed to theoretical innovation. Given the brief elaborations above on the Indian heritage and trajectory and the 'Indian way of democracy', it would seem inappropriate to use conventional social movement concepts, as they generally consider only the formal prevalent aspects of polity systems.

I argue that when concepts travel, they ought to be situated. Situated knowledge is the idea that all forms of knowledge reflect the particular conditions in which they are produced and at some level reflect the social identities and social locations of knowledge producers (Castree, Kitchin, and Rogers 2013). Situational knowledge is often embedded in culture, language, and vernacular practices and makes allusion to communities of practice. I argue that situating political opportunities to the Indian socio-political context – and particularly to the housing domain in Bangalore – has the power to be analytically sharp and provide a perspective from a precise location, to return the gaze, to look at other cases in a somewhat experimental comparative iterations (Robinson 2011). Methodologically, I engage in provincializing the political process model. Provincializing means 'identifying and empowering new loci of enunciation (Werner 2012) from which to speak back to' (Sheppard, Leitner, and Maringanti 2013, 895), thereby refining the analytical grasp of concepts and hence contributing to theory building. Such an approach also addresses the demand for more post-colonial integration into urban studies (Robinson 2011, 2).

I propose in this book an adaptation of the political process model to include informal dimensions that grasps the everyday interaction in post-colonial cities and ultimately co-shape mobilization attempts and outcomes.

On a theoretical level, the aim of the book is to expand the scope of social movement theory to post-colonial contexts, keeping the challenges elaborated above in view. Empirically, the goal is also to give more visibility to the acute problem of housing for the poor in urban areas and to understand the possibilities and limitations of differently resourced organizations to assert adequate housing.

Concretely, this books aims to answer the following questions within the context of the metropolitan city of Bangalore: *What are the 'real' existing conditions for differently resourced political and elite society organizations to mobilize on the issue of adequate housing?* In particular, the book investigates: *To which extent are political opportunities differential towards diversely resourced political and elite society organizations?* Political society organizations are slum-dwellers themselves mobilizing on an issue that directly concerns them while, on the other hand, elite society organizations mobilize *on behalf* of the slum-dwellers. Do differential political opportunities within the formal polity and informal circuits of corruption (including clientelism) translate into differences in accessibility? Focusing on Chatterjee's typology also leads me to ask whether *action repertoires of diversely resourced political and elite society organizations develop differently in response to the differential political opportunities?* This leads to look out for particular tactics constituting the action repertoire of the respective civil society organizations and also to delineate the discursive legitimation for their use. Having elaborated particular features of post-colonial contexts, this book examines: *To which extent do circuits of corruption skew conditions for mobilizing?*

The next section will explicate the theoretical framework to this investigation. It will lay out the main conceptual pillars. Some finer conceptual reasoning regarding elements treated in the subsequent chapters will be discussed where necessary.

Grasping conditions for mobilizing through multiple linkages

'Honey, I shrunk the field' – this is the subheading the authors McAdam and Schaffer-Boudet (2012) chose for their tour de force on the evolution of social movement scholarship. From considering social movements as irrational crowd behaviour in American psychology classes to the proliferation of associations, conferences, and publications, the field has come a long way. Nevertheless, the authors contend that the focus has become increasingly narrow concentrating on internal movement dynamics at considerable intellectual cost. Situating movements in a broader context of political and economic forces and actors at different scales has taken a back seat in recent years (ibid., 22). In my view, the scholarship has lost out on possibilities of inspiration and cross-fertilization from other relevant disciplines.

With the aim of revealing conditions for mobilizing in post-colonial urban India, I mobilize several bodies of literature and I argue in five points that my theoretical and subsequent methodological approach directly speaks to the current prevalent challenges of social movement scholarship. First, it is heavily biased towards North American and western Europe case studies (Thompson and Tapscott 2010; Thakur 2011; McAdam and Schaffer-Boudet 2012). Second, despite focusing on the political context, little of the existing literature addresses policy and policy processes. I will be relating mobilization conditions to a particular housing policy that was underway during my time of fieldwork. Third, political opportunities are often used in an oversimplified manner by using generic indicators and focusing merely on the formal blueprint of the polity rather than the 'real' and often informal and everyday ways in which politics takes place. Fourth, this leads to a static view of political opportunities losing focus on how opportunities vary not only across contexts but also across issues and types of movement organizations. I will be arguing that political opportunities present themselves differently to political and elite societies (Chatterjee 2004). Fifth, the major part of the literature is comprised of studies of successful mobilization and does not focus on failed, scattered, and small contentious acts (McAdam and Schaffer-Boudet 2012). We hence know less of why people *do not* mobilize despite holding strong grievances. This insight, though, is much required to create democratic and socially inclusive cities.

To pursue the investigation of conditions for social movement emergence, I propose a conceptual framework composed of two principal linkage mechanisms between, first, the macro level of socio-political systems and meso-level SMOs and, second, between formal polity and policy prescriptions and informal arrangements. The first linkage anchors itself into the conceptual toolbox of social movement theory, including the concepts of political opportunities, tactics, action repertoires, and social movement organization using a mediating mechanism – I will call this 'discursive repertoire' inspired by the work of Mohr and White (2008). I articulate the second linkage leaning on the work of Helmke and Levitsky (2004, 2006) on institutional interaction between the formal polity and informal arrangements. In this latter case the linking mechanism is articulated by the lack of accountability, creating incentives for informal practices, and at a discursive level, I will present governmentality as the bridging mechanism between formal and informal discourses. Both linkages will be substantiated with operationalized concepts where and when necessary in the subsequent chapters stemming from the literature from post-colonial, citizenship, corruption, and urban studies.

McAdam (1996, 26) presents a 'highly consensual list of dimensions of political opportunity': (*a*) The relative openness or closure of the institutionalized political system; (*b*) the stability or instability of that broad set of elite alignments that typically undergird a polity; (*c*) the presences or absences of elite allies; and (*d*) the state's capacity and propensity for repression. The concept has seen an array of operationalizations. To work out the operational dimensions, the scholarship conflates opportunities and sources of (Koopmans

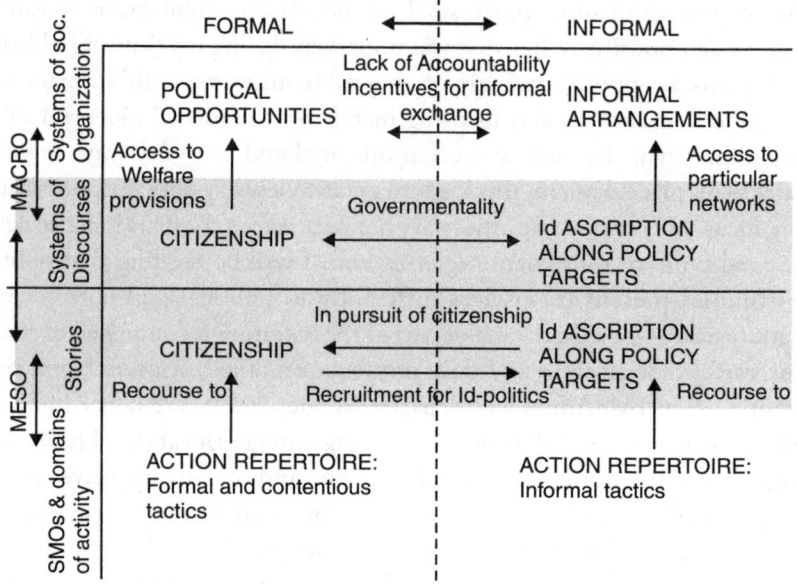

Figure 1.1 Theoretical framework

Source: Author.

2009, 96) and consequences of opportunities. A list of variables has often not been disproved, refined, or replaced, but simply added (Meyer 2004, 135). The list of additions based just on three articles containing reviews of the concept (Goodwin and Jasper 1999; Meyer 2004; Alimi 2009) is long (25 variables) and rather messy. These studies interrogate what political opportunities consist of, instead of asking *how* dimensions of political opportunities work upon meso-level agency.

This conceptual approach by linkages serves two purposes: First, it allows deciphering possible mechanisms that mediate between these two analytical levels and societal spheres. I am aware that this analytical split between the formal and informal is merely modelled. I write in a nuanced way in Chapter 2 and the following chapters that on the ground, everyday practices are much blurred and intertwined (Gupta 1995) and one can hardly discern between a formal and an informal sphere. But leaning on Helmke and Levitsky's theory on institutional interaction (as I will elaborate later), the analytical split is useful to trace the interaction that will explicate how movement emergence could be inhibited despite open formal political opportunities. The analytical distinction serves theory-building that this book also attempts.

Second, it also allows overcoming the pitfall of assuming that actors are homogeneously resourced, and it is hence apt to investigate how political opportunities work upon differently resourced collective actors in explaining their tactical choice. Choice of tactics is consolidated on the basis of sense-making of opportunities with the available resources and means of the movement organization.

Mohr and White (2008) model this interpretative space (sense-making) of everyday existence dually with the physical experience linked through social macro structures (ibid., 493). They split the interpretative space into two categories, one relating to the macro level that they call 'system of discourses' (ibid., 490) and the other situated at the meso level, which they call 'stories as patterned relation of meaning' (ibid., 498). System of discourses at macro-level incorporates values, meanings, and rhetoric that are perpetuated and reflected by institutions. This system of discourse dually relates to systems of social organization at the macro level. In the formal realm, citizenship gives discursive resources. In its narrowest definition, citizenship describes the legal relationship between the individual and the polity. For example, the institution of citizenship requires a social organization, such as the ministry of home affairs, but also represents a system of discourses on what, for example, dutiful citizens ought to be or do and the services, benefits, and rights they ought to receive as citizens. People can take recourse to such discourses to frame their claims.

The stories from the meso level stem from a network where meanings are shared through collective participation in repertoires of stories that give an interpretation of the system of discourses and the polity organization at the macro level. Social interactions at the meso level are organized through specific domains of activity (claiming housing in this case) around which specific identities may get triggered by active participation and ascription of a particular identity (van Zomeren et al. 2008) in social movement organization. It fosters a shared understanding that is embedded in a shared repertoire of stories as a patterned relation of meaning. For example, Mahesh's group assisted the community being evicted because of an upcoming metro line; they could buy time by knowing the official metro implementation guidelines, which stated that alternative housing had to be ready for communities being evicted. Hence, the community could be considered an 'infrastructure-impacted community'. The experience of this community builds a collective identity that is sharable, as their story travels across to other networks which may face similar situations. Such stories as 'patterned relations of meaning' triggering identities build up the propensity to mobilize and by conceiving particular tactics that clump up to action repertoires.

At the same time, action repertoires are then justified through these organizational stories. Repertoires of collective action are defined as the 'whole set of means a group has for making claims of different types on different actors' (Tilly 1986, 2 in van Zomeren et al. 2008). From the top down, the prevalent political opportunities comprise understandings of identified sets of prescribed, tolerated, and forbidden claim-making performances, along with the likely consequences of making such claims. From the bottom up on the other hand, the performances using chosen tactics represent important routines of emotionally and morally salient tactics (Jasper 1997, 237 in Diani and Della Porta, 2006) that clump into repertoires that describe the forms of claim-making available to any particular set of political actors, with likely consequences of making such claims (Tilly 2006). Tactics clumping into repertoires are characterized by different access conditions for variously resourced SMOs, due to differential sense-making mechanisms and resources.

Having described the macro–meso linkage in the formal sphere, I now go on to decipher the institutional interaction with the informal sphere. The macro–meso spheres and the discursive–social interaction spheres all constitute each other through relational duality (Mohr and White 2008).

The crux that Helmke and Levitsky (2006) have to offer is to understand the formal and the informal realms of interaction based on the differential functioning of formal institutions. They outline four reasons for the emergence of informality: (a) Incompleteness of the formal system. (b) Prescribed formal institutional change turning out to be too costly, thus informal institutions are created as 'second best option'. (c) Formal institutions are weak, meaning that rules and procedures are not enforced. (d) The creation of informal institutions to pursue publicly or morally unacceptable goals. These enumerated reasons equally represent the functions of informal institutions, which generally co-exist with the formal ones but creating either more effective or divergent outcomes.

Taking Helmke and Levitsky's type of outcomes further to articulate the formal–informal interaction at the institutional level of political opportunities, I argue that when formal institutions are ineffective or when the outcomes of informal institutions are more adequate, then there is a lack of accountability. A lack of accountability fosters incentives for corruption, which represents itself through inappropriate institutional design and practices. In this sense, accountability is a central element to understand the institutional interaction and how they may shape conditions of mobilization.

Accountability comprises answerability (providing an account) and enforceability (punishing poor or illegal performance) (Schedler 1999 in Goetz and Jenkins 2001). Accountability mechanisms operate either along a 'vertical' axis, where external mechanisms are used by non-state actors to hold policy makers to account. This type of accountability typically pertains to civil society participation through direct-democratic arena (Kriesi et al. 1995) or participation in elections to (re-)validate a candidate or punish him by electing him out. Another type of accountability is through a 'horizontal' axis. This type of mechanism articulates processes and arrangements for checks and balances internal to the state (O'Donnell 1999 in Goetz and Jenkins 2001) and hence compels effective institutional design.

For the latter type of accountability, Khan (1996) gives very pertinent insight on the importance of the institutional design of governmental bodies delivering crucial rights/entitlements. He outlines different constellations of state agencies (departments): First, where a single agency is the sole supplier of all relevant benefits; second, where multiple state departments compete in the provision of complementary benefits; and third, where multiple agencies supply all relevant benefits (ibid., 16). Based on the policy conclusions of the authors Shleifer-Vishny, he argues that corruption is best dealt with by increasing the competition among bureaucrats and allowing more agencies to supply similar benefits. This implies that the third option would be characterized as the best institutional structure and the second, in which complementary benefits are delivered, the worst as higher rents can be sought (ibid.), representing increased incentives for corruption.

At the level of the discursive repertoire, I argue that systems of governmentality represent resources to communities, as these systems have the power to ascribe communities particular identities (caste, class, gender, housing status, infrastructure impacted) corresponding to the definition of the targets of a particular policy. Zomeren et al. (2008, 509–510) explain how ascribed identity could turn into agency: When people come to realize that they belong to this newly formed group, their group-based perceptions and group-based emotions and action tendencies (for example, Mackie and Smith 2002; E. R. Smith 1993; Yzerbyt et al. 2003 in ibid.) are an integral part of this newly formed social identity. Thus, identity should predict collective action against both structural and incidental disadvantages. This newly formed identity may bridge the gap between the perception of injustice and collective action, politicize and hence motivate collective action by channelling broad social identities into more specific protest forms. This means that actual resources presented through polity arrangements of reservation enable identity processes through sense-making that in turn enable agency. As the empirical part will reveal, caste ascription in particular is used for political mobilization and informal transactions to qualify for benefits of certain policies. At the level of systems of discourses, the rationale of governmentality allows for resources to be actualized into stories of patterned meaning, as governmentality's goal itself is to lift a certain population with a particular identity ascription to universal benefits of citizenship as formally defined in the Indian Constitution.

Spotlight on a South Asian city: Breaking self-referential confines of social movement scholarship

Having elaborated on the theoretical lens employed in this book, what is the value of choosing a South Asian city and the issue of adequate housing for the theoretical objectives of this study in view of expanding social movement theory to grasp more accurately post-colonial contexts?

Taking a geographical location beyond the traditional social movement scholarship and a particular issue pervasive to the rapidly urbanizing cities of the Global South expands the scholarship to break away from its geographical confines in order to explore a new theoretical terrain and to include scholars who engage in building theory from the South. A theory from the South builds on the Southern experience 'of those, everywhere, whose livelihoods have been made precarious by geo-historical processes of colonialism and globalizing capitalism' (Sheppard et al. 2015). Scholars agree on one empirical fact, namely the Southern turn of urbanization. This turn is generating a 'veritable ecosystem of knowledge producers' (ibid.). On the one hand, there are scholars who adopt the view that the underlying assumptions about how urbanization operates, as learnt from Euro-American geographies, is also applicable across the post-colony, just that the particularities of such cities simply reflect the local context without disrupting core theoretical claims (ibid., 229). On the other hand, scholars rooted in an ontology of urban assemblage focus on the complexity and the everyday life of cities. The former critiques the latter of missing the meta-context of global political economic processes (ibid., 230). With the conceptual focus on political opportunities, articulated to suit a post-colonial context, this study aims to investigate the macro level of formal *and* informal context affecting claim-making embedded complex webs of socio-political dynamics. To do so, it articulates the opportunities from the national and state to the municipal level by considering formal–informal interactions that are to be understood from the everyday politics of citizens.

As McAdam and Schaffer-Boudet (2012) note in their book, the field of social movements has increasingly become self-referential in focusing on aspects internal to social movements itself and casts away external, contextual factors that shape movements. Moreover, the scholarship has not exhausted the scope of engaging with other scholarly fields, such as development and urban studies. These disciplines frequently engage with social movements as their object or context of study, but hardly refer to the particular vocabularies or mechanisms consolidated within the social movement scholarship. There is hence great scope for cross-fertilizing these knowledge bases.

I argue that the slum in an Indian metropolitan city represents a conjuncture of various social forces that social movement studies for the large part have failed to include. An increasing number of scholars are now engaging with the Southern turn of urban studies in an effort to understand the dynamics of the slum as a critical site that forges contemporary urbanism in the so-called Global South. The puzzle posed in this book is not limited only to India. The *UN-HABITAT State of the World's Cities Report* (2012/2013) revealed that there were 863 million slum-dwellers worldwide, meaning that every third urban dweller lived in a slum. The word 'slum' has indeed become an epistemological shorthand for tracking the cracks in the formal frameworks and for locating the transformations of the modern state (Rao 2006). The writings on slums are full of tales of contestations (Shatkin 2014; Dupont et al. 2016), but their conceptual framings hardly ever take recourse to social movement theory, but rather work with frameworks from political economy, urban governance, comparative urbanism, and policy analysis.

Rao (2006) points out that 'slum' becomes an important point of departure as an empirical and analytical category as it is located in the intersection of a whole range of changes whose specificity is no longer locatable within singular frameworks. I argue that to cross-fertilize social movement theory with other pertinent frameworks is promising to explain possibilities of social movement emergence, in particular in the area of policy analysis – an exercise that has been lacking (Thakur 2011). Within the literature of the Global South (Parnell and Oldfield 2014) the passage from slum as population and terrain to slum as theory is emerging. For long the slum was equated with the dysfunctional landscapes of Southern cities, but it also serves as an empirical and analytic point of departure for inquiries into the social and political life of and innovation in the city. Slum as theory calls to pay attention to the theoretical underpinnings of what appear to be the politics of location (Rao 2006, 231) informing how place matters in shaping geographies of theory as well as challenging geographies of authoritative knowledge (Roy 2008; Watson 2009; Yiftachel 2006, all in Bhan 2016) in a final goal to 'dislocate' the Euro-American centre of theory production (Bhan 2016, 13). Analogous to the urbanism literature, this book attempts to dislocate social movement literature that is anchored in a Euro-American inquiry into post-colonial contexts by probing its adequateness to explain politics and mobilization, and its emergence, sustenance, and decline.

Recognizing the multiple forces at play, the slum reveals different readings of the physicality and the life in the city. One such force that has been well studied is the one of global capital flows that orders spaces into a new territorial principle (Rao 2006; Sassen 2003; Brenner 2009). Another reading of these forces is that of nationalism, development, and modernity that are intersecting in the city (Prakash 2002 in Rao 2006, 226) having a particular impact on the instantiation of 'slums'. These readings compel scholars and urban practitioners to revise existing theories about the functioning of urban systems. The political process model being about the vulnerability of collective action to changes in the socio-political context at scale, the repercussions in the urban realm become relevant for social movement theorizing. The city of Bangalore being imbricated in global and local flows for being the hub of IT-services is an apt case for the exemplification of the conjecture of these forces.

How to study something that is absent?

The triggering, intuitive question on why a sustained movement on housing had not occurred in Bangalore came to me during the many summer trips to visit family in Bangalore. The cityscape was changing at an incredible pace. I saw fancy buildings, malls, and offices emerge, roads widened and an international airport opened – indeed Bangalore was gearing up to become world-class, reflecting the vision promoted by consultants from McKinsey and other companies. While new wealth through increased capital landing could be observed, pockets of shabby housing and undignified living persisted. Why were the so-called slum-dwellers not rising?

So, how does one sociologically study something that according to theory ought to occur but is absent? Yes, according to conventional social movement theory, all the elements were given for a sustained movement: grievances were held by a large population, the target to address the claim was identifiable, a diverse set of action repertoires had been experimented locally, Bangalore had a thriving civil society, the Indian Constitution and housing policies gave these populations a voice to participate in decision-making, and politics in recent years was rather fragmented – such that allies could be found – and yet, no movement! The answers lay clearly beyond these formal indicators prescribed by the political process model. I had to immerse myself into institutional and organizational logics, everyday rationales of slum-dwellers, and in the lived experience of policy and laws to find my answers.

To answer the research question this book takes a methodological approach of analysing macro-level political opportunities presented by, first, the general polity and, second, the housing policy by analysing formal legal and policy prescriptions through document analysis, expert interviews, and organizational narratives. It traces the interaction with informal institutions, which are informed by organizational narratives, expert interviews, observations on the field, and a press review. The interaction is spelled out by matching the data to claims made by Helmke and Levistky (2006) on institutional interaction. The meso-level organizational narratives of purposefully sampled SMOs were mainly gathered through semi-structured interviews and were triangulated with interviews with slum-dweller communities in which the housing process was underway and government officials from multiple agencies. Given the circumstances, I met with my interlocutors multiple times to create rapport and to get a chance to speak about with what, how, and why they engaged and mobilized the way they did. All in all, the insights that are described in this book stem from 50 odd qualitative interviews.

In this study, I employ a qualitative research design. Conventionally, studies on political opportunities are either cross-country comparisons or laid out in a longitudinal design. This case study introduces variation at an organizational level between differently resourced SMOs (operationalized through Chatterjee's concept of civil and political societies) within the same time–place context. Context is represented by the political opportunities (formal and informal) and the policy framework embodied by the scheme called 'Basic Services to the Urban Poor' (BSUP), which was one component of the Jawaharlal Nehru National Urban Renewal Mission (JNNURM) 2007–2012. The other factors inflicting variation in exploiting the political opportunities and consequently developing an action repertoire are, on the one hand, the amount of resources (material, social skill, relational) SMOs possess, as they determine the type of discourses and stories (at the discursive level) that relate to the opportunities perceived, and, on the other hand, the degree of visible co-optation by state or political forces and its practices, which reproduce entrenched patterns of interaction and hence hinder transformative agency.

Holding the institutional (formal and informal, general and housing) opportunities as constant and incorporating a double axis of variation result in a single-case design with four embedded units of analysis, in which Bangalore is the case and the SMOs the embedded units. Articulating resources and co-optation within a given context results in four quadrants as depicted in the Figure 1.2, which will be represented by the purposefully sampled SMOs that embody the characteristics of the amount of resources and degree of co-optation.

Constant: Formal & Informal political opportunities; general and specific to the housing domain

	Co-optation Yes	Co-optation No
Resources +		
Resources −		

Figure 1.2   Research design

Source: Author.

This book is the first to map systematically the political opportunities in India by deciphering opportunities in laws and policy from the Constitution to the state and municipal levels. The analytical approach also entails applying the theoretically derived dimensions to qualitative text that informed the informal opportunities and organizational rationale. Both strands of analyses were then related to each other to understand the formal–informal interaction by adopting a four-step procedure involving: description, analysis, interpretation, and explanation.

The majority of the fieldwork was conducted between 2009 and 2010 and insights from subsequent visits to the city and engagement with the evolution of the housing discourse in the country found their way into this book. At the time of fieldwork, political life in Bangalore was agitated. The city underwent an extended period of governor's rule, where an elected body to the government was not in place for three years. The BJP (Bharatiya Janata Party, a right-wing Hindu nationalist party) government came to power in March 2010 and underwent a confidence vote six months later. This vote was fiercely contested. Reports of horse-trading surfaced, and the government and the chief minister were alleged to have been supported by the mining mafia, which made available outrageous amounts of money to buy members of the opposition party in order to win the confidence vote.

The question that the book asks, and the socio-political impediments to mobilizing it uncovers, is highly relevant today on the fronts of democratic practice, urban pedagogy, equitable distribution of land, housing policy design, and citizenship. Claims for adequate housing are as imminent as in 2010. The *Census 2011* counted 9.6 million inhabitants in Bangalore (Government of India 2011). In 2016, the city's population is estimated at 11.5 million and projected to reach 20 million by 2031. The addition of 2 million people in six years is also highly visible in the horizontal and vertical expansion of the cityscape. Repeated droughts in the countryside, the dispossession of farmers through biased land transactions, and the lure of the city are contributing to the steady growth of the low-income segment in the city, often absorbed by the informal sector. Since the rise of the BJP in 2014, opportunities for civil society organizations are closing. There has been a crackdown on NGOs and a curb on foreign funding. The political leadership is facing accusations of suppressing critical civil society voices (Dhawan 2015; Vijetha 2015, both in Mawdsley and Roy Choudhury 2016). The Intelligence Bureau submitted a report to the Prime Minister's Office suggesting that Western states were strategically funding NGOs to raise 'people-centric' issues – such as human rights, violence against women, caste discrimination, religious freedom, and indigenous rights – in order to 'actively stall' Indian growth and development (Ranjan 2014 in Mawdsley and Choudhury 2016). The issue of housing for the urban poor embodies all these 'people-centric' issues and remains a politically explosive claim.

Structure of the argument

This book evidences the modalities and consequences of such housing policy design through qualitative data relating it to contextual factors of formal legal and policy opportunities to mobilize, in consideration of how corruption circuits possibly skew conditions for mobilizing.

By asking these theoretically innovative questions and a qualitative field-based approach to enquire into political opportunities, this book will bring empirical insights by articulating formal and informal opportunities prevalent in India. It shall serve future researchers and scholars as a basis to understand conditions for social movement emergence not only in India in general but also in other places where similar socio-political conditions are to be found. To my knowledge, it is the first attempt to chalk out the political opportunities for India in a nested manner with on-the-ground articulations of the opportunities and threats and specifically for the housing domain. The argument of the book is constructed such that the reader may engage with facets of the enquiry presented in single chapters. Lecturers may also find single chapters useful for their teaching purpose. Hopefully, this book lays out the road for further studies to engage with the dynamics between mobilization, everyday practices, corruption, and formal polity and policy design, taking the nature of local civil society seriously. It also aims to inspire urban practice by displaying the specific discursive and working operations of civil society organizations engaging in claim-making. Within the growing literature and discourses around the 'right to the city' this book hopes to make a contribution in depicting how the form of habitation itself and the type of constituency from where claims are launched shape access to substantial urban citizenship. As will be elaborated in the conclusion, this book hints at revamping our understanding of our notions of democracy and governance and points towards developing a critical urban public pedagogy to equip citizens to envision a more just and inclusive city.

Chapter 2 dissects the political opportunities prevalent in India in general and in Bangalore in particular. I demonstrate that a systematic application of the theoretically outlined dimensions of the political opportunities reveal operations of a state that are very particular not only to space and time but also to the specific actors engaging with it. Particular institutional design that is prone for informal practices are discussed in view of potential institutional interaction along with the features of formal polity. In sum, this chapter serves to delineate the prevalent political opportunities in which civil society organizations have to manoeuvre.

Chapter 3 works analogously to the previous chapter but focuses on the political opportunities represented in the field of housing policy for the urban poor. For this purpose, I analyse the only housing scheme that was available in the city of Bangalore at the time of fieldwork, the BSUP under the JNNURM. I also describe some important features of Indian land management and articulate the housing policy analysis at the Union and at the state levels. Along with Chapter 3, the chapters give the context for the claim-making activities of the selected civil society organizations on the issue of adequate housing.

Chapter 4 and 5 discuss the four embedded cases – the purposefully sampled civil society organizations. Chapter 5 includes two elite society organizations, whereas Chapter 6 discusses two political society organizations. The substantial data to this thesis consists of the interviews with and observations of the organizational members.

Chapter 6 answers the questions at the outset of this inquiry and describes the emergent insights and themes for upcoming research and governance practices, which also includes some conceptual and socio-political recommendations.

Finally, the reader will find an epilogue that contains a reflection on the research experience and a snapshot of the political and policy climate and narratives of 'policy affected communities' several years after the fieldwork that is at the base of this book.

Notes

1. Name changed.
2. In this study, I will use the term 'slum', as it is the term employed by the local actors, including the dwellers in Bangalore. In doing so, I am well aware that a 'slum' is what it is because of larger political, economic, and social forces, not confining explanations of its conditions to behavioural aspects of its inhabitants.
3. See http://www.censusindia.gov.in/2011census/hlo/SC_ST/sc/HH0201C-0000CRCD.pdf (accessed on 20 August 2019).

2

Indian democracy

Normative prescriptions and everyday practices

I was back at my desk in the beginning of 2011 trying to decrypt my notes from fieldwork, but little did I know that events relevant to my research interests would culminate in the 2011 Indian anti-corruption movement. The series of demonstrations and protests intended to establish a strong legislation and enforcement against perceived political corruption and introduce the Citizen's Ombudsman Bill with the purpose of appointing an independent body to investigate and enforce corruption cases. In the run up to the events in 2011 were a number of scams relating to land and housing. Scams also from Karnataka were feeding the movement against corruption: illegal mining, state-owned prime land allotted to family members of the chief minister, and scams over dwelling units constructed by the Karnataka Housing Board. This movement had a lot to say about the nature of the state resisting the anti-corruption bill suggested by civil society, the action repertoire from which the tactics were drawn, the particular segment of society it drew participants from, and the entrenched practices of corruption in the domain of land and housing. A list[1] enumerating the largest scams in 2010 in India featured 12 scams, 7 of them directly affecting the poor in some way, while 5 of them were directly related to housing.

The goal of this chapter is to pronounce a judgement on the political opportunities in India that considers the formal polity and informal modes of exchange circuits that includes corruption. I will attempt to carry out this judgement based on the nested nature of the federal state and by incorporating informal dimensions. To my knowledge such a comprehensive exercise on the Indian state has not yet been published and might be useful to a wider public interested in Indian social movements and politics. The question at the core is: Are the formal opportunities interacting with the informal ones facilitating or inhibiting mobilizations? To pronounce a judgement about the Indian state and its operation is not an easy task. Tilly, in his book *Regimes and Repertoires* (2006), argues that on balance India ought to be judged as a 'high capacity/democratic' regime.[2] In his words, this implies that one can 'expect to find few prescribed contentious performances; a medium range of tolerated performances; contention overlapping somewhat with prescribed and tolerated performances; high involvement of government agents in contention ..., and low levels of violence in contentious interaction' (ibid.). He makes this judgement with some reservation though, in observing that class and caste are transgressing inequalities, large patron–client structures within parties and regions being prevalent and armed rebellion in certain areas being persistent.

Gupta (2012, 53) argues that there is an important epistemological consideration that scholars must take into account when studying the Indian state. He says, '... all statements about the state assume that it is knowable in its fullness, that one can grasp it because its contours are clear and that its materiality as an institution is beyond doubt.' But he argues that it is not the case in India. This means that the ones investigating the Indian state ought to accept the partiality of their vision as a necessary starting point for analysis. In Gupta's sense, the state is rather a social imaginary that comes into being through practices and discourses (ibid., 56). Hence he makes the point that 'one ought to think the manner in which routinized practices enable such illusions, acts of magic, or fantasies to be created, sustained, and resisted' (ibid., 55) in treating the state as an analytical problem requiring explanation. In my analysis, I concretely meet his arguments in articulating the macro–meso linkages that takes recourse to discursive resources and organizational stories into both the formal and informal realms, by relating claim-making rationales targeted towards the state to specificities of different dimensions of state. I do this through the analysis of legal and policy documents. In addition, expert interviews, organizational narratives, press review, and field observation informed the picture of the formal and informal political opportunities. I then related the identified openings/closures of opportunities with the insights gained from interviews with civil society organizations, on how their tactical choice for claim-making, and the discursive justification for it, exploits the openings or challenges the closures. The macro level of my theoretical framework consists of 'systems of rhetoric' (discursive dimension) and 'systems of social organization' within the formal and informal realms.

The rationale for this chapter is, in a first step, to understand the imbrication of both systems at the macro level and to identify differential accessibility for members of political and elite societies and to further learn how these distinct societal segments take recourse to the systems of rhetoric. Second, I will operationalize six dimensions of the formal political opportunities based on the definition of Kriesi et al. (1995) and relate to informal practices prevalent and assess the degree of accountability that allows for formal–informal interaction according to Helmke and Levitsky (2006). Finally, I attempt to formulate a judgement on the prevailing political opportunities and gauge to what degree formal ones get skewed by informal exchange circuits. The articulation of the political opportunities will include analyses of the Union, state, and municipal levels.

The Indian Constitution as the discursive foundation

A good place to start is the Indian Constitution, which is the culmination of an emancipatory process departing from the colonial experience to formulating a nation-building vision. It lays the discursive foundation to systems of social organization. The Constitution is a body of laws, rules, conventions, and provisions. According to Abbas et al. (2010, 5), it deals with the nature and scope of authority of the state and the rights and obligations of the members of the state. This body of text functions as a fundamental law, meaning that the systems of social organization (governmental organs) owe their origin to it and derive their authority from it (Bakshi 2010, 2). The keystones of the Indian Constitution are the separation of powers and pluralism that is embraced in a particular form of citizenship.

Roy (2010, 7) points out pertinently that legal citizenship at the national level pledges to treat its members universally (equally) through recognition of difference and hence deploying resources to uplift such categories and promote their welfare at the local level. The universal implies that citizens of India enjoy guaranteed fundamental rights (Pylee 2007, 96). These fundamental rights (Part III of the Constitution) include legal rights of equality before law; equality of opportunity; right to life and personal liberty; and cultural, religious rights, and civil rights, such as freedom of speech, expression, conscience, belief, association, movement, residence, profession, and business. The latter rights are important for meaningful participation of the citizens in public life and the former legal rights are important for treating individuals as equal legal personalities, which is crucial to the concept of citizenship. Fundamental rights schemes rather than for the good of the exercise itself. Such a process hence becomes contra-productive to the purpose itself, as the set-up does not work towards striving proximity to the citizen.

The late inclusion of Constitutional provisions to municipal self-government along with the concurrent responsibilities of crucial items pertaining to the welfare of especially the poor has exacerbated specialized bureaucratic agencies at the state level, who decide upon issues of municipal concern. These deliver competing rights to the needy. But as welfare is part of the Concurrent list, states have specific schemes that are only accessible to those with origin in that particular state. This peculiarity has huge consequences for migrant workers of the low-income segment, who often have to rely on patronage networks to obtain identity proof in their host city.

In the case of Bangalore many such agencies called parastatals are responsible to service the city. The efficacy of such an organization of state responsibilities based on half-hearted imperatives of decentralization are difficult to judge in a generic way. But I did point out some features that hint towards the scope for incentives for corruption: First, when policies are designed at the Centre and prescribed top-down, there is a loss of accountability as the proximity to the citizen is lost. Second, when discretionary powers are given, an actor with such powers might act contrary to the common interests. Third, social welfare benefits are made even scarcer, as large proportions of the migrant urban poor do not have access to entitlements from state policies. Such scarcities of benefits for the migrants of the cities represent a comfortable breeding ground for patron–client and proof-gathering practices to avail such benefits.

I conclude that the dimension of 'de-/centralization' of political opportunities is not as favourable as the decentralization rhetoric proclaims, as it leans more towards centralization despite legislation that would encourage decentralization and devolution of powers. Thus, one can say that the intention of open political opportunity dimensions through favourable legislation for decentralization is present, but that fuzzy institutional arrangements at multiple levels give scope to incentives for corruption, which in turn can affect mobilizing conditions. The concretization of such effects will be discussed in the case studies presented in Chapters 4 and 5 and put in relation with findings of this chapter in the final conclusive chapter.

Nested legislature: Proportionally co-opted?

At the time of fieldwork in December 2010 in Bangalore, the alliance around Bharatiya Janata Party (BJP) had won the elections of 2009. At the state level, after elections. Even though access points to legislatures for political society members seem to exist, the means to actually get elected into that category will still have to be scrutinized. I learned through the activists and experts (personal communication, 2010) that while SC/ST citizens got into a legislative role through reservation, they became totally co-opted by more powerful party interests and could hardly act in the interests of the SC/ST population they actually were representing.

This bicameral model is replicated at the state level. In Karnataka, there are 75 members in the upper house. The lower house consists of 225 elected members representing the total number of constituencies (224) and 1 nominee from the Anglo-Indian community (Rajashekara 2007, in Abbas 2010). The lower house members are commonly called MLAs (members of legislative assembly) and get elected through simple plurality. Their mandate is for five years. The lower house has powers to call a motion of no confidence against the government. Members of the upper house are elected indirectly by a specific key and serve a six-year term, but one-third of the members are phased out from time to time.

The Karnataka Municipal Corporation Act specifies the functioning and the operation of the government. The corporation (municipal government for cities with populations above 20,000) consists of seats for between a minimum of 50 and 100 councillors directly elected for five years. A mayor and deputy mayor are elected from among the members for a year. He/she is the head of the deliberative wing. To serve the executive arm, a commissioner is appointed by the state government and is an administrative officer (Javeed 2007, 164). The mayoral office is supposed to be the 'democratic supremacy in urban governance', but is caught in 'the vortex of party politics and conflict' (ibid., 169). While the mayor is supposed to be elected from among the members of the corporation council, it is rather the party high command who selects and the corporation members accept. In this sense, the mayor's office has at times been used to appease the electorate on caste/communal issues. According to him, the deliberative wing under the mayor gains its importance through the varied roles of the councillors. They are mediators, linking the citizen and the administrator. But the bureaucrats (non-elected) see the councillors in 80 per cent of the cases as an 'unwanted interloper' (ibid., 170).

Historically, in Karnataka development of the political elite can be traced back to the colonial arrangement between the maharajas and the British of mainly placing Brahmins in key administrative positions (Laxman 2011). To leverage their political power and to keep mobilizations of non-Brahmins at bay, patron networks were fostered by the Brahmin political elite. The political cleavage had thus become one of Brahmins versus non-Brahmins. There was a clear dominance of two forward non-Brahmin castes, the Vokkaligas and the Lingayats, which were fractured within each of the castes, such that there were no political alliances fortified by organizational capacity to challenge the Brahmins. It was the onset of the Congress movement, which recruited widely beyond the Brahmin constituency, that weakened the supremacy of the Brahmins. The Congress firmly established itself in the newly formed Karnataka (1956) and it was only post the Emergency period in 1974 that the party made way for a chief minister hailing from the Janata Party. Tendencies in Karnataka's political life have been characterized thus: over-centralization of power, turning pro-poor policies into 'unprecedented harsh' anti-poor attitudes, supremacy of bureaucrats over politicians, meaning that politicians no longer received funds for financing projects in their constituencies and hence reduced opportunities to seek rents (Laxman 2011, ch. 4, 36).

Successive governments in Karnataka had aimed to appease almost every major interest group in the state and proposed manifestos that all resembled each other. It is the tendency of political vacuousness also put forward by one of the experts I interviewed, stating that when political vacuousness peaks, it has the ability to neutralize political actors with strong reform agendas stemming from movements (activist-expert, personal communication 2010).

Clubbed with an institutional design that lacks accountability and public scrutiny or minimal consultation on drafts of the bill, interest groups are not given space to voice their reservations about bills (Verma 2001). This is an important feature of the legislative system in view of my enquiry, as it leaves activists with mobilizing efforts outside the formal realm of participation. For the case of Karnataka, Heitzman (in Madon and Sahay 2001, 179) describes a strategy effectively used by the legislators to block access to information by not giving adequate time to pressure groups to mobilize their forces and oppose a bill. At the city level, being a councillor (representative) is generally considered to be a full-time job to attend to the populous constituencies of a metropolis of 9 million, but the councillors were 'only' paid allowances for attending meetings. Depending on the type of allowance, the remuneration was 200 to 400 rupees and amounted to about 4,000 rupees (personal communication, December 2010) a month. A remuneration of 4,000 rupees in Bangalore in 2010 was considered a pittance. Given this background, low renumeration for representatives reflects a structure of incentives for petty and grand corruption.

Climbing up a wrecked ladder: The monetization of representation

Given the diversity of people and issues in India, how has democracy arrived at political vacuousness? Starting with the Representation of People's Act (1951), it distinguishes those included in the adult suffrage – above 18 years of age and residing in the territory of India – from those who are disqualified (non-citizens, of unsound mind, connection with corrupt practices, offences in connection with elections, and non-residence). The scope of the conditionality of residence in the 'Handbook of the Election Commission' says that 'even persons living in sheds, and persons living on pavements without any roof are eligible for enrolment, provided they are ordinarily resident in the sheds or on pavements in a particular area, do not change the place of residence and are otherwise identifiable' (Haritas 2009, 53). A specification of the means of identification is indicated in the same document, which includes ration card or other civic documents that represent proof of residence (ibid.).

At the state level, the guidelines for holding elections to municipalities are specified in the Karnataka Municipalities Act 1964 (Chapter II). These specifications, among others, pertain to voter lists, eligibility and disqualification of candidates, election accounts, and means of repeals and conditions to declare an election void. Formally the conduct of an election is rather well regimented.

The State Election Commission is responsible for the maintenance of the voter's list (Art. 14). Article 15 states that unless disqualified on the grounds laid out in that Act, every person whose name is in the list may be qualified to be elected in the election of the ward. The list of disqualifications, which follows, is very long (four pages) and includes registered criminal case, offence of practising untouchability, and any involvement in corrupt practice. In terms of accountability of electoral campaigning, the Act (Art. 16A) specifies that every candidate is required to keep a separate and correct account of all expenditures in connection with the election. During the municipal elections, the State Election Commission sees to it that no corrupt practices takes place, that secrecy of voting is maintained, that officers do not influence voting, that the prohibition of canvassing in or near polling stations is observed, that penalties are imposed for disorderly conduct and other offences, and that ballot papers from polling stations are not removed (Art. 29–37). Article 41 foresees certain situations under which a councillor is liable to be removed from office.

All in all, one can say from studying the specifications of the modalities of representation that formally it is elaborated in great detail. The striking feature, though, is the concentration of the duties at the Union level embodied through the National Election Commission that organizes national and state elections. At first sight, this might seem to go against favourable conditions of political opportunities; on the other hand, representation is institutionally designed such that candidates compete at the state and Union levels. In this sense, the centralization of duties for both types of elections was intended to be the realm of a single body to avoid transaction costs, as all levels of elections are based on the same voter lists. When voter lists are constituted locally through means of formal documentation as ration cards, other civic documents, or residence proof and serve for elections even at the Union level, then its validity and up-to-date status are high priority. Especially, as Haritas (2009) outlines, when a considerable proportion of the urban poor population is inter-state migrants, 'illegally occupy' land, and hence cannot provide proof to correct the voter list or get included in it. The lack of proof makes them 'illegitimate' and has wide-reaching consequences as the following chapters will depict. The informality of living arrangements/land tenures and the representation of these people, who are politically the most mobilized segment of society, are at uncomfortable cross-roads, giving scope not to attend to correct voter lists in order to take leverage from a 'surplus urban poor population' that can be looped into informal circuits of exchange.

Scholars (ibid., 452) also point out the illegal manner in which election campaigns are funded to be an incentive for corruption. They identify that the Election Commission has laid down spending limits for the candidates of electoral competition, but though these limits have gone up in recent years, they remain unrealistically low – so low for modern India that campaigning could not be done at all, and therefore actually no official limits exist.

In an unpublished paper, Haritas (2010) – on the basis of information from an NGO staff and slum coordinators, as also the candidates themselves – revealed that political parties were selling party tickets for 10 million rupees each (about 170,000 euros), and that candidates were spending about 40 million rupees (680,800 euros) on elections.[6] While these figures were from personal communication and hence have to be taken cautiously, just the scale itself suffices to understand that election has acquired an investment rationale.

Such spending, it is presumed, would include the budget for vote buying. Excerpts from expert interviews conducted during fieldwork and the interviews with key civil society organization leaders reported that in the municipal election in 2010, it was common to expect 500 rupees for a vote from political parties. One of my interlocutors commented that in a joint family of 10 members, this amounted to 5,000 rupees at election time! This raises hence the question about the fund-raising practices of political parties in Karnataka, when they were able to distribute 500 rupees per vote! Based on the NGO's 'National Election Watch' report of electoral practices in Karnataka between 2007 and 2011,[7] it was disseminated in India's press that the Congress Party had raised an amount of 14,923,500,000 rupees for that entire period, followed by the BJP with an amount of 7,698,100,000 rupees and the local JD 46,300,000 rupees. While donations to the party amounted to 83.75 per cent for the BJP, the Congress Party's donations accounted for 12.31 per cent of the funds. The remaining was gathered mainly through the sale of party tickets. The JD entirely depended on donations. According to the report of *Citizen Matters*, mighty real estate firms were part of the big donors (Jacob 2012), a fact that has serious consequence on non-equitable allocation of urban land.

Making such huge investments not only leans towards the pure rational choice economic logic of having candidates to win elections by all means in order to recover the money spent during the electoral cycle, as also to be partly re-invested into the potential next cycle. But as Björkman (2014a, 618) argues, it also serves to shows 'how election-season exchange is, instead, constitutive of enduring networks of trust, sociality, and accountability'. Such rationales in my view explain the illustrative episodes as presented below.

During my fieldwork, I interviewed an SC woman standing as an independent candidate in her ward. She reveals an experience of blatant casteism, loss of loyalty of her own people due to overriding clientelistic loyalties, and corrupt modalities.

An SC independent candidate standing for municipal election without being able to spend much was difficult. Other candidates invested a lot of money during campaigns and twice as more to come to power. People didn't have enough awareness to understand their situation and the potential power of their vote. During election time all efforts of mobilizing and organizing of the Dalit organizations were gone in vain, as the poor went behind political parties in hope to be part of the power game or that they would get some alternative work during election time. Instead of doing hard physical work on the construction site, they get a new set of clothes, go canvassing and get a day's wage. When I went canvassing I was asked about my caste, upon hearing that I came from a lower caste, the response I got from middle-class people was that I couldn't represent them as they were from a different caste. Furthermore, I learnt that upper-caste candidates were considered a better fit for the job, as they were more educated.

During canvassing only a bunch of loyal people from the civil society organizations helped me and we wrapped the campaigning on a meagre 21,000 rupees. I know the exact number, as every two days I had to submit to the election commission and recalled the harassment of the officials against a poor SC woman like me, and as I had filed my candidature under the general category as an SC woman instead of under the SC/ST reserved category. The revelation I got through my candidature was how electoral power truly worked in India, when I was a witness to a booth capture.

At the end of the Election Day men in charge of the booth were inside the booth and on the basis of the electoral roll of that particular constituency having identified those who had not voted, they voted on behalf of those missing for the party, who had paid them most in that constituency. So if a candidate had enough resources to spend it on all relevant polling booths the election was over and decided beforehand. Even though monitoring people are sent to control the booths, even those are bought up. Even though upon seeing all this wrong-doing, I called the election commission, their response was to say that that particular booth did not come under their supervision and thus I had to call someone else, nobody ever came and checked and the election was announced successful. Witnessing such an episode, I realized that canvassing and campaigning were not necessary. In fact, I had observed that in my ward the councillor actually didn't canvass at all, the councillor elect was from BJP party. He was not even from the area, never stood for anything to be improved in the area, so people actually didn't know him and he was supposed to represent them. Once in a position of power it will stay in the lineage. I know an MLA who had to resign from his position to go to another post. That seat was not put up for electoral competition in the sense that he got a female relation elected and they were only proxies.

As in any other domain of politics and policy in India, there are guidelines and handbooks on every aspect of organizing and conducting an election, including campaign spending, but hardly anyone is monitored for compliance.

During election time, everything comes to a halt as people don't know. If government changes then priorities might change, transfers may happen and nobody will work anymore, just reverse their activity, in case of a different party winning. Even NGOs stop their work. I noticed that none of the civil society organizations puts up candidates, they shy away from political work and none of those organizations also supported my candidature.

It would be wrong to look at the event of the 'booth-capture' only as one instance of legislative corruption (Jain 2001). Rather, such an event must be reflected within the wider political context, within a logic of electoral cycle. The required networks of insiders to participate in such defection tells us that efforts and money invested to maintain such networks are consolidated over time and must be reiterated. Concretely, one needs to raise funds to 'buy up an election'. Breeding (2008), in her quantitative enquiry in Bangalore, found that 42 per cent of the respondents reported having had the experience with clientelism, meaning that they themselves or someone close had availed material benefits from a political leader. The highest prevalence of benefits being offered were social welfare at 42.18 per cent, 24 per cent in education, and 12.7 per cent in complex governance policy area. To bring together the resources necessary to distribute such goodies, it can be assumed that these could be collected over time through bribes (as speed money) and land transactions that stayed within a family. This means that lower-level clerks of the particular administration have to participate in corruption and legislators have the opportunity to divert public resources to finance their electoral candidature. Establishing such a circuit of corrupt exchanges consolidates the powerful candidate in regard to other contestants to win the election and annuls other avenues of repeal, as such agents would have to be maintained within the network.

Perceptions of corruption have become the content of everyday rhetoric (ibid.; Gupta 2005; Witsoe 2011; Doshi and Ranganathan 2018), in which people distinguish 'between the more corrupt and the less corrupt, the corrupt and efficient person and one who is both corrupt and inefficient. A person who is perceived to be corrupt by others can be voted to power by his constituents because he is seen to be responsive to their aspirations' (Guha and Raghuraman 2007, 454), so corrupt politicians in return then can be efficient to get things done for the poor, if the weight of the constituency is noteworthy. All in all, the imbricated formal dimensions of political opportunities on legislature, representation, and political alliance seem to be mixed at first sight. Even though polity design and unstable strategic alliances at the local level confirm the hypothesis for favourable political opportunities, I have to add valid concerns having considered the informal pendants to them and also the institutional arrangements, their historic genesis, and the power constellations. The anti-poor attitudes in the city of Bangalore, along with the entrenched political and informal practices, make it hard to make these dimensions work as favourable political opportunities for mobilization on behalf of and by the urban poor to access formal avenues of representation and legislative powers; at most I would say they make the outcomes unpredictable.

Bureaucracy: India's bent steel frame

At Independence, Nehru bought Indians into the idea that India's bureaucracy was its 'steel frame', which will guarantee stability and continuity after the

British Raj. But today, according to Das (2006), Indians believe that it is the bureaucracy that has become a prime obstacle to development.

Gupta (2012, 23) puts forward the thesis that despite India 'outdoing' itself in designing benevolent interventions in forms of policy to alleviate poverty, no matter how sincere the officials in charge of these are, the overt goal of helping the poor would be subverted by the very procedures of the bureaucracy. In his investigation he is particularly interested in why it is that a Weberian style bureaucracy that 'produces social indifference' (Hertzfeld 1993 in Gupta 2012, 24) achieves to produce arbitrary outcomes, when some beneficiaries achieve to get assistance and others do not.

Kriesi et al. (1995) clearly trace the non-linear causal relationship between accessibility/openness and the role of various actors and the determinants in the bureaucratic arena and highlight resource allocation, coherence of internal structure of the bureaucracy, and finally the structure of interlocutors to determine the openness of this dimension.

It is necessary to locate the realms of bureaucracy within the federal structure in reference to India's Constitution. This task is not straightforward as Baxi (2005, 544) highlights, as post-colonial Constitutions comprise a mix of texts of governance and texts of justice, where the latter type is rather slender. Within the context of my research, I will look out for the administrative roles pertaining to the administration of welfare benefits. As argued earlier, the urban poor are particularly dependent on the state to cover their basic needs, as they are subjectivated to be the target of policies (Chatterjee 2004) and in India in terms of governmentality the categories of reservation are specifically designed for the purpose of welfare allocation.

Part IV of the Constitution specifies the Directive Principles of State Policy. These provisions are not enforceable by any court, but they lay down the principles of governance of the country (Art. 37). The subsequent Article 38 states: 'The State shall strive to promote the welfare of the people by securing and protecting as effectively as it may a social order in which justice, social, economic and political, shall inform all the institution of the national life'. Particular attention is given to specified realms of welfare like means of livelihood, work, education, health, and the interests of the weaker sections (SC/ST) to be protected from injustice and exploitation. While states are given the prime duty to look after welfare, tasks of welfare also emerge in the Concurrent list. Furthermore, the Karnataka Municipalities Act features a long list of tasks under Article 91, among which many pertaining to welfare are qualified as 'discretionary functions of municipal councils'.

Independent India widened and strengthened the prevalent colonial administration to also include welfare. While all the departments were located at the state level, their control and coordination functions were located at the district level (historically given through colonial governance) and linked laterally to the coordinative control of the deputy commissioner. He is also designated as a major head of the department with disciplinary power over almost every department of the government. This allows him to supervise the entire administration of the district. In this sense, he represents the government at the district level (Chatterjee 2004).

In Karnataka, at the peak of JD's rule in 2004, all departments were organized into two vertical systems. Two-thirds of the departments were grouped into 'development departments', which included all departments pertaining to welfare, and the remaining one-third into 'regulatory departments'. The recent change in the system of reserving important departmental positions to different categories for a fixed term has, according to Jamdaar (2007), led to strange features, where 'inexperienced' women or SC/ST members are propelled to such positions and become puppets of other powerful actors (ibid.). Such developments has led to a crisis in administration in terms of lack of coordination, power being located in inexperienced hands, rampant and pervasive corruption coupled with lack of transparency and hence failing in the delivery of basic services, and, finally, lack of accountability and commensurate legal sanctions (ibid., 225). The lack of accountability is grave as the 'Karnataka Budget 2010–2011 Highlights'[8] (fieldwork in 2010) showed that the budget allocation towards the different departments providing welfare made up to 40 per cent of the total budget!

Mapping Khan's (1996) hypothesis to departmental organization in Karnataka, it is observable that welfare is organized across multiple departments, which are meant to deliver complementary benefits, but there are also agencies that supply similar rights, though to different categories of beneficiaries (SC/ST, religious minorities, and those based on economic income criteria). In Khan's sense, the organization of welfare allocation and administration in Karnataka along with the delivery of welfare at all three administrative levels represents the constellation that is most conducive for corrupt transfers.

The complexity of welfare designed through systems of governmentality gives rise to fierce competition and informal practices of 'proof-gathering' to be eligible for certain, sometimes intersecting categories to avail benefits from the state. Based on Chatterjee's (2004) elaborations, such benefits remain too few in regard to the large numbers seeking welfare benefits. The benefits become currency of political leverage that promote 'politics of access'.

The mechanisms of practices of 'proof-gathering' leading to 'politics of access' are best illustrated by an excerpt from an interview[9] conducted with a slum-dweller who functions as an agent 'to get things done' by gathering the necessary identify proofs to make a potential beneficiary eligible for rights supplied by a particular agency.

Interviewer (I): Is the councillor helping you to get personal loans from SY (Central government scheme for the urban poor to avail loans)?

Agent (A): Apparently he is signing the application form. He will do for them the way he does for us. He will not break his head too much for us. If not for votes from our area, that man would not have won in the elections. I have gone house to house to get votes for him, climbing up and down the stairs of these quarters. That's why I am sad and have decided not to support any political party and now I am working on my own.

I: What work do you do?

A: I help people get cash certificates, income certificates, birth and death certificates, etc.... I charge 100 rupees. The application costs 10 rupees, I spend another 20 for bus fare, and there to get the work done I have to give another 50 rupees to the Tappal section (the section that receives applications and stamps them as received), then I have to give another 20 to the officers, unless I spend this much the certificates will not be issued. Other than the 20 rupees that I get for bus fare, I don't get a naya paisa. If I go to apply for only one certificate I don't get anything. If I go to apply for 2 or 3 certificates, then only I will make some money with the extra bus charge. For ration card I charge 110 rupees, I have gotten around 500 ration cards done.

I: How do you manage that, do you know people there?

A: Yes, I know the food officer. I know the people in the ration card department, when I am there if I give 100 or 200 rupees to the officers there, they will immediately get a card done for us.

I: And what about voters' identity cards?

A: For that I don't charge any money. I just give them a form and ask them to get a copy of it. Once they come back with a copy, I fill it up for them, and I hand it over myself but I don't take money for that.

I: For ration cards you have to give money in the department?

A: Yes, now they ask for 500 rupees per ration card. It depends on the officers, there are some who are kind towards us poor people, so if we say, sir, we are poor please help us, they ask us for lesser amounts, 100 or 200 rupees, there are some who are there only for making money, they will refuse to help us. Now there are some officers who are very kind, they have made enough money and they don't need more, they will talk kindly to us poor people. Some of them will do it for us because they are afraid that we will complain to the MLA.

I charge only 150 for ration cards. The application form costs 10 rupees. And then I have to spend 20 for the bus charge. For this I have to go up and down at least 4–5 times. So tell me how much it costs if I have to go so many times? Now they have made the bus pass 40 rupees. From the 100 rupees that I take, if I spend 40 on bus charge and 10 on the application, I have about 50 remaining with me. There in the office, I have to treat officers to coffee and snacks, which is about 20 rupees. So I don't really earn much. But when I charge people, they say she has taken money. If you want something done urgently it costs 200–300 rupees, if you are ready to wait then it costs less. If you want something urgently people will not do it in the department unless you bribe them. So why not wait and get it rather than spend so much money.

I: Other than ration cards, you get birth and death certificates and ….

A: Caste certificates, income certificate. Income certificates that state the amount of family income. Caste certificates to state which caste you come from.

I: Caste certificates that is only for Hindus?

A: Hindus, SCs we get for all the castes.

I: Not for Christians?

A: Even for Christians we can get caste certificates. Who said there is no caste certificate for Christians. For children who are going to school, we can submit an application saying that our children are studying in this school and that they belong to so and so caste. Once the certificate is done, we use it to get ration cards and voters' id cards and other amenities.

I: For Christians then the certificate will say they are Christians?

A: Yes. If they are Muslims the certificate will say they are Muslims. For SCs the applicants have to come themselves and sign on their photos.

(…)

I: Ok, but she said she is Christian?

A: Yes, but she is an SC.

I: Is she a Christian SC?

A: No, she has made a certificate as SC.

I: Oh, was she an SC who has converted to Christianity?

A: No, she is a Christian, but she has got a caste certificate made that she is SC.

(...)

I: I wonder if she was an SC and then converted to Christianity?

A: Nowadays, when children are admitted to school itself, they say they are SCs.

I: Even if they are Christian they give it as SC?

A: Yes, they say they are SCs.

(...)

I: Is it because they have benefits?

A: Yes, they get everything free from the Government, they don't have to pay school fees, books, free higher education. They get subsidised loans. For us we have to pay full amount, they get subsidy.

This short extract indeed depicts powerfully the normalcy of corruption and the terms of interaction with the lower levels of bureaucracy solicited by the urban poor. In this sense, their engagement with the state is one of negotiating categories pertaining to proving one's identity to maximize governmental benefit. To make such 'politics by stealth possible', there is a clear lack of accountability. The extract displays efficacies that can be yielded through bribing in terms of access but also in terms of speed to get things done. In Baxi's (2005, 546) words, the renegotiation of these welfare benefits take place in 'critical social spaces for politics of identity and difference by introducing dissonances in lives of civil society and state'. These critical spaces are enabled through recourse to the Directive Principles of State Policy that are judicially not enforceable and through the placement of welfare in the Concurrent list (ibid.). These critical spaces that enable divergent outcomes and increased efficacies in the sense of Helmke and Levitsky (2006), but also arbitrary ones in the sense of Gupta (2012), leads me to conclude that the formal–informal interaction on the dimension of bureaucracy restrains access for the urban poor in the formal sense, but also creates opportunities for access and political network loyalty even though often with higher costs.

Mitra (2006) highlights the 'complex repertoire of politicians and administrators, acting in tandem through two-track strategies that sustain and enhance governance': political parties/coalitions establish, for one, a linkage between their organization and a particular social cleavage and, for the other, a linkage to the bureaucracy that enhances political dividend through arbitrary outcomes in distribution of welfare (ibid., 204). He concludes that in India formal institutions are necessary but not sufficient for governance (ibid, 205).

The flip side of this monumental bureaucracy delivering various benefits through numerous schemes based on diverse categories is that it creates distrust among the different segments of society (Smitha 2010; Uslaner 2008). The reason for it is that the poor have to woefully engage with the state through bureaucracy to access benefits targeted towards them, but as the middle and higher classes would be the ones financing these benefits, they feel discriminated in terms of non-reservations for them.

The 'world's most active', but 'uncertain' judiciary

The judiciary is conceived as the prevalent system of courts that interprets and applies the law in the name of the state, but the Indian judiciary also has the power to initiate new laws or restrain the legislature from law-making under the powerful provision of judicial review (Mehta 2005). Baar calls India the home to the 'world's most active judiciary' (Baar 1990), where judicial activism is an important avenue for citizens to voice their concerns (ibid.). While direct-democratic arenas as conceived by Kriesi et al. (1995) can facilitate a proactive political process in view of a country's legislation, the possibility of judicial activism is rather reactionary but does constitute a channel for repeal or claims for social justice. The police force is in charge of enforcement of the output of the judiciary in following up on prosecutions and the maintenance of law and order as determined by the law (Verma 2001). In the case of India, the police proves to have great capacity for repression in order to maintain law and order, but as I will argue also to repress for the ends of the non-legally mandated (Verma 2001).

Mehta (2005) in his piece entitled 'India's Judiciary: The Promise of Uncertainty' argues that the judiciary is a deeply paradoxical institution. On the one hand, the courts have become incredibly powerful through the creative interpretation of the Constitution in excising the power of judicial review. With this power it has limited the power of parliament to amend the Constitution and has become an institution of governance in absence of parliamentary legislation and has held bodies accountable (ibid., 159). In this sense, the judiciary is indeed the ultimate custodian of Constitutional values and accountability. On the other hand, he argues that except for the Supreme Court, most of the judiciary is in permanent crisis (ibid., 160).

India's judiciary consists of a three-tiered system of courts with the Supreme Court at the apex. Each state has a High Court and district-level courts. The High Courts are courts of first and second appeals in civil matters, have writ jurisdiction, and act as superintendents for subordinate courts (ibid., 159). Apart from the Constitutional tier, there is another and vastly larger tier of courts and tribunals that are staffed 'by hundreds of thousands of judges, officials, and lawyers, where ordinary Indians with everyday problems might seek remedy and protection' (Galanter 2009).

Some scholars describe the Indian Supreme Court as the 'most powerful court in the world' (ibid.), as it rules on cases involving Constitutional interpretation, and under Article 133 it exercises power over civil cases that involve a substantial question of law of general importance. It also has the power of writ jurisdiction over questions of fundamental rights and has the authority to issue advisory opinions (ibid., 159). The Constitutional remedies are both protective and remedial (ibid.). Dr Ambedkar, the chief architect of the Constitution, called Article 32 the very soul of the Constitution and envisioned the Constitution as a crucial weapon in the quest for equality within Indian society (ibid., 160). It is a right to move the Supreme Court for the enforcement of rights. Another notion of equality anchored in the Constitution is the one to be protected from discrimination. Article 17 proclaims untouchability as an offence. In pursuance of this provision, the Scheduled Castes and Scheduled Tribes (Prevention of Atrocities) Act was passed in 1989 (Pick and Dayaram, 2006, 290). Indian courts recognized the authority of caste communities to define their own terms of membership, but at the same time seeking to eradicate them. Indian courts came to understand that it was not possible to remake the social order without engaging those communities in the process of reform (ibid., 201).

Despite all the provisions of protecting the marginalized, the challenge of numbers is indeed a great one for the judiciary. Mehta states that 20 million cases were pending in Indian courts, of which 3.2 million were in High Courts (2005, 160). This may not be surprising when considering that India has only about ten-and-a-half judges per million of the population. This figure is among the lowest in the world. Accordingly, the entire expenditure on the judiciary is less than 0.3 per cent of the country's gross domestic product (GDP) (Mehta 2005, 181, his own sources not quoted). With the underfinancing of the judiciary, coupled with the fact that even the money allocated for modernizing its infrastructure has remained unspent, there is a growing corrosion at the operational level of the justice delivery system (ibid, 160). The reason for this is that the procurement procedures for governmental agencies are very complex (ibid., 182). Accumulations of procedural anomalies have created perverse incentives for judges and lawyers and are a major factor causing chaos for case management in Indian courts (ibid., 161). The role of the legal profession also plays a huge role in the view of Mehta (2005) and the legal expert I consulted. They are weakening the judiciary as their integrity factor has decreased and corruption has found its way into the courts. The expert (personal communication, 2010) said that the Bar was of low quality, as the cream of lawyers was siphoned off by corporate firms and that for court work only low-calibre lawyers and judges remained who were willing to be 'wined and dined' to turn them around (ibid.). The study by Transparency International (2005) found that among various domains, the judiciary, land administration, and the police were ranked 4, 5, and 6 respectively. In the judiciary among those who paid bribes, 41 per cent had influenced judgment, 31 per cent to speed up or delay judgment, and 28 per cent to get routine jobs done, such as the listing of a case or to get a copy of documents.

The instruments of the 'most activist judiciary' outlined below were called to life to democratize judicial activism and render the judiciary more accessible, especially to the poor. I have selected key Acts and present the spectrum of possibilities for formal tactical choices of legal repeals for civil society organizations in Bangalore. This is not an exhaustive list of Acts, but these were selected based on a press review that I undertook during the entire period of research and the lessons learnt from expert interviews. Box 2.1 gives a general overview of the Acts. In the empirical part of this volume (Chapters 4 and 5), where I present the civil society organizations, I will elaborate on which instruments were chosen as tactical choices and how these were embedded in the perception and experience of the particular state they were dealing with.

Box 2.1   Legal Instruments as Tactical Choice for Civil Society Organizations

Right to Information Act, 2005 (RTI)

Under the provision of the Act, any citizen can request information from the authority, which must be responded to within 30 days; if any delay occurs the Public Information Officer is fined. It also encourages the authorities to computerize the official records. Under this Act, the authorities are required to maintain adequate records and publish a list of duties and functions and information commissions at the Union and state levels have to be established to manage and monitor access to information.

The use of the Act is rather straightforward. A literate person has to specify one information requested, to which the authority must respond within 30 days. All requests have to be submitted in written form. One needs prior knowledge of what type of information is to be asked, to which department, and with what scope. The official website of the information commission does not present crucial information in Kannada (the Kannada link is redirected to the English webpage). Even the complaint form is available only in English.

Public Interest Litigation (PIL)

The purpose of establishing the PIL was to give new meaning to the enforceability of fundamental rights and to fight (a) governmental lawlessness and official deviance; (b) compensatory measures of rehabilitation from degrading treatment; (c) environmental degradation; (d) gender inequality and injustice; and (e) corruption in high places (Baxi 2005, 548).

Launching a PIL requires sending letters to justices drawing their attention to violation of the rights of the disadvantaged, dispossessed, and deprived sections of Indian society. The letters are usually based on media reports of violations of the rights of the vulnerable. Justices usually act upon them, thus inventing an epistolary jurisdiction, determining the facts at issue by the device of socio-legal commissions of enquiry and by orders and directions requiring state action (Baxi 2005, 548).

The issue addressed in the PIL letter has to be concerning a public issue or pertain to a social malaise. To formulate the letter, there is a need for literacy and knowing where to address it. Access to the poor might be restricted, often requiring an intermediary.

Scheduled Caste and Scheduled Tribe (Prevention of Atrocities) Act, 1989

This Act was passed by the Parliament of India in 1989 to prevent atrocities. It relates to Article 17 of the Constitution that intends to abolish 'untouchability' and proactively enable lives of dignity. This is the only legal instrument that relates directly to the penal code and hence would lead to prosecution.

The salient rules within the Act pertain to provisions of the criminal law for defined atrocities; provisions are made for relief and compensation for victims, and to establish special authorities for the implementation of the Act.

A complaint is filed in the form of an FIR (first information report) to the police. In theory, the use of this Act should be accessible to all. However, reports commonly emerge that victims are held back through force and threats against filing FIRs.

Karnataka Human Rights Commission (KHRC)

The purpose is to enquire into complaints of violation or negligence of human rights, intervene in court proceedings, review legal safeguards, undertake research, spread human rights literacy, and support civil society organizations in their quest to enhance human rights (KSHRC webpage, 2013).

The commission is constituted on the basis of the Protection of Human Rights Act, 1993. It has the powers of a civil court (KSHRC webpage, 2013)

To use this avenue of repeal, one has to have suffered a human rights violation or launch a complaint on behalf of someone having suffered it. It requires some knowledge of the legal provisions related to human rights to make sense of this instrument, and literary skills are needed as well to make a submission. The official website of the commission does not present any important information in Kannada.

Karnataka Lokayukta (KLA) (Ombudsman)

The Karnataka Lokayukta was created in 1986 and its role is to investigate complaints from citizens about public maladministration (Huss et al. 2011).

It is governed by the Prevention of Corruption Act, 1988, and by the Karnataka Lokayukta Act, 1986.

A complaint letter is to be addressed to the Lokayukta by a citizen. This avenue is open to all citizens who have the awareness on corruption and its societal impact and who are able to formulate a written letter. The legal expert highlights that to use this channel of complaint, the citizen ought to have the courage to be a whistleblower (legal expert, personal communication, 2010)

Lok Adalat: 'People's Court'

As courts and tribunals have massive problems of delay, cost, and ineffectiveness, the Lok Adalat offers an informal option. They specially cater to the weaker sections of society for petty contested cases (Galanter and Krishnan 2004, 799). The cases are called before a mediator or panel of mediators, whose members are typically retired judges or senior advocates (ibid.). Domains of litigation, which are considered 'petty', such as family issues, motor accidents, and wills for settlements, generally come under this court.

All parties seeking mediation or reconciliation in the matters mentioned above can access the court.

Indeed the criteria to use the instruments are pretty simple and straightforward. In most cases, a letter or a complaint form is enough to redress the concern. However, in a state where the poor have relatively low literacy indicators, the reliance on literacy for democratizing these instruments might skew their potential. Those who are illiterate would require an intermediary not only to formulate a complaint/grievance but, more importantly, to understand the institutional landscape and the requirements in the first place.

This skew in access is reinforced by the fact that some information is published only in English, a language that the poor generally do not have access to as government schools mostly teach in the vernacular language. Accordingly, it can rather be expected that educated members of elite society would take recourse to these legal instruments.

Another striking feature of these instruments is that with the exception of the Prevention of Atrocities Act, all other Acts do not refer directly to the Indian penal code. This means that the agencies do not have the authority to order a persecution through police forces directly. As the police are strongly imbricated with the political wing (Verma 2001), conviction and real consequence from the use of these legal instruments are rather rare (Narayana et al. 2011).

Police: Of duties, exigencies, co-optation, and capacity for repression

Repression is expected to have considerable effect on the action repertoire of civil society organizations and the capacity of repression that the state formally prescribes (Kriesi et al. 1995). Extremely high levels of repression will make collective action unattractive, but where lower levels of repression prevail, it is not clear whether mobilization will be reduced or radicalized. Auyero (2011) points out that there is almost a complete silence on participation of authorities in the perpetration of collective violence. He addresses this lacuna in the elaboration of the term 'gray zone' and calls attention to the existing continuities between state action, routine politics, and violence. He recalls that missing this area of study means missing much of what drives political action and non-action.

In the context of the maintenance of law and order in India, the question that arises is: 'Who is law and who is the order?' The evolution of the police has indeed gone from regimenting colonial subjects and collecting revenue to facing expressions of social and political rights after Independence. Nevertheless, it is the Indian Police Act of 1861 that governs the constitution and organization of the police force in all the Indian states until today (Verma 2009)! The law and order dichotomy is sharply emerging since the criminalization of politics and rampant corruption have turned most people away from their elected representatives (Verma 2001). On the flip side, political interference is paralysing the bureaucratic machinery and ruling parties are misusing the police for their partisan interests (ibid.). In this sense, political exigencies are taking precedence over professional management of government agencies. Verma argues that this would be the case for the police force as well. But such a state of affairs has immense implications for the country. The police is the enforcing arm of the legislation to keep under checks and balances the behaviours of actors regulated by it. The police force is hence supposed to be the guardian of rights and duties of citizens and public officials, the force ensuring some accountability of the government in investigating, and forwarding cases of wrongdoings for prosecution.

Unstable socio-economic conditions and politicization of the police force mean that its functioning has become more influenced by politics than by law or administrative guidelines (Verma 2001, 201). Scope for discretion represents an important condition for conduciveness of corruption and a source for the malfunctioning of the police. Indian laws and the penal code provide considerable discretionary judgements to police officers (ibid., 225). The police are given the authority to arrest even to prevent a harmful incident and it is prescribed that this discretion cannot be questioned (ibid.). Surprisingly, it is the lowest ranks that exercise the largest discretion. In the Indian police, constables are at the bottom of the hierarchy and form the bulk of the force. They enjoy little legal power and their roles are limited to very low-stake duties. Furthermore, they require very low educational qualifications (barely literate), their continuous training do not equip them with the necessary skills, and they are paid a pittance (ibid., 227). Nevertheless, they have a considerable amount of discretion as they are the first at the scene of an incident and are more in contact with the citizens. They get to decide if an incident merits further action or not (ibid.). Hence the classification of the incident entirely depends on the discretion of the police constable. In the context of elections, police exercise considerable discretion in making security arrangements for the election booths. They determine which booth would get heightened security and as 'all political parties have been criminalised and those get nominated who can forcibly win the elections', it makes police actions critical for the overall outcome of elections (ibid., 229). In this sense, politicians understand the importance of discretion and the use of police to exercise in their favour (ibid., 230).

There is no provision for local accountability. The only elected official to assert some control is the home minister, who is too remote for effective redressal of citizen's grievances (ibid., 237). The only mechanism in place, Verma describes, is the departmental inquiry. It involves a case when a public complaint against a police officer is placed in front of the head of the department and an inquiry might be ordered. The head then might order a minor or a major punishment and the 'guilty' officer has the right to appeal. But this procedure of departmental inquiry incorporates serious biases. It is not an independent inquiry and personal connections within the department might overrule serious allegations (ibid., 238). Other channels are the supervision of a civilian authority of the home department to act an external check and the independent judiciary. But in practice these controls, Verma states, are hardly operational and, if at all, highly ineffective.

With this background to the use of legal instruments as a tactical choice for civil society organizations, it becomes clearer that civil society organizations have to consider the effectiveness of enforcement, if at all, when selecting a particular tactic for activism. In regard to how this institution influences conditions for mobilizing, it is a double-edged sword: on the one hand, the police might not extend its cooperation to civil society organizations mobilizing on a cause and, on the other hand, the high level of corruptibility might tempt mobilizers to bribe them to win them over. But such an option is also open to politicians and other third parties that might oppose the efforts of some civil society organizations.

A report card on India's political opportunities

The aim of this chapter was to discern the political opportunities for social mobilizing given by the formal Indian polity and legal system interacting with prevailing informal arrangements and practices upon different accountability mechanisms.

A striking outcome of the analysis was to take note of the overlapping circuits of modalities of representation and the administrative exercise of the distribution of benefits through systems of governmentality. Hence while the separation of powers is formally inscribed, on the ground the circuits overlap and create particular inclusion–exclusion mechanisms that may contribute to the operations of the patronage democracy and its discourses. For example, a slum-dweller might formally be excluded from participating in an election because of migrant or undocumented status, but channels for inclusion exist informally for him. He might gather (fake) documents informally and then might be wooed by politicians for his vote, by including him into the voters' list.

Another striking feature is that there are competing logics of representation in the urban realm. While with my research question I am focusing on civil society organizations as intermediaries, the state has indeed 'acquired a manifold persona and an almost infinite capacity to generate legitimacy through its brokerage function' (Mitra 2006, 57). This brokerage not only blurs the separation of powers formally defined, but is also political capital representatives gain through the ability of local and regional elites to calculate outcomes as they negotiate their way through issues of welfare and identity and their ability to exploit institutional arrangements in an atmosphere of trust (ibid., 203). Hence even politicians and administrators deploy a complex repertoire to sustain the status quo and hold the poor in dependency at the intersection where citizens meet government officials. The enormous number of the poor and the vastness of the system of governmentality make the state a very important mediator to the welfare of the poor.

Analogously to Holston's (2008, 7) finding in the Brazilian context, the concrete instantiation of citizenship on the ground uses social differences (caste, gender, religion) to distribute different treatment to different categories of citizens. It thereby generates what he calls a 'gradation of rights among them' that leads to 'differentiated citizenship that uses such social qualifications to organise its political, civil and social dimensions and to regulate its distribution of powers. This scheme of citizenship is, in short a mechanism to distribute inequality'. Based on my analysis, this mechanism can be also inferred for the Indian context.

Against a post-colonial context, Baxi (2005) takes this observation further and pronounces himself on post-colonial legality in view of corruption and puts in relation many of the important concepts mobilized for the analysis of India's formal and informal political opportunities. In lieu of a final note to this chapter, I present his words:

> Postcolonial legality has proved itself versatile in its toleration of political corruption. Inadequate laws, insufficient investigation, politically debilitated prosecution, labyrinthine adjudication, witness intimidation, anemic law reform – all these combine to produce a legal and political culture rendering public accountability a casualty. Peoples' movements against corruption in public life, when not co-opted with 'moral crusades' against rival political parties or factions, are swiftly suppressed. Privileged criminality, of which corruption is an epitome, also bestows postcolonial legality with impermissible pluralism in the administration of criminal justice. Differential justice exists everywhere, but what distinguishes postcolonial law formation is its open espousal of regimes of impunity, perforated by an occasional 'truth commission' (Nino). In many a society, the bulk and generality of postcolonial 'citizens' are hapless victims of 'governance' beyond the pale of accountability. For them, the law itself assumes the face of fate. (Baxi 2005, 551)

Based on the elaborations above, here is my report card on India's political opportunities presented in a tabular manner (Table 2.2).

The table attempts to give an overview of whether political opportunities (formal/informal) are considered favourable or not. As it can be seen, all dimensions display interactions with informal channels. Even though the qualification of favourable/unfavourable is grossly simplistic, I nevertheless present the dimension in the format of a report card for the sake of analytical clarity. I hope that I have substantiated above that the nature of these analytical dimensions of the Indian state are much more complex and volatile. The score 1 means that the dimension is regarded largely favourable, judged against the hypothesis presented above and the discussion of informal interactions. The score 0 considers the dimension largely unfavourable, but displaying elements of openness through informal means.

Table 2.2 Report Card on India's Political Opportunities

Dimensions of General Political Opportunities	Judgement	Explanation	Informal interaction	Explanation
De-/Centralization	0	Only formal prescription, weak implementation	✓	Localization of corruption
Representation	1	Reservation for minority groups	✓	Clientelistic practices
Legislative system	0	Majoritarian system	✓	Co-optation of minority candidates
Political alliances	1	Proximity through regionalization of politics	✓	Identity politics
Administrative arena			✓	
Assistance in welfare	1	Plethora of available welfare policies	✓	Often poor have no knowledge
Inclusion in welfare	0	Exclusionary eligibility criteria	✓	Inclusion through bureaucratic corruption
Judiciary			✓	
Availability of Instruments	1	Plethora of available instruments of repeal	✓	Often poor have no knowledge
Efficiency	0	Exclusionary requirement for use and weak implementation	✓	Remains inaccessible for poor

Source: Author.

On the dimension of decentralization, I concluded that it was not favourable to mobilization, as it tended to be more centralized, despite prescribed decentralization. In this regard, Vijayalakshmi (2006) questioned the assumption that decentralization really leads to enhanced accountability and responsiveness of the governance system. Rather, on the contrary, she notes from her study that political and administrative decentralization can contribute to the localization of corruption, when vested interests are powerful in the absence of local accountability. This is a process that will have to be checked from the experiences of the civil society organizations. Hence the prescription of decentralization depending on local accountability practices may truly favour proximity, and therefore engagement from civil society organizations, or, contrary to expectations, it may make way for corruption that might informally include some (through patronage networks) and exclude others.

The balance sheet of the dimensions of representation, legislative system, and political alliances is mixed: the majoritarian logic to the election to the lower house is not favourable according to Kriesi et al.'s hypothesis (1995), but the minority provisions formally are in place, especially in regard to poorer groups. Along with the regionalization of political parties and the unstable political climate at the time of my fieldwork, this dimension represents favourable conditions for civil society organizations. However, on the whole, given the institutional arrangements and the particular clientelistic modalities of representation, it is hard to make this dimension work for the urban poor and their access to political powers, except through informal circuits.

The administrative machinery that instantiates governmentality (which includes public housing delivery) with its plethora of administrative categories and confusing institutional constellations represent resources that can either be used to claim entitlements contentiously from the state or such a claim can be operated informally through what I called 'politics of proof-gathering'. This means that a formal exclusion from a policy framework, when not matching the eligibility criteria to access the benefit, does not mean an exclusion from the benefit, as it can be accessed informally. Hence the judgement on the dimension of bureaucracy is that its openness depends on whether the claimant stems from an 'eligible category' or not, and if not, then access is not closed as informal channels might still be open.

The uniqueness of the Indian 'activist' judiciary was highlighted, but along with its shortcomings in terms of effective implementation and infrastructure, it makes this dimension seem to be open only rhetorically for the urban poor. In analysing the legal instruments available for appeal, I demonstrated that the disadvantaged resource base, especially in terms of social skill of the urban poor, makes this dimension hardly accessible to them. The police force and repression were found to be closely interlinked, when repression also can turn informal through the criminalization of politics.

All in all, formal and informal political opportunities represent a mixed bag for social movement organizations in India. The particular opportunities presented to claims addressing housing for the urban poor are discussed in the next chapter.

Provincializing democracy

McMillan (2008) takes up central hypotheses of democratization theory pertaining to the circumstances of a nation under which it has the best chances to establish a democracy. In his judgement, democracy in India was consolidated 'against all odds'. These unfavourable circumstances were low economic development, low levels of education, and contained urbanization. Also, the size and diversity of Indian society, characterized by Manor (in ibid., 734) as 'the most heterogenous and complex society on earth', can be seen as another obstacle. Furthermore, India's transition to democracy was also very unlikely because it took place in a period of national independence struggles worldwide. Despite these hurdles India ratified its Constitution in 1950 and held free and fair elections in 1951–1952 (ibid., 736).

This chapter attempted to map the openings/closures of prevalent political opportunities and concluded that everyday realities against the normative criteria of polity were unfavourable. But as Manor (ibid.) notes, Indian democracy remains vibrant and has indeed developed its own dynamics and logics. It is hence necessary to ponder the question of what these mechanisms of informal exchange circuits interacting with a sophisticated polity represent for the workings of India's democracy.

Despite informal exchange circuits being deviant to normative democratic theory, one should gauge their role in constituting India's democracy.

Randeria (2006, 103), for her development of the concept of what she calls 'entangled and uneven modernities', picks up on the idea of embracing plurality and selective appropriation of various aspects of Western models. So, in analogy to her reflection about modernity, it can be stated that *democracy* 'once pluralised, it becomes possible to conceptualise trajectories and outcomes that diverge from the ideal-typical historical experience of a handful of European societies'. The idea of a theoretically normative type of democracy that was adopted in the rest of the world must be replaced by a 'messier and complex picture' (ibid.). In this I follow Subramanian's 'call to "provincialize democracy," to see it ... as always the product of particular cultural histories' (2009, 22, in Björkman 2014a). Despite the generally negative connotations of informal exchange circuits assessed against normative democratic theory, I join scholars having a rather optimistic outlook on the capacities of India's democracy

Regarding governmentality, Dudley-Jenkins (2003, 170), in her empirical study about state simplifications, treats the question of whether reservations reinforce the categories they are meant to undermine. Her answer is that processes of implementing reservations can solidify boundaries, but at the same time she states that despite these rigid codifications people are not encapsulated by their classifications but rather defy them in many ways. In other words, these categories spark debate over reservation and mobilization on the basis of various intersecting identities that help to prevent the reification of categories. So, when the state changes the categories, protest groups resist. She concludes that even strong systems of official identification do not necessarily reinforce group identities but can be catalysts for challengers to these boundaries (ibid., 172). So, members of subordinate groups may reconstruct and utilize categories into a tool of empowerment (ibid.). Therefore, in Dudley-Jenkins' view, systems of governmentality are the end of the road for those targeted, but may be the vehicle for transformation itself.

Regarding the effectiveness of reservation in election seats, Pande (2003, 1133) comes to the conclusion that political reservation in Indian states has increased redistribution of resources in favour of the groups that benefit from political reservation. But also such increases have been accompanied by increases in overall spending and decreases in spending on specific domains such as education programmes. For her, reservation can enhance a group's influence on policy-making. She notes that legislators belonging to minority groups have used this influence to increase the incidence of targeted redistribution, but the crux of the affair is whether these redistributions towards targeted programmes improve the well-being of either the minority groups or the polity at large, and this remains an open question to her (ibid.). Having witnessed the modality and quality of implementation of the housing scheme in my case study, I would tendentially answer her question negatively.

Regarding patronage, Kitschelt (2000, 858) argues that clientelism is to be seen as the functional equivalent to 'welfare state appeasing the have-nots to abide by political orders that tremendously advantage the haves'. So, in other words, while clientelistic practices are indeed beneficial for the poor to avail something like welfare benefits, these do perpetuate the societal order. Alistair's (2008) verdict on the prevailing patronage democracy is similar, stating that it has provided for widespread participation across social groups, although it can also be seen to undermine effective implementation of government programmes and the neutrality of the administration (ibid., 746). Piliavsky (2014) argues that representative democracy in India not only co-exists with social hierarchies, but actually actively produces them and in direct conflict with egalitarian ideals of normative democratic theories. Yet she argues that the poor in South Asia are far more politically engaged and informed than the poor in Europe and America as in the latter case class conflicts are suppressed and they lack the ethnoreligious heterogeneity of the post-colonial world (Chandra 2015). She calls for acknowledging that patronage networks are inherently political and, contrary to common assumption, they are not only present where the state fails, but are part of the most vibrant and huge democracy in the world (Piliavsky 2014). Patronage, in her writing, is seen as a living moral idiom that carries much of the life of South Asian politics and also helps to overcome the gridlock of liberal political heuristics to see the local actors' own normative imagination to understand the region's own political sense (ibid., 4).

Björkman (2014a) concludes about the cash-infused electoral season in Mumbai that 'politics might be construed as significantly more "representative" than the politics of many "Western" democracies' in the way networks concern the content of 'representation' by constructing particular semiotic and strategic contexts that co-constitute identity and claims of enduring significance. In her contribution with Witsoe (2018), the authors highlight the co-constitution of patronage networks with regional economy that sources the finance for establishing these networks in the first place.

Overall, it can be said that these informal exchange circuits based on the mobilization of particular identities are constitutive of Indian democracy. Piliavsky goes as far as hinting that corruption might be a key mechanism of India's electoral participation (2014). The inclusion of circuits of informal exchange to analyse social movement emergence results in conceiving particular modes of situated urban practice and possible pedagogy while engaging with communities, state officials and their entourage, and other actors that influence policy and governance.

Notes

1. See http://www.bhrashtachar.com/2010.html.
2. Government capacity includes amount of prescribed performances and degree of government agent's involvement in contention (ibid.). Extent of democracy includes range of tolerated performances and levels of violence in contentious action.
3. 1 lakh = 100,000; 1 crore = 10 million.

4. Available at https://www.india.gov.in/my-government/constitution-india/constitution-india-full-text.

5. I will suggest this statement in the next chapter through the analysis of a specific housing policy that was underway during my fieldwork.

6. Euro equivalent calculated at the July 2018 exchange rate of 58.7 rupees per euro. The amounts have been rounded off.

7. See http://adrindia.org/sites/default/files/Karnataka%20political%20parties%20donations%20final%202%20.pdf (accessed on 22 August 2019).

8. Available at http://finance.kar.nic.in/bud2010/budhig10e.pdf (accessed on 22 August 2019).

9. This interview was conducted by Dr Kaveri Haritas (2010) in scope of her own work and kindly shared with me.

3

Governmentality of housing and the politics of access

The expression of India's awareness of the urban age was embodied by the launch of the Jawaharlal Nehru National Urban Renewal Mission (JNNURM) by the prime minister of India on 3 December 2005 in New Delhi. The prime minister's speech started with the observation that in India an increasing share of its population now lived in urban areas, against the long-held myth that 'India lived in its villages' as long cherished by the Mahatma himself. The need to invest was justified by the rapid urbanization that has 'not only outpaced infrastructure development, but has also brought in its train a terrible downside – the downside of proliferating slums, the downside of increasing homelessness, the downside of growing urban poverty and crime, of relentless march of pollution and ecological damage'. Within the second paragraph, he enumerated all the factors to convince India that a 'massive challenge' lay ahead. The need for renewal was also argued recognizing the fact that the urban economy 'has become an important driver of economic growth. It also bridges between the domestic economy and the global market'. In regard to the urban poor, the statement was made that urban governance had failed to address the needs of the urban poor and that they had to be made 'increasingly bankable'. At least from the prime minister's speech these were the principle objectives of the mission and he went on to present some of its novel components. In his speech he described India's urbanization process exhibiting two unaligned developments: cities being the main pillars for the positive economic development and cities being also the source of vulnerability for their citizens due to slums and infrastructure pressures. So, this mission was about bringing the economic, social, and physical development in line with today's exigencies of a 'world-class city' with the means of making funds available from the Centre on conditions that a list of reforms would be implemented by state governments.

At the time of my fieldwork, the only public scheme that was making available houses to the urban poor was the JNNURM, which in Bangalore was to be implemented through the parastatal Karnataka Slum Development Board (KSDB) and the Bruhat Bengaluru Mahanagara Palike (BBMP, or the Bangalore municipal corporation).

The previous chapter set out to analytically describe the complex conditions to mobilize – appreciating the nested context of the city of Bangalore, the relevant dimensions of the state , and the institutional interactions also with informal exchange circuits. In this chapter, an analogous approach is applied to the policy domain of public housing for the urban poor. As outlined in the methodological elaborations in Chapter 1, the empirical enquiry is mainly based on legal and policy texts, secondary literature, and expert interviews. The interest of this chapter is to uncover the conditions for mobilizing to access public housing on behalf of (by elite society organization) or by the urban poor and to pronounce a judgement on the features of the policy framework in view of its openness/closedness to participation, engagement, and contention from organizations of both segments of civil society: what/where are the access points, who qualifies or is eligible to access, to what extent is there scope for incentives for corruption given by policy design, and to gauge the lack of accountability/monitoring.

This chapter is structured in three main parts: First, the analysis of the modality of the JNNURM and its component of Basic Services to the Urban Poor (BSUP) represent the core analytical content of this chapter. Second, the implementation at the city level and the local policy context of slums in Bangalore will be presented. Finally, based on the findings I call for thinking and practicing within vernacular modes of governance.

JNNURM: Ambivalent intentions of toothless tiger

Six years after the launch of the mission, Sivaramkrishnan (2011) published the book *Re-visioning Indian Cities: The Urban Renewal Mission*. It makes a good job of evaluating the mission and gives plenty of insights into the mechanics of this central scheme from his scholarly perspective, as also through the insights he has gained in being part of the technical advisory group to the mission.

As an introduction to the main argument in this chapter, the policy and discursive background and the mission itself will be described . The main argument of this part builds upon the evaluative elements that Sivaramkrishnan (ibid.) presents, which will be rearranged within the operationalized dimensions of the political opportunities to discuss the hypothesis derived from the theoretical framework. The particular scenario of the case of Karnataka will be of interest to then make further sense of the mobilizing conditions of the local groups. The analysis of the macro–micro and formal–informal linkages at national and local levels will result in a conclusion about the terms of openness and closure and the differential impact of the specific housing political opportunities in urban Bangalore at the time of the fieldwork.

Discourse, policy background, and the institutional set-up of JNNURM

This is the mission statement to be found in the overview document of the JNNURM website:

> Mission Statement: The aim is to encourage reforms and fast track planned development of identified cities. Focus is to be on efficiency in urban infrastructure and service delivery mechanisms, community participation, and accountability of ULBs/Parastatal agencies towards citizens.

This mission statement includes key terms that are almost all antonyms to current practices in urban planning and governance in India. Cities in India hardly follow planning guidelines; thus, they are hardly fast-tracked. Because of this unplanned nature, the infrastructure and service delivery is highly inefficient in most places, and community participation and accountability of urban local bodies (ULBs) actually goes against the procedural habits of bureaucrats and technocrats (Benjamin 2000; Roy 2002; Barta and Pokharel 2009). One may think that the desolate state of urban affairs in India today makes it legitimate to state such objectives in the mission statement of this intended urban renewal. Indeed, Indian cities have a long way to go. What happens when a fast-tracked neoliberal imperative collides on stubborn post-colonial structures of governmentality? As this section will show, it produces an important lag between the imperatives and the structures built to implement them and the actual routinized practices that inhabit these structures.

The success and failings of the national renewal mission have been discussed and debated in the public sphere. In this section it is of particular interest to explain its evolution in light of these colliding worlds. The elaborations here shall show to what degree the good and legitimate intentions of the mission statement are compatible with the realities of urban governance mechanics in India and how they affect conditions to engage with the state.

The stated objectives derive rather naturally from today's imperative of a globalized race for world-class cities that tries to accumulate and concentrate global capital as the model city of the twenty-first century (Sassen 2003) but the flavour that the implementation of these objectives get derive from a very specific type of discourse stemming from international consulting firms, such as McKinsey, spreading vocabulary, models, expectations, and procedures of implementations (Zérah, 2009, 862; McKenna et al. 2003). In 2003 (before the launch of JNNURM), McKinsey produced a report for Mumbai proposing to transform Mumbai into another Shanghai. This report was taken up by the state government and it became formal policy. The recommendations given then resemble very much the prisms of the mission launched two years later. In 2010 (after the launch of the mission), the same firm presented a report. The latter depicted the gap in India's investments in urban areas and services and stated the possibility of turning around the state of affairs in urban India by investing the appropriate amount[1] of funds and introducing governance reforms. The recommendations had an overhauling tone of neoliberal approaches, which pushed to corporatize public agencies and foster public–private partnership, including all good governance concepts. While in a vacuum of particular political dynamics these recommendations might be appropriate, their adequacy and prescribed pace of implementation are not reflected or discussed.

Adopting any of these recommendations meant building upon urban governance structures that were complex, vast, and had their own dynamics that had evolved from colonial to post-colonial times. One can observe that the policy background to the JNNURM (Sivaramkrishnan 2011, ch. 1) is characterized by the phases of institution-building in the early post-Independence era and the onset of a political culture based on patronage (Kanchan 2003). This led to the proliferation of new rights, to uphold the political balance between all sets of clients (Khan, 1996), and thus also requiring to create new institutions to manage and deliver these rights. The accurate representation of these tendencies of the Indian developmental state is the depiction of the evolution of the urban poverty alleviation schemes from the mid-1950s to the end of the 1990s (Supriti et al. 2002 in Sivaramkrishnan 2011, 49): various schemes replacing each other, and frequent renaming of the schemes and the managing authorities. Such system of governmentality for poverty alleviation at the local level and its messy evolution was markedly influenced by the developmental doctrines promoted by the industrialized countries. The JNNURM's institutional set-up incorporates the present jumble of authorities and schemes and at the same time it strives to implement models of cities that have had a very different path of genesis and evolution and that stand higher in the recognition of a 'world class city'. Such antagonisms between 'old structures', institutional relations, and practices of novel elements of neoliberal management and the dictate of developmental acceleration are reflected within the set-up and the functioning of the JNNURM.

Institutional set-up of the JNNURM

Within the mission, 63 cities were eligible; there were three tiers of cities selected on the criteria of the population size (Government of India 2011) inhabiting them: Tier A cities inhabited by more than 4 million people, Tier B between 1 and 4 million, and Tier C cities, which were selected for their politico-administrative, religious, historic, and touristic significance. Bangalore was included in the Tier A cities. The core reforms that these eligible cities had to implement to access the funds were measures for decentralization (74th Constitutional amendment), adoption of an accrual-based double entry system of accounting, making available quarterly performance information to all stakeholders, and implementing community participation and disclosure law.

The budget for the incentives for urban renewal and the prescribed reforms at the commencement of the mission was projected at 1,20,536 crore rupees over the seven years of the mission duration or annually 17,219.5 crore rupees for those 63 cities (JNNURM, Overview document, Ministry of Urban Development [MoUD]). These financial incentives were targeted, on the one hand, at the sub-mission for urban infrastructure and governance and, on the other, at the sub-mission for the basic services to the urban poor. While the former served to improve/renew the physical infrastructure of the city, including sanitation, water supply, roads, and transportation, and was administered by the Ministry of Urban Development (MoUD), the latter was administered by the Ministry of Housing and Urban Poverty Alleviation (MHUPA) and focused on providing shelter and basic services to the urban poor. The means to implement these sub-missions effectively were prescribed through a strategy that included the tasks to be fulfilled by the state governments: (*a*) preparation of city development plans (CDP) to communicate the vision for the city and also to specify through which policies, agencies, and financial means the vision should be implemented; (*b*) preparation of detailed project reports that flowed from the CDPs; (*c*) the release and leverage of funds from the Central and state governments which had to flow to the state-level nodal agency as loan or grant-cum-loan or as grant to fund the identified projects and in order to catalyse investments also from other resources; and (*d*) promotion of incorporation of 'private sector efficiencies' throughout the project life-cycle through public–private partnerships (JNNURM overview document, MoUD).

Matching the current institutional set-up, the sub-missions were rolled out through two separate ministries: the sub-mission for Urban Infrastructure and Governance (UIG) through the MoUD and the sub-mission for the Basic Services to the Urban Poor (BSUP) through the MHUPA. The focus will be more on the BSUP sub-mission for the purpose of the investigation in this book, seeking to explore the institutional openings for citizens to access and engage with the state for the purpose of claiming adequate housing.

What is in it for the urban poor?

The BSUP had its companion called the Integrated Housing and Slum Development Programme (IHSDP), which was the reincarnation of the National Slum Development Programme introduced in 1996–1997 for the purpose of providing basic services to slum-dwellers. This programme subsumed other previous programmes that were focusing on Dalits and their housing needs. While the BSUP covered the JNNURM listed cities, the IHSDP covered all towns and cities where slums were identified (Sivaramkrishnan 2011, 24). The BSUP component preceded the formal launch of the National Housing and Habitat Policy of 2007, but the premises were the same. Both policy documents took off from a positive note building on previous public efforts to improve housing. Both policies declared to seek to provide a 'garland of 7 entitlements' to the urban poor, which include security of tenure, affordable housing, water, sanitation, health, education, and social security in low-income settlements in the mission cities (ibid., 50). Other objectives were to provide housing near their place of occupation, securing effective linkages between asset creation and asset management, and scaling up delivery of such amenities and provisions with an emphasis on universal access to the urban poor. Inadmissible projects were those pertaining to power, telecom, wage employment, and creation of employment opportunities, and also land costs in general were not be financed. Where detailed project reports (DPRs) had to be prepared by the implementing agencies, the components on health, education, and social security were funded through a convergence of schemes and budgetary provisions available (MUHPA, 2009 modified guidelines for BSUP). The funding was split in a 50–50 per cent share between the Centre and the state/ULB/parastatal, including beneficiary contribution, which was 12 per cent and 10 per cent for SC/ST/OBC. The funds were released upon the agreed implementation of the mandatory and optional reforms. The prescribed reforms ranged from implementation of technical innovation in governance processes, redesigning administrative procedures towards decentralization, and legal revisions, to creating a more inclusive approach to urban governance.

The largesse of the JNNURM nourished the perception of the public that it was a package from the Central government in the belated recognition that something had to be urgently done about the urban mess in the country (Sivaramkrishnan 2011, 157). The mission mode was a recent coinage to distinguish itself from the numerous previous, sometimes uncoordinated schemes to address urban issues and to imply that this one was scaled up and more integral to realign the cities' development on the right, planned track. The new rhetoric of the 'mission' indeed integrated some novel institutional elements to manage, sustain, and administer its provisions and prescriptions. These elements were: a complex project sanctioning process, service-benchmarking, the Peer Experience and Reflective Learning Programme (PEARL) networking platform, leveraging of the Members of Parliament Local Area Development (MPLAD) scheme, the independent review and monitoring agency (IRMA), disclosure regime, incorporation of advisory groups at Central and local levels, and mechanisms for social audit and participation. Such innovations created more institutional structures, further complexifying them and representing a challenge to those implementing these innovations without proper capacity building to carry them out in an efficient way. The discussion of such a tendency and what kind of political opportunities this mission represented for citizens to engage with the state follows in the next sub-section.

Structures as shells, their impact as empty promises

Within this sub-section, the JNNURM will be analysed on the basis of the dimensions established by the operationalization of the political opportunities. These dimensions will be described in the context of the mission and their interaction with the informal dimensions will be discussed. This shall allow me to determine what kind of political opportunities in the domain of housing the civil society organizations were facing in the city of Bangalore at the time of my fieldwork. Based on the hypothesis drawn from the theoretical framework, this section will discuss how the dimensions of formal and informal interact to not only represent biased avenues of participation but also certain incentives for corruption at the national and local levels. First, I will give a descriptive account of the mechanical workings of the mission and how the set-up of this mission reflects Shleifer-Vishny's (in Khan 1996, 17) classification of corruption. Second, the housing resources and access avenues for the urban poor will be discussed to determine the resource facet of the political opportunities according to Koopmans et al. (2005). Then follow reflections on the tensions between decentralized prescriptions and centralized habits, along with the hypothesis that the more centralized the handling of processes the less accessible they remain. The means for a more inclusive and participatory approach will be outlined to be followed by elaborations on political alliance formation within the deployment of the mission according to Kriesi et al.'s hypothesis. Finally, this sub-section will end with some concluding remarks on whether the political opportunities on housing shall be considered as rather open or closed and on which terms at the national level.

Mechanics of JNNURM: Responsibilities, processes, and outcomes

In this sub-section, the institutional set-up of the mission and the gap between formally prescribed modalities and the actual practices will be scrutinized. This shall allow me to assess to which extent the set-up represents a possible incentive for corruption. Based on the Shleifer-Vishny model (Khan 1996), the hypothesis to verify is: the more the number of competing agencies , each supplying complementary rights, the higher the level of bribe and the higher the overall collection of bribes (Khan 1996).

The starting point to deploy the JNNURM funds to the selected cities, which were decided upon centrally, are the CDPs that need to be submitted by the state governments in order to receive funds from the scheme (Sivaramkrishnan 2011, 21). To review these plans a Central Sanctioning and Monitoring Committee (CSMC) was established chaired by the secretary of the MoUD and initially planned to include the secretary of the MHUPA as well. After some time, the meetings of the committee were held separately; UIG projects were reviewed by the MoUD and those for providing BSUP by the MHUPA. A state-level replica of the sanctioning committee had the task of reviewing the DPRs prepared by the ULBs and other parastatal agencies at the state level. The credo for the appraisal process at the Centre was speed of sanction; thus the quality of appraisal tended to be less than thorough. Criteria such as whether the DPRs flowed out of the CDPs or considerations of energy efficiency were not spelt out either (ibid., 37).

This artificial split of the mission was given as a 'quasi-political and bureaucratic compulsion' of maintaining two separate ministries, which hindered the much-needed convergence of policy and programme to deliver services at the municipal level for the needs of the city and those of the poor (ibid., 60). Because of this split, as Sivaramkrishnan (ibid.) reports, the officials showed little enthusiasm to interact, this fact being reflected in the mid-term appraisal of a fragmented structure at the Centre, repeating itself at the state level (ibid.). The two ministries represented, in the scope of urban renewal, competing agencies supplying complementary rights (namely one for UIG and the other for BSUP) which in Shleifer-Vishny's model (in Khan 1996, 17) made possible high levels of bribes because of the lack of coordination between the agencies, which was then replicated at the local level. The consequence of speedy sanctioning, the practised modalities to avail the funds, and the incentives for corruption was that the mission was not designed in a coherent way. There was no scope for public participation, re-evaluation, and, most of all, there was no time given to the local actors to take all steps necessary for a consultative process of urban planning. The carrot-and-stick principle implied luring the state governments with funds without asking for the quality of the urban vision that could be truly inclusive and sustainable. The incentives for corruption were nourished through the lack of coordination between the two ministries. For example, one sanitation project could be submitted by the state government under UIG and the same again under BSUP; with little communication between the two ministries, the same project could possibly be granted twice, and with only the 'spent money' as the monitoring criterion, the grant could well be used for other purposes.

As a conclusion one can say that the reforms prescribed participatory approaches to urban planning but as the submitting deadlines were sharp and the sanctioning process speedy, there was not much scope for participation. The artificial split of the mission allows for loopholes to serve as incentives for corruption.

For the monitoring of the sanctioned projects, a tripartite memorandum was the starting point for the exercise. The states engaged themselves to report the progress usually every quarter, whereas the ministries employed units from national educational institutes to do the task (ibid., 102). In most centrally sponsored schemes, the results are measured more in terms of expenditures and less in terms of physical progress and quality of construction – hence the same principle also applied for the JNNURM. Review meetings were held every month to evaluate the projects sanctioned, their costs, release of funds from the Centre and from the state, and the utilization certificates, which just indicated whether the money received had been spent. Within JNNURM a further initiative was to be set up: the involvement of an independent review and monitoring agency (IRMA) to review all phases of construction including user satisfaction in the final stage (ibid., 84). Sivaramkrishnan (ibid.) notes that by April 2010 IRMA reported on 240 projects, all of the reporting concentrated only on the physical outcomes of the projects. It did not give information on non-physical aspects of participation, quality of implementation, and benefits to the public, despite the mission being clearly aimed at improving such processes as well (ibid.). As for the BSUP sub-mission, the ministry's report presented that, as of September 2010, 812,000 dwelling units were completed or 'under construction' out of the 1,532,000 sanctioned. It did not indicate how many of those had been allotted and occupied by the beneficiaries (ibid., 50). To improve the quality of performance and reviewing, the JNNURM set the service-benchmarking initiative, since many norms contained in various municipal laws stemmed from British times. It sought to determine minimal standards of performance, which then could be institutionalized as part of the service delivery of the agency. While the reliability of the data was very low, it was indeed a good initiative to monitor the delivery commitment . The consequence of poor monitoring for participation and the incentives for corruption were that there was no follow-up on the criteria of participatory planning and it remained only a formality. It was up to the citizens themselves to get vocal to be part of the decision-making processes. Poor monitoring when large money transfers are in question facilitates the practices of corruption, especially in a transfer from the Centre. While the intention of the mission was to bring transparency in regard to planning, decentralization, accountability in urban governance systems, and hence make political opportunities open, the institutional set-up, practices, and incentives for corruption, did not allow substantial engagement from the public.

Housing resources and access for the urban poor

According to the progress review of September 2010, the distribution of costs between the two missions in the city of Bangalore was 2,305.3 crore rupees of approved cost for UIG projects and 510.8 crore rupees for BSUP. In Bangalore it was projected that 11,603 dwelling units at a unit cost of 125,000 rupees would be constructed during the mission period.

Within the modified guidelines for BSUP (2009, 13) one of the outcomes expected was that 'all urban poor people will be able to obtain access to a basic level or urban services'. This expected outcome seems to be a bit unrealistic considering that the coverage of slum redevelopment in Bangalore under JNNURM was 54 slums (KSDB, 2010) when Bangalore houses about 20 per cent of its population in 542 slums (out of which 246 were declared under KSDB) (KSDB 2010, 3). Improved housing being available only to a few, what were the entitlement criteria for the allotment? There was no transparent criteria list to how the 54 slums were chosen. Even when asked orally, the officials of the KSDB did not give a consistent answer. A unit cost was budgeted for 125,000 rupees for which 50 per cent was endorsed by Central funds and 50 per cent from the state of Karnataka, which included 12 per cent beneficiary contribution. The criteria for eligibility were minimum proven five years of residence, possession of ration card and voter identity card, and a caste certificate to avail a decrease of 2 per cent in beneficiary contribution (ibid.). An identified beneficiary was given a biometric card making him/her eligible for a unit. From the mandatory reform agenda, the participation bill was still to be ratified in the state legislature and there were other backlogs in the reform catalogue, hence the funds from the Centre had stopped to flow. To remedy these shortcomings a draft participation bill was presented, to which civil society organizations reacted strongly. Another measure was to enhance capacity within the KSDB. As the BSUP included a participatory appraisal and consultation for the implementation of the housing scheme as well as a 'holistic' approach to housing, a project implementation unit was set up with professionals of social science background to undertake these non-technical (in terms of engineering) tasks.

After the houses were allotted, the urban poor did not get legal titles, and the scheme did not address security of tenure. It is known from the housing literature that security of tenure is an important factor that enables the urban poor to prosper, having their dwelling as an asset. The slum-dwellers are given 'only' the right to reside with no claim to the land or the permission to alter the construction as their families grow. This means that further generations of one slum-dweller family are not given the leverage of the parents being allotted a house under this scheme. The consequence of important loopholes in the guidelines coupled with the poor monitoring of the local activities within its own realm of the state is not favourable to open political opportunities for claiming housing provision for the urban poor. The loopholes allow for partnering with slum-patrons who can have vested political or monetary interests, by influencing the selection of slum, its beneficiary families, and the manner of services to be provided. The possible influence of such actors drag in informal practices of a whole patron–client network that pulls along the power play of the elected commissioners, the members of legislative assemblies (MLAs), and their political powers into the mechanics of the implementation of the BSUP scheme. It turns out to be not favourable for the urban poor as will be depicted in the following empirical chapters and in the elaborations on Karnataka's scenario of the JNNURM.

The overall implementation of the scheme was to be overseen by the state nodal agency, which was the Karnataka Urban Infrastructure Development Finance Corporation (KUIDFC). The KUIDFC was a special purpose parastatal created to liaise between lenders (both multilateral and private) and municipalities. It was staffed mainly by business and management school graduates, engineers, and other technocrats. The KUIDFC hired project consultants, oversaw projects, and negotiated loans. Its role was to assist the ULBs to place proposals in front of the sanctioning committees, manage grants, and release funds to the ULBs (Ranganathan 2008, 7).

Kamath (2012) presents some lessons from her enquiry into the case studies of BSUP implementation in Bangalore by the other agency, the municipal corporation BBMP. The issues she highlighted pertain to the identification of beneficiaries, security of tenure, and power asymmetries and contestation.

Decentralized prescriptions and centralized habits

The less decentralized urban governance is, the less accessible are the forums of decision-making, and the less favourable such processes are to constituting open political opportunities (Kriesi et al. 1995). This hypothesis shall be verified with the processes constituting the JNNURM. One of its central objectives was the mandatory reform of implementing decentralization measures as envisaged by the 74th Constitutional amendment enacted in 1992 to strengthen the role of local bodies to perform effectively as vibrant democratic units of self-government. This amendment was supposed to facilitate the Constitutional provision in the 7th Schedule of the State list – that it was the state's responsibility to constitute the municipal corporation with the powers of self-government (7th Schedule, Art. 5, Constitution of India). The whole exercise of the urban renewal under JNNURM embodies a paradox. While decentralized local self-government was the wished for outcome, the means to do so were centralized decision-making in Delhi, which was against the very concept of self-government. The design of the JNNURM was the brainchild of 'one group of officials in Delhi, partial consultations with another group in the state capital and a nodding discourse with a few cities' (Sivaramkrishnan 2011, xxv).

The reflection of certain reluctances at the local level against the Central imposition was to be seen in the decline of 35 per cent of the budget allocation for the year of 2010–2011. This was due to the cities' failure to implement various prescribed reforms and thus not receiving the third and fourth conditional instalments from the Centre. The implementation of decentralized measures was further complicated in the current institutional set-up of urban governance, where parastatals are administratively located at the state level, but delivering crucial urban services at the city level. This fact had created more ambiguity as the JNNURM guidelines equated parastatals with an elected ULB (ibid., 94). The consequence of such fuzzy guidelines from the Centre was that states could continue undermining the role of ULBs and use the lack of capacity for planning and implementation functions as a pretext (ibid., 95).

Another reason for the states' reluctance to give planning authority to the cities was that it would involve giving up control over land resources. Control over land use meant possessing power over land conversions, which in turn lead to control over a valuable asset exercised by departments of the state or parastatals and thus accountable to the ministers in charge. As accountability remained at the same level, discretion over land issues and the potential profitability they bring could go less noticed, which was widely abused (ibid., 160). Urban land scams had been numerous, especially in Karnataka.

The attitudes of the state officials together with the ambiguous procedural guidelines from the Centre had led to a series of disconnects articulating the tensions between the prescribed decentralization to be more accountable to the citizen through means of greater inclusion of the elected bodies and centralized practices. To leverage the JNNURM funds, the selected cities had to prepare CDPs. The guidelines, though, did not stipulate that the ULBs had to be made responsible under the implementation of the 74th amendment (which is a mandatory reform). With the dictate of rapid implementation and an early start to establish a funding relationship, many consultants were hired to work out the CDPs, against the vision of a participatory process of urban planning. In most cases, the municipalities did not understand or discuss the CDPs in the municipal councils but rather just endorsed the CDPs to make way for the preparation of the detailed project reports (ibid., 78). In general, the CDPs were supposed to include singular projects, for which DPRs were submitted to the sanctioning committee. Here again ad hocism and speed led to many DPRs not flowing out from the CDPs. In many cases, consultants just polished up previous projects to match the requirements of the sanctioning committee. Within such procedures and a not thorough enough appraisal process, stakeholder consultation and participatory planning remained a myth or at most just a formality (ibid., 80). The credo of speed was also a convenient way to undermine any participation from below the level of parastatals. In fact, parastatals engaged as managing authorities and created documents that the ULBs were supposed to prepare. One must note that parastatals are not elected bodies. The implementation of the projects once sanctioned was entrusted with the parastatals themselves, as they knew the matter, having prepared the proposals (ibid.). Sivaramkrishnan (2011) notes that through the JNNURM the alienation of the city governments from the ongoing projects was further amplified, even though a real opportunity existed to reverse the trend by properly implementing the 74th Constitutional amendment.

These disconnects have serious implications for political opportunities: citizens have hardly had any chance to influence decision-making at any level, or through any body to contribute to the envisioning of their cities. The continuing practice of Central decision-making inhibits proximity of the citizen to the elected representative, thus restraining avenues of engagement with the state in the formal realm. This concretely meant that elected representatives at the ULB level would be four times closer than state representatives, as a city councilor represented on average 40,000–50,000 people, whereas a representative of a state assembly represents 200,000 people. Informal practices around the central–decentral tensions only supported processes that serve access to particular groups for their vested interests in particular projects, at the cost of the political power of the bureaucrat. For example, for the selection of slums under the BSUP scheme of JNNURM, there were no formalized rational criteria for slum selection (personal communication, KSDB officer, 2009).

Intentions of inclusive planning

The leading assumptions given by the literature (Kriesi et al. 1995; Devas 2001) regarding open political opportunities and inclusive planning are that the more proportional the representation mechanisms are made in any forum, the more accessible political opportunities are, and thus more open. Other direct-democratic arenas make political opportunities favourable when these exist in forms of institutionalized participatory mechanisms. Some of these were indeed novel formal elements built into the mission. The relevant reforms and some participatory means within the mission will be presented here and evaluated for the degree to which they contributed in opening political opportunities. Some of the reforms were part of the mandatory ones and included the enactment of the participation law providing for area *sabha*s (assembly) below the municipal ward and the enactment of public disclosure laws. Other more participatory arenas for the functioning of the mission were the technical advisory groups (TAGs), the city-level technical advisory group (CTAG), the city volunteer technical committee (CVTC), the community participation fund, and the mechanisms of social audits. These efforts were an important departure from the previous more conservative view that participation of the people at the local level should be informal and needed not to be provided for (Sivaramkrishnan 2011, 140). Even though the commitment to a local democratic structure was laudable, 'a structure however is only a necessary but not a sufficient condition for empowerment' (ibid., 95). The process of political acceptance from the authorities of increased citizens' participation was less than enthusiastic on many fronts, and for those usually excluded from participation it was a welcome promise. In the following, I will articulate to what extent this promise was substantiated with action and recognition and to what extent it remained unfulfilled. First, I will discuss one of the pillars of the reform catalogue, namely the implementation of the 74th Constitutional amendment through the proposed community participation bill, followed by the discussion of the various participatory arenas envisaged in the mission. This section will conclude with the proposed disclosure law and its related legislations.

Within the framework of mandatory reform to receive Central funds, the Centre offered a model draft to implement a participation law that aimed to institutionalize a three-tier model of citizen participation and create area *sabha*s at the polling-booth level in urban areas in order to involve citizens in municipal functions. The municipality is subdivided into wards which nominate each a representative to the municipal governments. These wards are then subdivided into 'areas', which is the polling-booth level. The model participation bill (called the Nagara Raj Bill) prescribed that the body of people inscribed in the electoral roll of an area, which constitutes the area *sabha*, elect an area *sabha* representative. At this level, the model bill did not recommend any reservation for SCs/STs, and only registered voters are eligible, again excluding many migrant workers and pavement- and slum-dwellers from participation (Haritas 2009, 64; CASSUM n.d., 2). The functions and rights of this forum were: to assist with municipal work, provide and mobilize voluntary labour, generate proposals and assist with legitimizing beneficiary-oriented schemes, promote harmony and unity, co-operate with the ward committee, be informed about decisions of the municipal corporation and the ward *sabha* and municipal activities taking place in the area. These representatives together form the ward committee (two-thirds) along with other persons nominated by the municipality representing civil society. The functions and rights of the ward committee were similar to those of the area *sabha*, structurally located between the area *sabha* and the municipal government and being involved in all planning activities (including finances) affecting the ward. The participation bill, hence, institutionalized a third tier of representatives to municipal governance. The representatives from the area *sabha* (third tier) would be thus representing 5,000 people against the current 50,000 in urban areas represented by a councillor (CASSUM n.d., 1). In general, this suggestion was laudable to make municipal activities more participative and accountable to its citizen in increasing electoral proximity. Nevertheless, there were some issues concerning the form of implementation suggested. At the Constitutional level, Prasad Idiculla (Centre for Budget and Policy Studies, 2010) noted that there are two inconsistencies: First, the provision for the third tier of the area *sabha* was not included in the Constitution, unlike for the *gram sabha* (rural areas). It only mentioned that ward committees must be constituted where the population is over 3 lakhs. Furthermore, the 'model' bill suggested by the Centre could not be a valid reference, as according to the 7th Schedule of the Constitution, local government was exclusively a state subject. He noted that the whole incentive from the Centre to make mandatory the passing of such a bill to receive funds was against India's federal spirit. One major loophole in the model was the possibility of election or nomination of the area representative. If the 'State Election Commission, or the agency appointed in its place by the State government, fails for any reason whatsoever' (Model Nagara Raj Bill, Ministry of Urban Development, 7) to conduct the election, the ward councillor shall initiate a call for nomination. If this was missed as well by the councillor, it was the state government which had to proceed with the nomination of area representatives. There were two problematic issues with these procedural prescriptions: First, the power of the state government to appoint a person to the lowest local level was severely encroaching upon the sphere of local government. Second, the whole arrangement represented a scope for manipulation of affairs by a state–councillor nexus, which could lead to a situation where the government could nominate 'its' representative, especially in areas, where real estate was a highly valuable asset. The suggested composition of the ward committee could also be problematic, where not more than 10 persons representing civil society[2] from the ward had to be nominated by the municipality (ibid, 10). The need to nominate such persons was not clear as they could be elected as well, and, when needed, experts could always be included in separate advisory committees. Third, in the proposed model the state governments retained the power to determine the territorial limits of the area *sabha*s. It was highly likely that such a process would not be transparent and various vested interests would influence the demarcations (CASSUM n.d., 1). Fourth, a linguistic loophole in the legal language had kept open the scope for arbitrary decisions. The language of the Constitutional (Amendment) Article 243S is 'wards committee' rather than 'ward committee'. This linguistic nuance makes the difference in the institutional set-up of a three-tier local government. Many states have interpreted Article 243S as requiring groups of wards for creation of wards committees rather than one for each so that the number of these committees can be kept to a minimum (Sivaramkrishnan 2011, 141). The former understanding would not contribute to more electoral proximity, but rather only add one more layer of institutional complexity.

Along with the bill, the JNNURM provided for a community participation fund (CPF) in support of the Community Participation Law. It was available for various small-scale projects, which costs 100,000 rupees or less. These projects were to be designed and executed by community organizations, creating capacities to effectively improve their living environment. The community had to contribute 10 per cent of the project cost or 5 per cent in case of projects involving the urban poor. The projects had to be submitted through one or more area *sabha*s by community-based organizations that included residents' welfare associations (middle class), neighbourhood groups, youth clubs, and market committees as representatives of urban communities (JNNURM UIG, Toolkit for CPF, 3). Surprisingly, self-help groups (formed frequently by the poor) through which financial benefits were received through other schemes were not eligible. This meant that capacities being built through another scheme could not be used for the sake of infrastructure development of their own environment. This was especially surprising in view of the complex process described in the toolkit to avail these funds (Toolkit for community participation, MoUD). A lucid project-management language was used to describe the procedural conditionality involving four stages beginning from community consultation to project appraisal and sanction, project implementation, and monitoring impact and evaluation. How could the urban poor, lacking such specific incorporated resources, meet all the procedural conditionalities? Within these unmatching prerequisites, the role of non-governmental organizations (NGOs) was envisaged. The toolkit suggests that as communities needed local capacities on many fronts they could seek support of NGOs throughout the project process and NGOs could play a critical role in ensuring communities to come together. Hence it was not the local authority providing for capacity building, but rather the NGOs that were expected to participate in this mission and act as brokers enabling access for the communities by providing the resources the communities lack in order to avail the benefits of a scheme.

The projects had to be first appraised by the TAG even though it was not an elected body. The TAG was a novel element and consisted of a non-official group to guide and assist in the process and monitor the overall progress of the mission. Its terms of reference were to advise all levels of government in steering, planning, and implementing. The members of the TAG were individuals of high standing and reputation, including Professor Sivaramkrishnan. In his own words (2011, 150), a major problem with this group was its effectiveness. The evaluative element incorporated in its task could only be carried out with the cooperation and active support of the two ministries involved, which was lacking in his view. So, their focus was left to setting up CTAGs and CVTCs and the preparation and processing of the CPF (as mentioned earlier). Even though these various groups were conceived as open arenas to influence decision-making in urban governance by citizens, it remained only open to those with 'technical' expertise, meaning that only highly educated, networked, and powerful individuals were able to participate. Again, these citizen groups were not free from the powers of the authorities for their composition. In the case of the CVTC, its composition could be finalized by the municipal commissioner with the consent of the mayor, councillors, and other elected representatives. The chairpersons of the CVTCs then would be the members of the CTAG. Furthermore, a recognized NGO from the state would serve as an anchor institution. The resources given for organizational overheads and logistics are a mere 100,000 rupees per mission city. The efficacy of this well-intended complex set-up could be questioned in view of its potential influence when the city governments themselves were marginalized by the state governments. Unfortunately, these technical and voluntary groups for this mission remained only empty shells as they were set up three to four years after the commencement of the mission, when most projects were sanctioned and underway (Sivaramkrishnan 2011, 153).

The much-embraced idea of institutionalizing public participation in urban planning and the urban vision remained rather exclusionary of those not possessing technical expertise, English language fluency, and the incorporated resources to engage with such networks of highly qualified, educated middle/ upper-class bureaucrats or politicians. The ad hoc manner of setting up the mission and the inverse timing of procedures make these novel participatory structures remain hollow without any impact on the political and governance culture of Indian cities.

Within the same spirit of public participation and public accountability, another key mandatory reform was to establish a disclosure regime in matters of municipal governance. As it could be taken from the JNNURM guidelines to the 'public disclosure law' (JNNURM 2012), the core objectives of the public disclosure law were to provide appropriate financial and operational information on various municipal services to citizens and other stakeholders, to promote efficiency and consistency in the delivery of public goods and services of the municipality, and to enable comparison over time and space disseminating information in a structured, regular, and standardized manner. The remainder of the document delineated the rationale and the steps of implementation. While the document at first sight seemed to be a coherent read, Sivaramkrishnan (2011, 147) rightly points out that there was a fundamental confusion: When throughout the document the proposed regime was spoken of in regard to the municipalities, serious doubts arise about the applicability of the proposed law, as it was not clear whether parastatals and their services were in its purview or not. If it did not apply to the parastatals, then indeed the purpose was lost. It was also not mentioned how the proposed law related to other laws dealing with municipal services. Within the current scenario in India's urban landscape where the scope for the autonomous governance by ULBs was manipulated and marginalized, what was the use of creating a law applicable to the municipalities when they were only a puppet of the state, the one taking all important decisions on finances and operations?

Another measure to assure transparency was the introduction of the social audit in BSUP and Integrated Housing and Slum Development Programme (IHDSP) components. The MHUPA had published the document titled *Social Audit Methodology and Operational Manual for BSUP and IHDSP Projects* (December 2011) (Ministry of Housing and Urban Poverty Alleviation 2011). This toolkit was thus available six years after the start of the mission. This gives us a glimpse of the priority given to measures to work towards inclusive planning and participation. The principle objectives of the social audit were: to assess the physical and financial gaps between the needs and the resources, to create awareness among beneficiaries, to increase efficacy and transparency, to scrutinize decisions, to popularize good governance, and to demand accountability (ibid., 3). The document describing the means to attain these objectives was rather vague, just mentioning key words without detailing the exact procedure, while at the same time it used a very technical language. Viewing the proposed social audit methodology as a possible opening of the housing specific political opportunities, especially in regard to the urban poor, and also with the scope to curb corruption, there were some issues indicating that it remained not so open as the term 'social audit' itself suggests: Even though there was talk of institutionalizing the audit, the document suggested that works will be selected from a sanctioned list of projects that the ULB was implementing. The social audit was used in its singular form stating that the 'social audit should focus on a single sub-component at a time' (ibid., 6). This fact made us question the impact of social auditing if it was happening only in a scattered way. The key stakeholders to be identified and consulted were the beneficiaries, the elected representatives, government officials (including state and Union levels), civil society organizations, and the media (ibid., 7). With all these stakeholders having equal weightage and knowing that there often was a nexus between politicians (elected) and bureaucrats, what was the voice of the beneficiary community in such a set-up? Furthermore, the implementation of the social audit required putting in place a complex institutional structure from top management to those working at the grassroots. At the national level, a core advisory committee was to be set up, which excluded activists. Its tasks included appointing an independent facilitating agency at the state level on the basis of bidding. The state-level advisory board, which included the mayor, the municipal commissioner, the chief engineers, and other concerned staff, had to be present at the meeting. Finally, at the city level, local partnerships with NGOs and community-based organizations (CBOs) and departments were also given a role . The impact of social audit so far had not been much debated publicly, perhaps because they had hardly been institutionalized and the results made public.

Both means of assuring transparency and accountability – the social audit and the public disclosure law – inscribed themselves within the legislation of the right to information.

After having analysed the procedural and implementation details of the proposed measures for inclusive planning and participation, the intentions of the JNNURM architects seem ambivalent. Particular loopholes in the legislation/formulation of the guidelines or model law drafts permitted the continuation of old practices in a more hidden but legitimate manner. The timing of these measures also raises the question of the real intentions behind the prescriptions for inclusiveness and participation; while the CDPs and the

DPRs were rushed through the jungle of committees at the beginning of the mission, these more 'soft measures', which shall demonstrate traits of the 'good governance' paradigm, indeed only served as demonstrative rhetoric rather than the real political will to induce change and provide for a better quality of life for all in India's cities.

Salience of political alliances

Having spelled out the possible openings within the JNNURM, it is visible that there were efforts to involve all levels of administration and representation. As the JNNURM mainly represented the flowing of funds on particular conditionalities, within the political culture and reality of urban India, it was clear that the basis to claim those funds and to allocate them remained a highly political issue and an arena of competition and contestation. To access these funds there were competing parties. From the perspective of the urban poor, the mobilization to get the BSUP scheme into their locality only depended on the political mobilization of the higher levels and the electoral vote banks they represented. As the cities for inclusion into the JNNURM were not decided upon their needs, but rather their economic importance and potential (Sivaramkrishnan 2011, 18), it could be assumed that not very clear criteria would have governed the allocation to fund projects within the cities. With this background, it was thus important to consider the electoral geography within urban areas. Possible political alliances for claim-making was crucial for the success of the mobilizers according to the political process theory. The more parties, the more chances to find allies, the more probable it was to bring the claim to the agenda and thus to facilitate a favourable outcome to the mobilization effort (Kriesi et al. 1995). There were special power-sharing arrangements, which posed special challenges to the reform agenda that the JNNURM preached, especially in view of the gap between the prescribed and the resilience of the political practices. Even though Indian democracy is constitutionally committed to the separation of powers, in 1993 a controversial scheme called MPLAD scheme was launched. It basically enabled the member of parliament (MP) 'to recommend works of developmental nature for creation of durable community infrastructure based on locally felt needs' (Sivaramkrishnan 2011, 184). This mechanism thus entangled the legislative and the executive sphere and was legitimized through a Supreme Court judgment in 2010 (ibid.). This scheme made public funds available at the discretion of the individual judgement of one MP instead of representative bodies at different levels. Such an arrangement incentivized the political representatives even more to dispense patronage and encourage vote banking within a constituency. Thus, in situations when MPs and MLAs wanted to have a substantial say in municipal matters, the MPLAD scheme was an impediment and inversely paralleled the proclaimed goals of inclusive planning. It was left to the state nodal agencies to involve the political spectrum covering parliament, assembly, and municipal representatives (ibid., 185). Without effective monitoring, where the real needs of the city's areas and its communities were accounted for, even Central funds could be easily instrumentalized. Such incoherent, parallel power-sharing arrangements are typical of the incentive for corruption, behind which corrupt acts can be legitimized through one or the other institutional provisions. Hence the political alliance possible through the MPLAD scheme made the participatory platforms proposed in the JNNURM design void.

Beyond rationales of execution, the mission established the PEARL initiative. Its aim was to create networks among the JNNURM cities and to disseminate knowledge in the form of experiences within the groups of cities. Again, there was the provision for NGOs along with other actors (ULBs, consultancy organizations) to act as knowledge managers (ibid., 132). However, the usurpation of the independence of the NGOs into the mechanics of governmental initiatives was visible. Sivaramkrishnan (ibid.) concluded that the efforts of this initiative had been fruitful to establish a network of professionals and city managers and share technical knowledge, but had failed to grasp the more complex features of the reform agenda such as public participation, disclosure, and effective platforms for decentralization. Moreover, the PEARL initiative had failed to bring in the political spectrum in its knowledge-sharing activities.

One can say that the political alliances made possible through the architecture of the JNNURM benefitted more the already powerful ones, they being able to deploy their political power for accumulation of more political and economic power (which feed each other) rather than enabling and empowering the poor to participate in the shaping of their city.

Favourable rhetorics, convenient loopholes, and arbitrary access

To pronounce a judgement on what type of political opportunities the JNNURM represented, is not a straightforward task. While the rhetoric, guidelines, toolkits, and the model drafts for bills to be enacted at the state level seemed to speak a language of inclusiveness of and proximity to the citizen, also with special regard to the urban poor, a closer look at the documentation and the implementation practices revealed a different story. On the one hand, the vocabulary was loaded with good governance terms in official written documents and oral proclamations, but the loopholes within the Centrally proposed legislation were imprecise in regard to crucial elements, such that the actors in charge of implementation could legitimately retain the status quo. The source of these loopholes stemmed from the discrepancy between the formally prescribed and the informally practised and the interpretative flexibility of formal laws at the different administrative levels. For example, while the primacy of local/municipal bodies for urban governance was constitutionally given and promoted by the mission itself, state governments still had set up and retained a strong hand over municipal affairs through non-representative parastatal agencies instead of municipal governments. So, when a model bill from the Centre addressed municipal governments, the piece of legislation was an exercise in futility, as in reality decisions were taken by the parastatal agencies. The analysis of the mission for its openness considering the dimension of centralization/decentralization (Kriesi et al. 1995) of the political opportunities came to a bizarre conclusion, as there was some systematicity to such loopholes to retain powers centrally, while preaching decentralization (participation bill, public disclosure bill). In similar ways, the argument was true for the dimensions of representation and the presence of direct-democratic arenas (ibid.). Modalities for representation within the 74th amendment were imprecise, such that processes could be manipulated to lead to top-down nominations. Implicitly, a novel form of representation of a particular section of society was induced into the implementation/procedural guidelines. The official language of the mission distinguished between CBOs and NGOs, which were generally middle-class led and possess enough capacity to interact with the authorities. This novel form of representation involved, on the one hand, middle-class NGOs taking up a representative function for the urban poor communities and, on the other hand, the same NGOs being co-opted into the activities of the state and consequently being responsible to state authorities. The basic prerequisite to interact formally with the state was information about how to go about it. Such basic prerequisites were hardly available to the urban poor communities due to the technical language and unrealistic qualifying criteria, where they had to relay their needs and possible claims to the more resourced NGOs. Direct-democratic arenas designed within the mission were exclusive of them, based on the same grounds. This differential accessibility created a dependency of political society organizations on elite society members. If such a dependency was not resisted, it created in a way a double co-optation. First, the elite society organizations, when co-opted, reproduced the socio-political context, and when political society organizations had to depend on elite society organizations, they could in turn get co-opted by them, reproducing not only the socio-political context but also the circuits to which elite society organizations belonged, for example the donor-funding circuits.

Preaching bottom-up processes while prescribing them top-down remained highly conflictual and confusing. It became pretty clear that the principal priority of the mission was to physically change the face of urban India rapidly, where social processes and demands for accountability took a back seat.

Strong incentives for corruption were the most probable, according to the Vishny and Sheifler model (in Khan 1996), when two or more agencies delivered complementary rights in an uncoordinated manner. The institutional set-up of the mission with the artificial split between the infrastructure and the services to the urban poor component replicated exactly that model. Professor Sivaramkrishnan in his role of a scholar and a TAG member witnessed the predicted unwillingness to collaborate from both ministries involved. Along with the undeniable patronage democracy existing in India (Kanchan 2003) and the possibility of existing political alliance structures reifying themselves within the mission's bureaucratic structures and processes (for example, the MPLAD scheme), a corruption incentive structure exists and prevails.

Even though the dimensions of accessibility to adequate housing and available resources for it had gained new dimensions in the public sphere, it needed to be put in context. For example, in the city of Bangalore it was the only public housing scheme for the urban poor existing during the time of my fieldwork and given the number of slum inhabitants in the city its effect was only scattered.

Many points of critique were articulated against the mission; they were indeed grave as the opportunity to actually bring substantial change in Indian cities had been missed. Nevertheless, it had created an unprecedented awareness for urbanization. The JNNURM was a toothless tiger after all. It was a tiger because it was aggressive with the 'premise of being fast-tracked' because it endeavoured to turn around the state of urban India within the mission's duration (after China's example); it was big, complex, and further complicated urban governance affairs. It remained toothless because the envisaged measures were ad hoc, not thought through; the institutional structures built were empty shells; because capacities to understand the vision of 'world class cities' not only as an outcome but also as a process and to implement it were lacking; and current practices were not given the time nor the resources to evolve and align with the formally expected prescriptions. The turning of these two sets of unparalleled wheels – one of the formally prescribed with the overhaul of neoliberal arrangements and the other within the logics of governmentality, patronage democracy, and overreaching informal practices – for the moment did not benefit the disenfranchised poor in enabling their 'right to the city' in Henri Lefebvre's terms (2003). This means that the JNNURM represented rhetorically open political opportunities, while in reality, especially for the urban poor, it remained a closed 'invited space of participation'. This meant that claiming adequate housing with all its relative urban services had to happen through contention.

'Vernacular' instead of 'good'

Tracing the prevailing mismatch between formal policy prescriptions and the everyday practices on the ground, and possibly deliberate loopholes in policy, leads to the questioning of the doctrine of 'good governance', on which the policy language was based. Good governance was majorly elaborated in the context of international development cooperation. It has become the sole point of reference on which any critique of the state is based. This normative concept was defined by the World Bank (1992 in Blundo and Le Meur 2009) as 'the manner in which power is exercised in the management of a country's economic and social resources for development'. It refers to a political regime that respects human and civil rights and can rely on an effective, competent, responsible and incorrupt, capacitated bureaucracy to implement its measures (ibid., 1). The authors continue to state that the notion is inherently paradoxical 'as it recommends a vigorous civil society to counter-balance and control a state which is always suspected of various shortcoming, but also leaves unspoken the specific role of social forces in this process, tending to concentrate on the production of technical rules for the efficient administration of public services' (ibid.). Such agendas of technocratic 'new public administration' are depoliticizing (Corbridge et al. 2005, 187).

It was exactly this paradox and trend that I identified in the analysis of the BSUP that lets me conclude that it was a 'toothless tiger after all'. What such imposition of 'good governance' rhetoric does is to stress the hegemonic nature of development narratives without analysing actual practices on the ground. This hegemonic nature is reflected in the inappropriate underlying assumption of 'good governance' – that governmental actors would work towards the normative ideals of democracy (Teorell 2007). But prevalent discourses and institutional incentives for corruption and entrenched informal practices make governance actors prone to indulging in informal circuits of exchange that characterize everyday transactions. Corbridge et al. (2005) come up with a perspective that is geared to thinking of politics 'as a continuum of practical and not always additive actions around the construction of social and economic relationships and forms of rule'. In other words, they recommend acknowledging and considering the indigenous and entrenched forms of existing social relationships. Resulting from this recommendation arise two questions. First, how can then such acknowledgement and consideration of particular localized processes and rationales enter models of governance? Second, what difference would it make? Regarding the first interrogation, Sundaresan (2017, 10) recommends the inclusion of cultural geographies into the analysis of governance. This means taking seriously practices that consolidate in particular places governing culture and shaping particular outcomes. To characterize governance as vernacular instead of good represents the idea that 'mechanisms of social governance in practice take very specific forms in their rationalities, technologies, actors and processes in particular places in relation to the governing structures and processes of the modern nation state' (ibid.).

To include such mechanisms into governance models, one needs to recognize that place matters and that social relationships articulate around communities that in urban areas are strongly constituted by space (Bourke 2009). The urban communities that I met during my fieldwork were heterogenous in terms of caste, religion, and occupation, but they still constituted one community in one certain locality. What was constitutive of their relations was the commonality of their status and place of habitation in the city, either in form of tenure, access to urban amenities and services or depending on what networks they belonged to. This contradicts the handling of systems of governmentality that targets individuals through a catalogue of eligibility criteria to be beneficiaries of social housing entitlements, for example. I argue that a model of 'vernacular governance' needs to create a link between individual rights of citizenship as articulated in the Constitution of India and the rights and sovereignty of a community that is constituted by space or the city. In such a model, the notion of community will have to be revisited in terms of space and access to the city. An endeavour to formulate and co-construct a model for 'vernacular governance' would have to incorporate an anthropological approach of enquiry to learn with the community and its relationships, and assist in building capacity for community members to express, communicate, and coordinate and engage in a participatory process of decision-making.

Regarding the second question – what kind of difference such a conceptualization of governance would bring about – I would like to unpack a study by Breeding (2012). She explored whether developmental projects that account for informal practices from the outset of the project design have better development outcomes. These practices are clientelism, rent-seeking, cultural practices, norms, and other traditions. She assessed a random sample of 200 World Bank projects and 50 country programmes during the period between 2004 and 2010. Results suggested that development outcome ratings had improved in projects that identified informal practices from the outset.

The rhetoric of good governance could be equated to a Weberian ideal-typical model, its sanitized language void of local politics also serving to tuck away bad governance, especially if the metrics to measure governance outcomes are conceptualized in a simplistic manner to cover up unattained goals.

The next two chapters present the experience of elite and political society organizations that were facilitating, brokering, or challenging BSUP implementation in slum communities in Bangalore. These chapters discuss the differential political opportunities (formal and informal) they face, the action repertoire they developed in response, and the discursive repertoire they deployed.

Notes

1. USD 2.2 trillion over the next 20 years in India's cities (McKinsey Global Institute, 2010).
2. It is noted that civil society means non-government organizations or associations or persons, established, constituted, or registered under any law for the time being in force and working for social welfare, and includes any community-based organization, professional institution and civic, health, educational, social, or cultural body, or any trade or industrial organization and such other association or body as the municipality may decide.

Mobilization on behalf of the urban poor

Who mobilized on behalf of the urban poor on the issue of adequate housing? Why and how would they do it? What would the rationale be? Within the Basic Services for the Urban Poor (BSUP) component of the Jawaharlal Nehru National Urban Renewal Mission (JNNURM), a role was foreseen for elite society organizations. How would they live up to it? The policy assumed that slum communities lacked skills and resources to be the interlocutors for the implementation of the housing policy and envisaged a critical role for civil society organizations. The toolkit suggested that civil society organizations could play a critical role in facilitating communities to come together. Hence it is not the local authority providing for capacity building, but rather civil society organizations that were expected to cooperate in this mission and act as brokers between the policy beneficiaries and the implementing agency.

Housing was indeed a domain in which civil society organizations hardly engaged because of the contested nature of urban land and space and the high funding and expertise required (Sen 1998). Most of the city's civil society organization listings did not even include housing as a category. Since the initial days of embarking on to this research endeavour with a clear organizational focus, I closely watched the press and a preparatory fieldwork phase helped to grasp 'low-intensity thermodynamics' of the housing domain and its actors. I had identified two organizations of interest.

I met my interviewee of the first organization at a junction in a rather well-to-do neighbourhood. The junction framed a little triangular patch of land, which was bordered with homes made of low-quality materials with tarpaulin roofs. Amidst this patch of self-constructed homes rose a three-storeyed concrete structure. This was one of the first BSUP project sites underway in Bangalore at the time of my fieldwork. My interlocutor was one of the project coordinators for the elite society organization called CIVIC. CIVIC was one of the oldest civil society organizations in Bangalore, which had made its name in organizing citizen consultations and raising awareness on urban governance issues. She held a degree in social work and was specialized in the domain of health. She came here once a week to visit the community of around 112 families. CIVIC took particular interest in this locality to understand the mechanics of BSUP and to assist the community. They were more versed in interacting with middle-class residents' welfare organizations, but due to new funding priorities devoted themselves recently to urban poor communities.

A few days later, a tall man along with a trimly dressed woman were waiting for me in a southern neighbourhood. He had been working for over 20 years in housing initiatives across the city and she was a fieldworker recruited at the slum, a fieldworker recruited at the slum. She had assisted her community since the since the 1980s, when her locality first became the target of the subsequent housing policies. Both worked for the elite society organization called AVAS. It was the only elite society organization in Bangalore to have worked on housing with the urban poor explicitly. Their initiatives on the issue dated back to the 1980s and they had received national recognition for their in situ participatory approach with the communities involved. The founder of the organization came from a rich industrial family who had married into the family of Karnataka's first chief minister. I had learned from press reports that the founder was appointed to a newly formed non-constitutional government body, which was called ABIDe (Agenda for Bangalore Infrastructure Development).

These were the two organizations that would give me insights into the conditions for mobilizing for elite society organizations that mobilized *on behalf* of the urban poor. I argue along with Chatterjee (2004) that civil society of post-colonial countries, including India, was segmented due to colonial governance practices that prevailed in the current systems of governmentality. He distinguished between political society and civil society. The former had an inherent political relationship with the state because of their status as subjects and targets of policy. The latter he called civil society (and I call elite society), who are given equal rights and freedom as they are not dependent on the state and are not ascribed policy targets (ibid., 38). Relational resources influence the tactical choices elite society organizations make (Pichardo 1998; Bourdreau 1996). Elite society organizations are more likely to have elite involvement through their specific networks and thereby create elite audiences; they will be unlikely to support or ally with organizations that embraced radical tactics or goals. Hence one can expect that elite society organizations engage in non-radical tactics. Their tactics could include making use of formal means such as legal means of appeal, participation in direct-democratic arenas or else contentious tactics such as protests, but displaying tolerated performances. In this chapter, I present these two organizations and their struggle to mobilize on the issue of adequate housing *on behalf* of the urban poor.

I first give a short introduction to the organization and present for each case an episode of contention, which is illustrative of the way the organization operates and the socio-political context they face. An episode of contention 'can be defined as a period of emergent, sustained contentious interaction between actors utilising new and innovative forms of action vis-á-vis one another' (Fligstein and McAdam 2011, 9). An episode is characterized by a shared sense of uncertainty/crisis regarding the rules and power relations that reinforces the perceptions of threat and opportunity that lead the parties to engage in sustained mobilization by incumbents and challengers (Fligstein and McAdam 2012, 1). The following analysis of the political opportunities they face, the action repertoire they develop, and the discursive repertoire they employ to justify their actions are based on the data corpus consisting of numerous rounds of semi-structured interviews with organizational members and their interlocutors, document and press analysis, informant's inputs, and observations gathered during my fieldwork.

Claims for accountability through the state's own tools

CIVIC, standing for 'Citizen's Voluntary Initiative for the City', was one of the oldest civil society and most visible organizations working on governance and civic issues in Bangalore. At the time of my fieldwork CIVIC consisted of eight trustees, one executive trustee, one head coordinator, and five project coordinators. Given the personal background of the staff and the leadership, CIVIC was endowed with international funding and social skill resources. All of them had earned some educational credentials, most of them having a Master's in Social Work. Written communication among them was often in English. The professional backgrounds of the leaders were prominently from the private sector. The members of CIVIC were not experts in urban governance but 'they try to work as informed citizens to the best of their knowledge' (interview with CIVIC members, Bangalore, 2011).

The activities of CIVIC were manifold, diverse, and were organized along the logic of project management and funding cycles. The activities ranged from research, evaluation, monitoring, interacting with the urban poor communities and the department's staff, creating visibility in the press, awareness building (with the creation of relevant material), and networking. CIVIC mainly facilitated discussions and brainstorming at the city level and later got involved with residents' welfare associations (RWAs), which were generally composed of the middle class. Their aim was to create awareness and organizational capacities among the middle-class RWA to understand and implement the 74th amendment. CIVIC played an important and pioneering role in its formulation for Karnataka. 'It had never spoiled its hands' (ibid.) by working with the urban poor. Acknowledgement that there was a need for substance to formulate systemic changes based on 'field' experiences triggered the change in focus of the organization during the round of funding between 2009 and 2011, which was supported by the funders to encourage more visible impact of their work. CIVIC's experience with working in slum communities was only about two years old at the time of the fieldwork.

CIVIC worked in one particular slum community in which BSUP was underway. They also involved themselves in governance processes within the ward by involving other habitants as well. They had taken the role of facilitating interaction between them and the government officials in creating platforms for grievance redress. CIVIC had maintained a routine of visiting the slum communities once a week to be in touch with the events on the ground, striving to keep the right balance between advising them and not interfering too much with community dynamics. Not getting too involved was the rationale. When they did advise the communities on how to go about matters of concern to them, they tried not to take ownership of the action, except when they were organizing an event.

In the following, I present the contentious episode involving the locality in which Bangalore's first BSUP in situ redevelopment project occurred with CIVIC's involvement. The episode depicts the implementation of the policy, the political opportunities they faced, and the tactical choice of CIVIC to mobilize on behalf of the community. After briefly discussing the episode, I move on to decrypt CIVIC's perception of the political opportunities and action and discursive repertoire.

Episode: The quest for transit housing

Upon consultation with their NGO network, CIVIC selected one specific slum in which JNNURM BSUP housing implementation was going on. At the moment when CIVIC stepped in, this BSUP housing project was just kicking off, which was part of the second JNNURM funding phase. Karnataka Slum Development

Board (KSDB) was in charge of implementation. At that time CIVIC encountered a community of urban poor having their occupation in domestic work, astrology, and begging and was hardly informed and scared about their future prospects on that land, which they had been occupying for over 30 years. The slum board had initiated the scheme without ever calling for a public meeting. Apparently a few engineers from the slum board had stepped into the slum and told the occupants to vacate within four days. If they did not comply they would lose their houses. Due to the lack of information and assurance, the dwellers did not want to vacate for the construction to start, fearing that they could not come back. So CIVIC at that time was the first to call for a community meeting, to communicate their lessons learned from the collected project toolkit (GOI, JNNURM) and the detailed project reports produced by the KSDB. In the following, they requested the commissioner to come to the community and explain a list of 16 points that needed clarification. The commissioner sent the Technical Director, who was an engineer. During the meeting, CIVIC presented the discrepancies between the prescribed toolkit, the detailed project reports, and the concerns of the community, asking him to answer and take a position. The engineer did answer the technical questions, which was within his capacity and left all other points of the list to be addressed by the commissioner. The commissioner could assure the slum-dwellers that they would get a house, as they were given a biometric card – a proof of eligibility. That was the first time they heard about the purpose of the cards distributed previously. CIVIC pushed KSDB to establish some terms of reference with the community, but at the time I interviewed them, such a thing had still not happened. CIVIC formed a beneficiary committee (as prescribed in the toolkit), the members being suggested by the community itself. With this then newly formed committee they went to meet the commissioner. The relevant question of lacking transit housing was acknowledged, but the commissioner still requested the slum-dwellers to vacate part of the land for the construction to start, while promising them to find transit accommodation within a week. Upon that request from the commissioner, CIVIC advised the community not to vacate the land, to demand transit housing first, and in case the bulldozer struck to protest and halt the demolition. The slum-dwellers had agreed on this action plan. To the surprise of CIVIC, two-thirds of the community had acted exactly the opposite way, justifying that they were frightened about not getting an apartment if they delayed the work. At the same time, the middle/upper-middle class of that area got active in redeeming the fact that these slum-dwellers had by then set camp on the street and feared more families would join such an 'eyesore'. They thus complained to the police. CIVIC narrates that when middle-class residents got to know that CIVIC was working in that community they sought some support from CIVIC to find some transit accommodation in a joint effort – but finally without any success. So, the community were on the streets when the construction started. By the time monsoon set in, the situation became unbearable. That is when CIVIC filed a complaint with the Human Rights Commission. As they are a toothless body, no impact was visible from that action. CIVIC also filed one with the Information Commission; the commissioner acted under the provision of 'threat against life and liberty' of the RTI [Right to Information] and urged for a meeting with the KSDB and ordered, 'You must give transit housing' in his capacity of former chief secretary. The response from KSDB was that within Phase II of the project, no budget was allocated for that purpose. The proposal of at least endowing them with cash to be able to rent a place met with the same response. Ultimately no other kind of accommodation could be found, so as soon as one building was up, the 114 families cramped into one incomplete apartment complex, resulting in double or even three-fold occupancy of each unit. At that time, other three buildings were still supposed to be built and their completion was pushed beyond any reasonable assessments as elected politicians (MLAs) started to intervene. One local MLA and then the councillor stopped the work by demanding 5 per cent of 'their cut' from the contractors. The contractors being fed up of such harassment stopped the work and slowed it down considerably due to dearth of funds. CIVIC launched RTI suits reminding that as per guidelines it had to be completed in a maximum of 15 months. The other partner organization who was working with the community and who had got the slum declared intervened, as the chairman of the Slum Boards happened to be an MLA who was from a constituency where this partner organization was very active. So, they spoke to him and the chairman then threatened the contractor to cancel his contract. At the time of fieldwork, this was the story I encountered with this community.

Figure 4.1   CIVIC Episode 'The quest for transit housing' (2009)

This was CIVIC's first experience of working with the urban poor. With a sharp understanding of the contrast between the guidelines and toolkit of the BSUP and the implementation on the ground, their evolved action repertoire served to claim accountability from the government for the delivery of housing to the community. They pursued their activities to assist the community with the constant goal of developing an intervention model based on rigorous research, community interaction, and keeping the state accountable to its own ends and means. Their research and the resulting understanding of the BSUP policy was sound, their action repertoire to claim accountability was evolved, but the community interactions were less experienced.

I visited the community to triangulate the contents (transit housing episode). I could witness that CIVIC's interventions were hardly known to the community. They were constantly referring to the leaders to talk about CIVIC. They seemed resigned and uninformed of the course of the events of the housing implementation. Even though CIVIC would be present once a week and took up the information dissemination of the project, it seemed that the community 'only' consumed the information and no capacity building for agency had occurred. In the perception of CIVIC the poor had no experience in taking consensual decisions or in speaking in one voice and sticking to the decisions they took. In their view, this condition was amplified by the poor's 'livelihood issues, as they can't leave their jobs'. CIVIC was conscious of the precarity of their housing situation and learned that the poor would compromise the claim-making exercises to safeguard their chances of securing a public housing unit.

Given these conditions, CIVIC argued that they would have to do the 'hand-holding' in the beginning to 'empower' them and then to 'learn to let go'. 'You should build capacity in them; not build dependency on yourself' (ibid.). CIVIC prescribed more radical tactics for the community in order to resist government action than they would deploy themselves. For example, in the episode 'In quest of transit housing', CIVIC suggested that the community should protest and resist evicting the site before they got transit accommodation. While they suggested such action, they did not take part in it, as the coordinators only visited 'the site' once a week.

CIVIC had little experience and KSDB sent only engineers with technical knowledge to deal with the engineering exercise, but the expertise to conduct community participatory processes was lacking.

Cracking open the 'supposed to do democracy'

Probably one of the most striking strengths of CIVIC was their capacity to dig out or to patiently track institutional openings that existed and did not come to public light. Most government orders were published in the official gazette and still needed to be asked for and were not publicly accessible over the Internet, for example. It was through CIVIC's perseverance that official proceedings and prescription of deliberative arenas within the different departments were made known. Hence their ambitions of upscaling their work could be focused on the output of their research findings they pursued also through RTI.

In regard to the housing impacted communities, CIVIC did observe that it was increasingly difficult for the poor to gain access as they lacked the skills to use the means of appeal. Other reasons for restricted access in their view was: First, no information was given by implementing agencies and officers about the scheme potentially affecting the lives of the urban poor. Second, no platform was present where officials would be accessible to take questions or redress grievances. Third, formally elected representatives – the councillors – were hardly available to the population and did not use their power to allocate public money towards the community. Finally, the pressures of bureaucratic corruption around welfare benefits represented another obstacle for the poor to access the systems of governmentality. The openings of the political opportunities presented themselves to CIVIC through their style of interaction with the government in staying polite and not using violent language. Such organizational behaviour allowed them to broker access on behalf of the urban poor. Impediments to their activity were community leaders and elected members that wanted to monopolize their power.

On avenues for different forms of participation, CIVIC made it its business to be informed and to demand information. There was, first, conventional electoral political participation. Second, platforms or arenas of consultative decision-making and deliberation, which were supposed to exist, including those that were not thought of. Third was regarding the provision for participation in legislation drafting and budget allocation. These interactive spaces were shaped by contextual political dynamics, including informal ones (as described in the episodes) that shaped the avenues for elite society organizations. For conventional political participation, the form of habitation itself made the slum-dwellers into denizens. Many had migrated to the city/ state and were not enrolled into electoral rolls, especially if their slum was not declared. Before the 2008 assembly elections, CIVIC had brought to notice the messy and faulty state of electoral rolls and, in a pilot, had demonstrated the task of cleaning up the list. Political parties kept migrant slum-dwellers as unregistered voters, but still got them to vote by buying their vote on names that were not valid anymore, for which faulty electoral rolls came in handy. An expansion of the pilot was curbed as the bureaucrat supporting the endeavour was transferred off. Various arenas for participation and deliberation were provided for in the legal government orders, but the concerned departments were not really functional: the ward committees prescribed by the 74th amendment; the grievance redressal systems at levels of service delivery prescribed by the Department of Personnel and Administrative Reforms; the government orders about monitoring systems that shall be in place; platforms for interactions between the service providers and citizens; even the 'Jana Spandana' (citizen outreach) provided by the municipal corporation (BBMP) had an online system where grievances could be registered. CIVIC deplored the lack of provision for mechanisms of accountability in the JNNURM guidelines. CIVIC pointed out that communities could be brought to participate, but the government officers were often uninformed and they could only count on the goodwill of the implementing officers and their supervisor. There was no formal way they could demand them to come for grievance redressal. Participation in legislation drafting and budget allocation was also characterized by fragmented guidelines and loopholes in CIVIC's view.

The governance model in place in Bangalore was perceived by CIVIC as ad hocism to the detriment of careful planning, non-monitoring of the processes, doing for the sake of money, working only in a reactive mode, and attending to only those who 'cry to be given the milk'. It was a governance process that was very volatile and blurred around the superposition of administrative bureaucratic processes that were not independent from the electoral cycle. One CIVIC member quoted the following example to illustrate the superposition: 'One MLA sends 10,000 applications filled up of BPL (below-poverty-line) cards to the public distribution system (of basic goods) and tells the commissioner "you give cards to these 10,000 application, instead of the bureaucrat"' (interview, Bangalore, 2011). The non-existent job charts of the bureaucrats or the elected representatives amplified the possibility of such superposition. CIVIC experienced that there was no institutional capacity for any social exercise and no systematic way of governing. Having a governance model that got the work done through tendering from the market forces to catch the lowest bidding contractor, along with corruptive demands, decreased the quality of public delivery, as was also the case in CIVIC's housing episode.

Avenues for policy-prescribed participation were not functional for the larger part and governance mechanisms were unpredictable. So how could the concerns of the poor get represented? The patterns based on the data of semi-structured interviews reveal different logics of representation. One was obviously the logic of conventional political representation. Another was a certain competition of actors to represent the poor. But the question remained: towards whom was the representation intended? The so-called conventional political representation did not seem so conventional to CIVIC as witnessed in their experience of faulty electoral rolls. Buying the votes presupposed that funds were available. In this regard CIVIC observed, 'Political party in power make money so that with that money it can sustain itself in the next cycle.' (ibid.) In their view the political parties have had the choice between two paths – either to do good work and get re-elected or to distribute money and get elected (ibid.). In their view, Karnataka had opted for the second choice as 'political parties are also made of individuals and the greed has taken over from an incline' (ibid.). According to them, such a state of affairs affected the poor particularly badly because 'there is no political voice, second they can't stand up on their own because of economic, educational, social status.... Unless the present polity makes up its mind not to go to them once in 5 years but to really uplift the poor across the community, caste whatever, I see no hope'. Based on such belief they reflected that political parties wished to keep them as vote banks. In consequence, the poor would keep going to them begging for services. This way they could control that section for their political interests to be safeguarded (ibid.). At the same time, the dilemma remained that even though in a democracy all citizens were eligible to stand as a candidate, elected representatives in their view had to have some minimal credentials: sufficient formal education to understand the complexities of cities along with confirmed managerial skills. So, the elected members who could also become policy makers were not professionals; they were supposed to serve the interests of the people, which they did not either.

It was not only the 'legitimate' elected representatives who claimed to represent the urban poor but also their 'own' community leaders. CIVIC referred to slum leaders as doing 'politics inside the slum ... interfering same like the elected representatives' (ibid.). CIVIC witnessed in numerous instances different forms of corruption functioning at all levels which considerably shaped the possibilities of CIVIC's intervention within a community. Through their narration different mechanisms influencing CIVIC's choice of tactics could be chalked out. Corruption indirectly affected their work. Indirect effects were through the entrenched practices that were facilitated by prevalent incentives for corruption of fragmented and uncoordinated governmental agencies of a policy scheme. These practices were maintained to be non-transparent and blurred all possibilities of accountability by not informing the beneficiaries, having documentation only in English and not in the vernacular language, not informing about services that government agencies were supposed to deliver, government officials being unidentifiable (not wearing name tags), and not promoting any prescribed measures of deliberative participation or citizen's involvement. Another indirect effect was the involvement of corrupt practices within the community itself. One CIVIC member narrated that within the community in which the housing episode took place, members were corrupt themselves in gathering false certification to avail entitlements from the bureaucracy of the public distribution system. This system did not check or reprimand such mechanisms of false proof-gathering. There was corruption on both sides of the equation, namely by the implementing agents of governmentality systems and by the beneficiaries. The community could not blow the whistle on the corrupt official, as there was the threat that the same official might blow the whistle on the community that would rip them off of any potential benefits.

CIVIC was also involved in helping women access a livelihood scheme. They were not allowed to participate as they were refusing to pay a bribe. CIVIC collected complaints, in which one corrupt official was explicitly mentioned. That official sent out goons to tackle those in the community who had blown the whistle on him, but they accused CIVIC. Their experience of cleansing electoral rolls also displayed elements of informal repression in the form of internal repression (transfer of government staff). Clean rolls would have made vote banking and other election-related corrupt practices more difficult.

Such effects of corruption made CIVIC members intervene cautiously on behalf of the organization, but also in their personal endeavours of being responsible citizens. The same way as government anonymized its services (no name tags of officials), CIVIC also resorted to anonymizing grievances and not using their letterhead. In this sense, it is not surprising that out of security concerns CIVIC was not too present in the community where BSUP was underway. As a measure of caution, CIVIC only wrote and published its concerns of civic and governance issues in English. Those deploying informal repression would not read those papers. The CIVIC staff had experienced very strong informal threats against themselves and their families. The lesson learnt was to keep initiatives and voice at bay not wanting to risk personal safety. It seemed that the choice of people to interact with and also the choice of tactics struck a delicate balance between being visibly effective, to be able to showcase to the donor, and employing means that kept them safe from informal repression.

'RTI is our god'

CIVIC's action repertoire was characteristically moderate. They tried to work from within the system and focus more on governance processes. At the centre of their action was the Right to Information (RTI) Act and the creation of public platforms for grievance redressal, also in order to 'shame' the government. These two approaches were perceived to be an effective way of getting things done.

Using formal means of appeal available to demand accountability and participation space was the rationale of CIVIC's action repertoire. Even though each of these instruments was differently impactful, they used a range of legal remedy instruments: the Human Rights Commission to get transit housing for the slum-dwellers; Jana Spandana (citizen's outreach platform), which was supposed to be held at regular intervals by the municipal corporation; Supreme Court judgments that could be used as a reminder of things the government ought to be doing; and most of all the RTI Act. The use of RTI was not only an efficient tool to demand accountability but also one that was considered safe to use. The provisions of the 74th Constitutional amendment (third tier for formal representation) was more about spreading awareness, rather than making use of it.

CIVIC's aim was clearly to promote a decentralized agenda for governance, such that local problems could be solved locally. They were demonstrating that all grievance redressal channels could converge at the ward level, as prescribed by the 74th amendment. They aimed to institutionalize certain public components – platforms of grievance redressal and participation, putting up citizens' charters at government service points, and demanding that each officer should have a job charter – made CIVIC's external strategies characteristically public. Government orders prescribed holding of grievance redressal platform in some departments (for example, health and education) once a month. CIVIC facilitated the first meeting to show how it could be done. Concretely, this meant they had the funds to pay for the logistics of the events they organized: in the case of grievance redressal meetings, they rented a hall, arranged for transportation of the slum community, and also for the food and other logistics of the event.

At times they consciously invited the media to report on their events and sometimes even regretted when a grievance redressal meeting that had been an eye-opener did not get the public attention it deserved. They used English newspapers to disseminate the lessons learnt.

Since the introduction of the RTI Act (2005), the mode of functioning of CIVIC had drastically changed. While previously they were 'only' facilitating city-wide discussions, brain-storming, and training sessions mainly with the middle class, they had recently taken to a more activist style of direct interaction with the state departments. The actions taken ranged from filing an RTI suit, submitting minutes of a grievance redress meeting, and filing a complaint with the human rights officer. Interactions with government agencies were conducted with the aim of bridging the gaps between what was foreseen in the guidelines and on-the-ground realities. RTI was an important tool in this endeavour. Having the tactic of RTI at the centre of their repertoire served multiple purposes according to CIVIC: 'RTI is god, that's all.' Different dimensions of these purposes can be outlined. It served as a research tool to know what the government was 'supposed to do' by digging into government orders (published only internally in gazettes) and job charts (non-existent for most cases). Second, once such information was in hand, CIVIC pursued a course of action and could hold the government accountable. Using the same logic CIVIC persisted in following up with the government through RTI. Third, RTI allowed them also to have an insight into the contractual relationships of the government with contractors and other elite society organizations that carried out particular social exercises (surveys and so on). Filing RTI suits to meet all these ends amounted to each coordinator of CIVIC having to manage about 60 to 70 RTI suits. Each suit consisted of a request for one particular information, upon which generally a follow-up suit had to be launched, for which CIVIC members have coined the phrase 'RTI gives birth to the next baby' (translated from Kannada). With such extensive use of RTI, CIVIC had been accused of harassing through the means of RTI. CIVIC argued that RTI was the only safe weapon to protect from repression when formulated sensibly in an anonymous manner questioning the system and not an individual. Filing RTI suits was thought to be the most efficient way to deal with the government so as to force open participation, transparency, and accountability and to scale up such efforts to the state level in future.

CIVIC made a clear distinction between a political and a non-political agenda; they claimed that the 'political agenda is out of CIVIC' – a claim that was not unambiguous. Despite this claim, during the last election along with other elite society organizations they engaged in an action called 'meet the candidate'. The goal of such a platform was to introduce the candidates standing for election to the ward inhabitants. The candidates responded differently; while some came and spoke, others felt no such need as they would have been operating on their own terms. CIVIC also urged the candidates to commit that they would put all transactions made in a public domain. CIVIC deplored that not a single candidate committed and questioned their true interest in the elections. This was the main effort in which CIVIC was engaged in to counter clientelism in the poorer communities. They reflected that indeed actions were needed to bring awareness.

Taking the democratic polity and policy literally

The experiences of CIVIC that constituted their discursive repertoire related to different actors in the scene and to different societal forces. They observed that there were so many symptoms appearing from a dysfunctional system and they were conscious how people could get conditioned through them. Such conditioning had led to the fact that they esteemed that ethics were all convenience-based and that a social ethic was completely missing. Within such a context, it was all the more difficult to play a whistle-blowing role. They perceived a clear demarcation of activist elite society organizations and those who were not. In Bangalore, this segmentation among elite society organizations was strongly felt. CIVIC deplored that, in general, others spoke about a 'right-based' approach, but in reality they actually did not practise it, since they did not know how to demand their rights and not bother to pay a bribe for convenience. In their experience a 'pure rights' approach, taking it literally, could actually hurt. CIVIC tried to stick to their understanding of such an approach. Claiming rights in the socio-political context of Bangalore became a balancing act, as they observed that in fact 'everything is in policy. If all things are implemented according to the policy why would India be like this?'

Taking the formally written words of the Constitution literally, CIVIC observed that though the Constitution stated that people were the masters, 'we have become the servants'. To enable a more proactive citizenry, CIVIC believed that it was crucial that collective action had to enter public consciousness. Despite the fact that CIVIC invested immense resources to create an environment conducive to a larger role of the citizen (platforms, citizen charters, and so on), they deplored the 'pathetic' ways of Bangalore's citizens and the tendency to not challenge the status quo and tolerate wrongdoing. Given the socio-political context and the 'apathetic' nature of Bangalore's citizens, members of CIVIC asked themselves: 'Where was the institution to groom second generation politicians?' In their view, a political process that would support a vision of democratic accountability and welfare would be in grooming and finding alternative candidates. Independents had to be standing up as an alternative to the common political parties. Committing publicly to accountability could trigger politicians choosing to deliver good work in order to get elected instead of making money to reinvest in the next election. The upcoming middle-class party called Loksatta was not validated as a real option as in their view it did not really seem to understand governance processes. They concluded that an elected representative ought to be like the 'area CEO', thus a professional or at least a very good manager with high grasping capacities. Within the bureaucratic realm, they thought that a public grievance platform would give the citizen a voice to claim benefits from the welfare state. The nature of state and systems of governmentality were not questioned. Their vision fitted the formal framework given by the current Constitution. Interestingly, even though CIVIC's action repertoire was rather moderate in working from within the system with given formal tools, one key organizational member believed that 'there has to be a revolution inside the party, inside the polity. There has to be a second generation of politicians who are capable of understanding development in its totality'. CIVIC did confer legitimacy to a movement mode, reminding that even though they were a closed trust, they were mobilized within a vast network of elite society organizations and about 400 RWAs.

Housing process in decades

AVAS (Association for Voluntary Action and Service) was registered as a trust in Bangalore in 1980. It defined itself as a service organization. In Bangalore, AVAS was known to be the only elite society organization with long and substantial experience in housing for the urban poor. When I encountered AVAS, they were working in various slum communities, most of them having had a relationship with AVAS almost since its inception. Housing for the urban poor was still a priority area for the organization but they were also in the process of diversifying, restructuring, and formalizing other domains (youth, education, health) in which they were active. In contrast to CIVIC, AVAS had many years of experience in housing processes and invested considerable effort in building up the community.

AVAS started with the visionary zeal of the organization's founder, who came from a privileged family and always wanted to do social work as a way of life. Fighting forceful evictions and demolitions that were underway at that time in Bangalore was on the activism agenda. AVAS emerged from that experience. With initial donor funding, AVAS recruited many committed members who were still working with AVAS even after 30 years. In 2010, AVAS started a process of diversification with the goal of making the various domains independent. The idea was to make the main AVAS coordinators take ownership of the sub-organizations, with AVAS thus becoming the umbrella organization. The domain of housing was supposed to be renamed as HERO: 'Housing Empowerment Resource Organization'.

Given the strong focus on communities, the core strategy of AVAS had evolved through lessons from the field incorporating holistic approaches and had remained principled, such as not giving or accepting bribes and remaining transparent about the organizational proceedings and accounts. They not only disseminated awareness about housing but also made it a point to inform the community about good practices and attitudes. This meant that their activities in housing also had the aim of spreading awareness on health, confidence-building, collective saving, accounting skills, and information on government programmes and schemes. It also included administrative skills to get things done, face officers, and to confront bribing expectation. A major shift in strategy was the restructuring of the organization towards new focus areas of intervention. On the whole, having gained experiences from the field in diverse communities, AVAS assessed that they had created enough different types of models to impact policy. This was also a reason why the founder agreed to become a member of the ABIDe committee.

Episode: About community and its leaders

In a community living near a lake in southern Bangalore, land issues were not so smooth. The community was settled on municipal land, but had not got it declared, as it was a low-lying land very prone to flooding and could not be rehabilitated in situ. Thus, the municipality had to allot an alternative land. The community insisted on demanding a site nearby. To do so that allotted land had to be handed over to the KSDB, which was responsible for declaration and rehabilitation of slum-dwellers on the basis of a government order. Furthermore, dynamics within the community were not straightforward. After a long struggle to assert the land, development was not happening. Each time the government sent for some work to be done, the leaders along with their political connections diverted the funds such that the work never got completed. AVAS experienced the limits of capacity building within this community, learning that if people were not able to oppose their own leaders not much room was left for positive development. This even after spreading awareness on how power networks worked in detriment to their quest. Nevertheless, AVAS still highlighted knowing some well-intentioned slum-leaders who got work done on behalf of the community and who were taking money from the community in order to bear the loss in their income for the cause. Through the precursor government scheme to the BSUP called VAMBAY, construction was carried out on one part of the land. The soil on that land was very loose and guzzled up more money than planned, resulting in a dearth of funds. When AVAS stepped in to participate in the community's efforts to claim the necessary services such as water, sanitation, and electricity, the leaders would interfere. They wanted to collect money from each family, so the service would come through them. The threat of not getting a house at all silenced the people. AVAS topped the scheme's money with its own funds to complete the project, but it still could not be completed. The construction site was turned into a new concrete 'slum', which was incomplete and without urban services. On the second part of the land, four-storeyed buildings were supposed to be constructed. For 17 years the community resisted it, wanting only a ground-floor housing (where increments according to family growth could be added). They even declined land offered in other places, where ground-floor housing would have been possible. AVAS went up to Delhi for their cause. At first KSDB did not succumb and fenced off the site for the four-storeyed block, leaving space for commercial purposes in a public–private partnership (PPP) logic. The community protested and AVAS paid for the transport to hold a protest in front of KSDB. Upon knowing that funds were available through BSUP JNNURM, AVAS along with the elected MLA got the scheme into this locality. By the time BSUP started in this second part, the community had learned to monitor the work and contacted AVAS for their need to claim services in a systematic manner and without bribing (as the community organizer confirmed). However, in the first part of the land, even with additional funds from BSUP for completion, no tendered contractor was willing to risk a loss, as building material got regularly stolen from the site.

Figure 4.2   AVAS Episode 'About community and its leaders', upcoming ground-floor + 1 houses.

Source: Author.

This episode of contention depicts the difficult constellation within the community which leads to an incomplete housing and unsatisfactory outcome. This episode contextualized in the BSUP implementation starkly contrasts the award-winning housing outcomes they were involved with in previous efforts.

The particularity of this episode is that the community is 'policy affected' at the outset of the BSUP implementation. Based on previous interventions in slum communities, AVAS held that a land issue had the potential to unite people. In this episode, however, it was visible that housing silenced and possibly disrupted the community immersed in a web of divergent interests. Brokering, AVAS had to skilfully manage the diverse interests of actors that were part of a political-economic nexus that was picked up through the PPP-modelled governance framework. Despite AVAS's efforts of stretching this episode for 20 years by topping up financial resources through private means whenever necessary, this episode shows how heavy the very local context bears upon the housing outcome.

Members of AVAS narrated this episode with some bitterness, as it contrasted heavily with other interventions that had far more positive outcomes. They made me visit a neighbourhood that was constructed with brick and mortar and now integrated into the city's fabric. It was named 'people's power'. Here too their commitment stretched over two decades. AVAS spent great effort in creating substantial financial resources within the community itself by initiating saving schemes to enable their housing and to maintain it. Demonstration as a rationale was not only towards the government in housing implementation, but also towards society's view of the urban poor in challenging the commonly held belief that they were not reliable and not bankable. AVAS was able to convince a bank to lend the credit directly to the members of the community instead of routing through a 'respectable NGO' and indeed the members had paid back in time. The capacity built in the community also paid off in resisting donor imposition.

On a skill level, they started with building self-confidence, not to perceive themselves as inferior and knowing how to speak up. AVAS's understanding of the lacuna in their capacities was due to the lack of education, so they claimed that in holding meetings after meetings, 'whatever they learn from our meetings is what they have. As we know more things we are able to talk much more'. On the economic front, the communities were taught how to effectively save towards owning a home. Such an exercise included awareness on gender relations, drug misuse, building leadership in the community to hold it together, and managing the money collectively. They also included accounting and file-management skills that had to be identified within the community to serve collectively. The process led them to form a community-based organization (CBO), which was registered and had a bank account opened. Creating awareness on the political front was an ongoing process, sensitizing the community not only about their collective strength but also about the political context, to which slum-dwellers were prey to election logics of the politicians.

Through their 30-year-long commitment in urban poor communities and having been critical to housing outcomes, members of AVAS found it legitimate to have received the recognition of 'expert' on the matter of the urban poor and to be able to speak on behalf of them in the non-constitutional body ABIDe that the then chief minister called into being. So, the perception of co-optation did not occur to them at all and they were actually regretful that the body was not functional during that time. The founder wanted to use the ABIDe platform to build strategic alliances to diffuse lessons learned through AVAS and impact policy. AVAS did not budge and patiently followed democratic procedures, not expecting any favours from the government – at times taking in brokering positions and at times presenting themselves as challengers.

Patiently dealing with an unresponsive state

The striking feature in the narratives about the political opportunities among AVAS members was the temporal changes they observed. They recall that the kind of social work done 25 years back and the manner of social development in 2010 were totally different. In their opinion, even though institutional legal opportunities to engage with the state had scaled up through the RTI Act and the ratification of the 74th amendment and the sort, like CIVIC, they questioned the extent to which the poor could actually make use of them. At the policy level, they acknowledged the existence of specific policies designed for the urban poor and particular provisions for participation by the beneficiaries (as in the JNNURM BSUP). The reality, though, was that accessing these provisions was hardly possible or they were not implemented at all. For example, to avail the CBO programme, the implementing agency would ask for an audit report of the CBO. 'Which slum-dweller CBO will have audit reports?' – one coordinator asked. Holistic community approaches within the housing scheme of the JNNURM BSUP were not included and the minimal standards of 'participation' were void due to the lack of implementation by the concerned officers. One coordinator rightfully questioned: What was the use of the government holding hygiene awareness programmes when sewage and water connections were not given to the completed houses? So, such exercises were just about the tick marking of the guidelines to avail more funds from the Centre in the case of BSUP projects. On the other hand, they stated that they were not able to voice like before, as there were hardly any places to protest in the city and, second, because permissions to hold protest were difficult to obtain. Institutional openings for participation had become available but were designed in an ambiguous way. Hence, in their perception, political opportunities were becoming increasingly closed and access was highly dependent on what strategic alliances could be formed with key government actors and how one was able to persevere.

Members of AVAS clearly distinguished between officers of the bureaucracy and elected representatives. In their view, the latter ones were 'used' by the AVAS coordinators only if there was an absolute need for it. Otherwise they were happy to continue their work with the communities without them, as the elected representatives would serve the interests of the middle and upper classes who could anyway buy the services they needed. They recalled that often the elected representatives needed to be reminded of their duties and responsibilities. The bureaucrats and the executive branch of the government, namely the commissioner, was very important. Through him all the lower officers could be held accountable once cooperation was assured from the commissioner. Engaging in housing projects in the community, AVAS could foresee the amount of 'horatta' (running around) they would have to do depending on which government agency the land belonged to. During a period with good alliances to the Bengaluru Development Authority (BDA), fairly less of 'running around' would occur, as they were perceived to be systematic. The communities held in great esteem the fact that AVAS held accounts and meticulously organized the files to be submitted to the agency.

Narratives on logics of representations were manifold when talking to AVAS members: First, seeing themselves as representatives (ABIDe). Second, questioning the means of political representation through elections. Third, informal representation within communities. The formal way of political representation would be to elect someone. But illegitimate means of vote buying and giving away undue favours deployed by the politicians turned the political context into roping loops of dependency. Though the councillors did not perform their duties, they ensured their stranglehold over the communities, claiming that they were their representatives, and disliked it when elite society organizations like AVAS collaborated with those communities, even when the work done was useful. Other actors competing over 'representation' of slum communities were their own leaders with political connections and other elite society organizations who worked in slums and were by recent policies called upon to represent the poor.

In the perception of AVAS, corruption had increased enormously. They claimed to always have incorporated fighting corruption in their action repertoire. The means to do so were numerous. First, they engaged in networks that fought corruption and they claimed never to have succumbed to bribing incentives. Once their case was attended to the bureaucracy they would insist and persevere until the job was done. This took 10 times longer, but through such an approach they claimed to have built their reputation. In consequence, the bureaucrats would not even attempt to ask AVAS staff for a bribe. On the other hand, they did know that when people went on their own the same bureaucrats would ask the community members for a bribe. The slum-dwellers finally would end up paying, as they could not leave their livelihoods repeatedly. AVAS observed that there were many actors to corruption. First and foremost, it was the bureaucrats.

Corrupt slum-leaders that did not contribute to the unity of the community perpetuated corrupt practices within the community. So, when there was no unity in the community and when they were clashing among themselves, then exploitative leadership had more scope. If one took the leaders on, then along with the political backing the mafia would come along as well. They said that as long as people did not oppose such leaders by coming together, there was not much an elite society organization could do, as learned from the same episode cited here. AVAS also narrated the case of one community where the leader was good and genuinely did the follow up with the land issue. AVAS acknowledged in this case that it was not possible for a male leader to run around for the issues of the slum without providing the family with some sort of income and thus justified the fact that he did take some money from the community.

Another set of actors they quoted were other elite society organizations in the role of the implementing agencies of some government scheme. They cited instances when they had won the public tender and the elite society organizations would ask for commissions from the contractor. Within such a constellation there was competition to get a cut from the contractor's 'public resources' between the implementing elite society organization, the local area representatives (councillor, MLA), and the slum-leaders as well. All this would result in very poor quality of work or even having to stop the construction due to a dearth of funds. Regarding proof-gathering, one coordinator said, when a caste certificate was needed and a dweller succeeded in getting a false one, they would go back to the community and make them aware of the importance of not lying, but of mutual trust.

The third group of actors were the landlords who resorted to threatening informal repression often having the backing of the police. For private landowners, land was always at the heart of their interaction with the slum-dwellers. They would have bought it some time back as an asset and not cared for it, until they realized that their land, on which dwellers had squatted, was supposed to get declared. As the KSDB was not able to pay compensation at market price (personal communication, KSDB legal advisor, December 2012), the landowners had three choices for action. Either they took it to court. This would take many years and the probability of losing or getting an alternate land allocated was rather high (ibid.), or they would let go in exchange of a meagre compensation, or they resorted to violence against the squatters to vacate the land. The investment they made to hire goons in view of the worth of the land was negligible. So, slum-dwellers squatting on private but available land were very vulnerable to violence. The threats were as extreme as 'the landlord said, we will throw acid on you, cut your limbs, set fire on the huts'. The only instance where the police instructed by the commissioner was on the side of the slum-dwellers was when they had cleared all the right documentation and the landlord was still harassing them.

Members of AVAS all said that the overall social situation and politics was fully polluted, that votes were being sold for saris, *biryani*, money, and jewellery. They made efforts to spread awareness about the weight of their vote. They said that it was not necessary to resist the goodies, but that they had to vote for the best candidate regardless of the goodies and then stand their ground on demanding work getting done using their bargaining power. But politicians were smart about luring them, so during election time AVAS held many community meetings.

The salient narrative by AVAS regarding housing was about scarcity: of available urban land and about scarcity of public housing for the urban poor. Land was the most crucial issue and determined the duration of the whole housing process, which was highly dependent on the cooperation of the government. They deplored that the government did not seem to understand the complexity of the issues of the poor and went ahead with unsuitable approaches such as rehabilitating them far away or displacing them before providing adequate services such as water, electricity, and transport.

AVAS's members had a very detailed understanding of the issue of land. At the heart of the issue of asserting land for the urban poor was the intense fight over it by a diverse set of actors. Land, as argued in the previous section, represented a gold-mine, whether it is at the centre of the city or at the developing periphery. The fact that there were numerous actors involved in the competition made the targets shift for the claimants. Even when the counterpart was the government, it did not necessarily mean that there was a clear, singular target. Urban land belonging to the government meant that there was a high degree of fragmentation in the ownership between the numerous government agencies, as presented in the episode 'About community and its leaders' where the land was transferred from the municipality BBMP to the parastatal KSDB. Such a shift in target implied that community members and brokers such as AVAS had to renegotiate their relationships with new allies.

When dwellers wanted to secure the land they squatted on and the land belonged to a private owner, the conflict could get nasty, as the owners were presented with the prospect of losing property, that is, a financial asset. In such a case, market mechanisms and the primacy of money played an important role. The legal officer at KSDB (personal communication, 2010) assured me that when private land owners put a case into court against the squatters, as it is a matter of shelter for the poor and 'only' a matter of investment for the owner, generally the case was ruled in favour of the squatters, while the owners were paid a compensation. But as the land prices in Bangalore had rocketed sky-high, KSDB had the capacity to pay only a compensation way below the market price. Furthermore, court cases could go on for years. Such reasons pushed the land owners to bypass formal institutions and take it in their own hand, resorting to bribing the police and to informal repression against the squatters.

Another less tangible target that emerges in AVAS's narrative is the globalized corporate entity in the forms of malls that occupy space in the centre as well as in the periphery. In the case of Bangalore, IT corporate firms populate important corridors. The head of the organization stated that in such a context development work on behalf of the poor had become very difficult, as such targets were intangible and the process of land allocation highly opaque.

In their view the urban poor were in a dilemma, as a scheme like the BSUP JNNURM would only happen, if at all, once in a lifetime. So, either they grabbed the opportunity that their community got and be content with the way delivery had taken place or they demanded to get it in a sustainable way with amenities and participation. The second choice, though, would put them in a challenger position, which would make relations difficult with government officials. The episode 'About community and its leaders' also depicts that there is a limit to claiming as well, especially when state authorities do it as a Centrally prescribed exercise. While AVAS along with the community did achieve to get BSUP into their slum, claims to the right type of house, which included balconies and proper door and window frames, were beyond the intended provisions. The beneficiaries did invest a considerable amount of their own money to refurbish it on their own terms. Opting for the second choice to get housing on their own terms, the episodes depicted that the community had to have the capacity for intense involvement, even to bear violence.

All in all, AVAS's narratives paint a picture of the government lacking responsiveness. Dearth of budget could be the final excuse to stop a housing project, without considering that the urban poor would have cleared the land for in situ housing, for example, and would have to bear prolonged undignified living waiting for their houses to be constructed. In many instances, they had to pick up the shovel themselves and take forward the work. In their experience, land was the crux of the issue for speedy housing implementation and responsive cooperation from government agencies. When there was no litigation and government land had been allotted, then further procedures were predictable. When land issues were not resolved, the responsiveness of the government to the plight of the poor could be lacking or could go against them, tying up with private parties.

The relationship of the government to the slum-dweller was not only seen in the capacity to deliver services but also in highlighting and encouraging the dwellers to pay their taxes. This would allow them to be able to declare that they were corporation taxpayers and thus to claim the services they were due to get. Paying their tax was the final milestone in the pursuit of the evidence by the urban poor to demonstrate citizenship, legitimizing in some way land allocation by the government. The same speaker talked about the misunderstood concept of citizenship, which often boiled down to communalism that was in general decreasing in cosmopolitan Bangalore, but which got ignited at times of social unrest given the water issues, reservation in education, or even Hindu–Muslim riots.

Across all interviews with members of AVAS, there was hardly any mention of caste whatsoever. They referred to the communities as the poor, the urban poor, or the slum communities. There was also no narrative on the origins of the lack of resources of those communities.

Tailor-made tactics

AVAS's action repertoire was rather diverse and tailor-made to the communities' quest. The organization being active in housing since the 1980s, its action repertoire had evolved according to the housing approaches of the government over the years. Their strategy had always been to engage with the community as well as the government and to convince both parties towards the best solution for the poor given the constraints of a fast-growing city. On the one hand, convincing the community involved visiting them very frequently and making them aware of various issues and their inter-connectedness while, on the other hand, convincing the government agents involved the deployment of their considerable resources and presenting them with facts that were derived from self-conducted household surveys. The tactics they employed ranged from organizing rallies, protest, sit-ins, writing letters, and interacting with all levels of officers to filing court cases, launching RTI suits, and facilitating meetings with officials. They did not have one central tool, which was at the centre of their strategy (like RTI for CIVIC). But one can say that previously their action repertoire was more radical (especially in the 1980s, when housing approaches for the urban poor mainly consisted of evictions and demolitions) and that it had become more about persevering with the officials about the claim of the community in recent times. The key members of AVAS claimed that even though resisting bribing and corruption had always been incorporated in their strategy, recently they had to witness high expectations of bribes. Therefore, they admitted that procedures took 'ten times longer'. But as they had built up their reputation that they would not pay a bribe, the files concerning the communities they worked with would be processed. Such an approach demanded a lot of patience and perseverance.

AVAS's key organizational members narrated that they used formal channels like anyone else to interact with government officers and that every time they took along the slum-dwellers. In this way, the slum-dwellers got an exposure to the ways of dealing with the state in an official way. Going along with a recognized elite society organization such as AVAS also gave the slum-dwellers some leverage on account of the respect they got, rather than going alone. An AVAS member narrated, 'With us, in these offices they are asked to take a seat. If they go on their own they are not even offered a seat.' In regard to formality it was rather them who demanded formality in the dealings of the governments, especially when allotment was at stake. They narrated an instance where only after getting an official allotment letter that the slum-dwellers cleared the land for an in situ housing project to start.

Over the course of all these years, AVAS had taken recourse to legal instruments. In the 1980s, along with women's movements, they went up to the Supreme Court to get a stay order on demolitions, based on which they spread awareness among the dwellers on how to fight demolitions with the authority of the supreme instance of India's judiciary. In their experience, taking the poor along to the court got them different responses from the judges; while some acknowledged their plea in the presence of the poor, others complained why an NGO capable of presenting their case brought the poor along, causing them to lose a day's wage. The availability of RTI encouraged their strategy of not succumbing to bribe expectations. In recent years, they made use of the possibility of getting information through RTI and they also gave awareness to the poor about it.

Contentious activities of AVAS started even before the organization was formalized in the form as it was known at the time of fieldwork, especially through the organization of the rally that roped in some communities. That rally was remembered with great pride, especially in view of such rallies being hardly possible in recent times due to administrative hurdles and lack of space. One member recalled that in an instance when the permission was actually given to hold a much smaller rally, the judge had sent the police to deliver a warning that such an attempt should not occur again. Where earlier they could organize city-wise protests, today mobilizations limited themselves to getting together communities slum-wise.

Holding public consultations and one-day workshops, along with creating committees on issues affecting the poor, were also part of the activities of AVAS for which they involved officers as well. The use of media was not mentioned much in their narrations; they did not actively seek media attention except for opening ceremonies of layouts they had been involved in. As they invited political heavyweights, media got drawn into it automatically, giving them good visibility and attention.

AVAS spread awareness about the political process and tried to convince the communities to start a CBO at the slum level and explained the benefits of having united visibility (through letterheads, for example), cultivating unity and a collective identity. In some cases, AVAS had facilitated the candidature of slum-leaders, who reflected: 'why take money from someone, why not stand in elections', and they had won as independent candidates.

Navigating imperatives of community and networks by learning policy on behalf of the urban poor

'Everything is in policy, if all things are implemented according to the policy, why would India be like this?' – members of CIVIC stated. This statement by CIVIC is analogous to the research question at the heart of this book – theoretically, 'everything is present to give rise to a social movement on the cause of housing, but then why isn't there one?' Taking CIVIC and AVAS, the only two elite society organizations engaged in housing, under scrutiny revealed what could be the impeding factors for a social movement emergence.

In this section, I aim to discuss some emergent and important insights from these two cases that illuminate the conditions for mobilizing.

Both organizations had mobilized *on behalf* of the urban poor and acted as brokers between the implementing agencies and the community as prescribed by the BSUP policy to translate the policy requirement and to help the community come together. CIVIC and AVAS had a different experience base to take this role of policy brokers. AVAS had a long-standing experience in working with the urban poor; CIVIC was a novice to working with them. However, CIVIC had long experience in urban governance and stayed loyal to their core strength of tracking and claiming accountability from the government. They did this through their prime weapon – the RTI – this tactical choice did not allow the community in which they were working to own up the claim-making in the context of the government's 'supposed to do' rationale with its own tools and within the project management cycle.

In contrast, AVAS had detailed knowledge of the housing process within impoverished communities of Bangalore and also had faith in them. This buildup of mutual faith had resulted in long-standing commitment until the entire completion of the housing project, including the bureaucratic procedures, which in one community lasted 18 years. The long duration was especially striking where the tenure of land was a concern. At the same time, this very long alliance with some communities proved AVAS's difficulty of letting go of them – a fact that lets me question the extent of the social skill resources infused in the community. In my visit to one of the communities with a successful housing outcome, I could witness that even though community members were well versed with formal procedures and had done their due in facing the government agencies, it was still the AVAS coordinator compiling and keeping the books to submit the final application for the land. AVAS had hence imparted the importance of certain skills for collective well-being but it seemed they were still the ones who were executing those most of the time.

So, what does mobilizing 'on behalf of' within a context of policy really mean? From the experience of these two elite society organizations, it means to veer around loopholes in democratic practice and manoeuvre between the policy prescriptions and actual practices on the ground. It also means to be ahead of the economics of representational politics, mechanisms of corruption, and gauge shifting targets to address their claims.

The BSUP policy is an example of how the inclusion of the urban poor in Bangalore's housing landscape became compromised into a rhetorical promise. On the other hand, its loopholes and the lack of monitoring and accountability enabled the officials to work the funds into their pockets and further make use of clientelistic practices. The scheme allowed space for voices to be expressed from the bottom-up through a given format, precisely by agents such as CIVIC and AVAS. Participatory planning was not understood and facilitated by the government, nor had the government prepared the community for the engagement. Both organizations could assist with this process only in a limited manner. Hence the interests of the community was only being articulated in an reactive mode to policy processes on the ground that were at times driven by agendas stemming from the Centre, area MLAs, or community leaders. The interest representation of the policy-impacted community over the longer term through electoral politics also had grim perspectives, as the electoral mechanism reified itself to use money as the means to a political end.

An electoral candidate standing for election not only had to spend money on the campaign and to hire crowds to rally, but also to maintain performative and socio-political networks that infused everyday life beyond election day. Election season is hence constitutive of enduring networks of trust and sociability (Björkman 2014a). Such exclusive constitutive relationships sow strong vertical patron–client linkages that incorporate exclusion mechanisms and inhibit horizontal weak ties, instrumental for mobilization efforts (Miaz and Requejo 2004, 9; Klandersmans and Oegama 1987). Buying votes from the reserve army of unregistered voters in slum communities, as the CIVIC experience revealed, become crucial in an election. A web of actors seem to be deployed and maintained to keep the communities in a status that would make them run to the representatives for betterment of some services. The representatives, it seems, however, would never completely deliver, so that the community would have to keep running to them for betterment. Hence urban service delivery and routine endowments of entitlements get intertwined with electoral logic and patron–client networks. There is thus a void in representing and promoting the 'real' interest of the urban poor. With the void comes also space for manipulation. The relationship between the electoral candidate, slum-leaders, and elite society organizations could be very conflictual, as such organizations cut across the clients to which they were catering to. Such economic rationale of electoral politics could potentially lead to fragmenting the poor into the networks of different actors, undermining the collective unity needed for mobilization.

These entrenched networks also cut across prescriptions of good governance, widely proclaimed by consultants, civil society groups, and international organizations such as the World Bank. The general assumption to such prescriptions is that actors of governance are benevolent and operate in a space devoid of power relations. The mismatch between such prescriptions and the actual practices on the ground reflect that there is not even sufficient understanding of the poor by the state and hardly any political will, nor possibility to comply with formal prescriptions on all fronts because of entrenched practices that embody a fertile ground for incentives for corruption, especially when big and expensive infrastructure projects are underway.

From the two cases and the wider insights from the general and housing political opportunities, six mechanisms of corruption emerged: First, corrupt forms of bribe collection fund informal repression against whistle-blowers or unwanted interruptions by being able to hire goons. Second, when implementing officials and members of the community (informal proof-gathering) are both corrupt, then none of them will blow the whistle, as both parties will have to risk the threat of being exposed. Third, informal repression not only was to be found against the population, but was also a mechanism internal to the system itself through an erratic system of transfers of (well-meaning) officials. Fourth, corrupt practices were as subtle as withholding information, publishing in English, and not displaying departmental services and name-tags of officials. Fifth, corruption led to anonymization of the agents involved in the corrupt process and also to the anonymization of whistle-blowing efforts. Sixth, informal institutions such as corruption led to an amplification of the degree of moderateness/radicalness of the action repertoire. In the case of CIVIC, it was tendentially to become more moderate and less offensive. In sum, these mechanisms contribute to making formal conditions more unfavourable for claim-making.

In regard to the action repertoire, both organizations stated that they attempted to build models of interventions that could be scaled up and disseminated through their own elite society networks, as in the case of CIVIC, or through governmental efforts, as in the case of AVAS (as a member of ABIDe). But the very local nature of engagement in one locality stemmed from the multitude of possible targets (and shifts) in that particular milieu, which deployed their own actors, cultures, and logics. In consequence, this meant indeed that models of deploying tactics of action repertoire could hardly be diffused. It rather asked for a very flexible handling of the community, targets, and repertoire.

One important feature of AVAS's action repertoire was their aim to enrol community members into formal procedures as a way to engage with the government and also to claim substantial citizenship proactively (for example, paying tax, registering CBOs, and opening bank accounts). Such performances cut through the logics of governmentality, where slum-dwellers were kept as 'merely' recipients of benefits. In such a logic they could hardly assert a 'right to benefits', as these were scarce and functioned as political currency. In fulfilling to some extent their duties as citizens, they gained more leverage to claim substantial citizenship rights, even though they were articulated through similar welfare mechanisms of governmentality. Hence, the discourse of citizenship had a basis of reciprocity rather than the discourse of benefits. This way the poor also gained more credibility to demonstrate their worthiness of being bankable, which would further cut through informal circuits of exploitative loan sharks.

One crucial bone of contention was the issue of land tenure and the shifting targets to assert the land. In the experience of AVAS, the specificity of the target for claim-making had scaled up and become hardly identifiable. Global corporate entities asserted land either in the centre or at the periphery of the city (Goldman 2011). The poor stood a meagre chance to assert the tenure of land against such mighty entities towards which the state was most favourable in loyalty of a neoliberal development paradigm. In their view, this new dimension of global financial circuits intersecting with the local land market had added one more competitor and decreased the access to land for the urban poor. Other competitors were wealthy private land owners (including government staff) and government agencies, resulting in fragmentation of the authority over land and thus making the targets shift for claim-making for the urban poor.

To veer around the conditions that influenced the economic rationale of electoral politics, informal repression, corruption mechanisms, shifting targets, and mismatches between policy and on-the-ground practices, a detailed knowledge of society–state dynamics and the housing process was needed – a learning that evolved over time from a particular vantage point. Both organizations sourced their discursive repertoire to justify their action repertoire from universal identities such as citizenship for CIVIC and human service for AVAS. In their narratives, never did they mention caste; they acknowledged the existence of this stratification system, but saw it as a mistake of the past that one had to deal with. But never did their action repertoire address caste issues. In CIVIC's case, the community was seen as a beneficiary of a policy that was not implemented according to the guidelines. AVAS viewed their work as human service neutral of caste ascriptions and the larger mechanisms at work that put such communities in poverty-struck situations in the first place. The socio-historical backgrounds of the main trustees and founders of both organizations influenced the epistemic foundations of their work, which I argue also influences their learning. McFarlane (2011) argues that leaning is always a process of translation and highlights the importance of intermediaries in the production of knowledge of which intermediaries are constitutive, because it also depends on the way knowledge is reconstructed and coordinated by those translating. In this sense, CIVIC and AVAS have translated their understanding of policy from a vantage point different from the experience of a low-caste community living in the city. This is a remarkable difference from the possibility of translating knowledge by political society organizations, as I will depict in the next chapter. However, as I will argue in the final chapter, this difference in learning and its resulting pedagogy of the urban has the potential to draw upon the complementary strengths of elite and political society organizations to engage constructively with the state and contribute to innovation in the much-needed domain of political organization in the quest for adequate housing in the Global South, as Monkkonen (2018) argues.

Mobilizations by the urban poor

It was a hot day. I was standing at the edge of a deep ditch and gazing at the other side where these matchbox houses – the way it was called – rose from the steep slope. I was at the south-western periphery of the city and seeing the largest instantiation of housing under the Basic Services for the Urban Poor (BSUP). Mahesh was right, BSUP was just about reproducing the same old patterns of keeping the urban poor and the Dalits out of the city, beyond the deep ditch.

Mahesh was one of the leading young activists of the political society organization named Slum Janara Kriya Vedike (SJKV), which means slum people's association. Their activities mainly focused on capacitating the communities to claim land or to formalize land-tenure for their communities. In general, to improve habitat conditions for urban poor communities. The activities ranged from using moderate formal and polite means of interaction with state agencies to radical contentious tactics such as protests and roadblocking. The slum locality in which the SJKV was active in mobilizing and the BSUP constructions were underway was on the city's side of the ditch. This BSUP intervention was the only one to be just a ground-floor housing. Even though densifying low-income settlements was the rationale, the targeted community with the assistance of the SJKV had managed to claim ground-floor housing. Such social housing is known to be beneficial for low-income households, as incremental building becomes possible as the family expands.

In contrast, in one of the denser areas in southern Bangalore, one of the largest BSUP housing projects was coming up in situ with 1,500 dwelling units in a ground plus four storeyed structure. In this locality, several civil society organizations were active; among them was the Dalit Panthers of India (DPI). DPI is an all-India organization that was born in the state of Maharashtra in 1972. It was started by Dalit writers countering the crimes against Dalits and stood for total emancipation and political domination (Shakit 1993, 630). It borrowed its name from the Black Panther Party – a movement that was started in the 1960s by African-Americans in the United States. Within India, there were organizations in several states that were active under the banner of DPI. The group I had the opportunity to interview had consciously come to work under the name of DPI. This group earlier was called KJS – Karnataka Janara Sangha (Karnataka's people association). They chose to join DPI as they felt that there was a need for a source of overarching unity, which they found in the strong leadership of DPI. They referred to the leader of Tamil Nadu, whom they revered as a good and simple person, even though he had become a member of parliament (MP) as a Dalit.

These were the two organizations that would give me insights into the conditions for mobilizing for political society organizations that mobilized *for their own realization of adequate housing.*

In regard to the research design, given the low amounts of resources SJKV and DPI possessed, it was assumed that the formal political opportunities would hardly be accessible. They would thus employ an action repertoire of contentious tactics, based on a mediating discursive repertoire about denizens being in pursuit of citizenship. DPI was an organization that was visibly a co-opted one, as I established by talking to various actors and informants: Within the unclean dynamics in one particular slum which was supposed to be razed to make way for a shopping mall, the slum leaders were charging 500-rupee memberships to join DPI, whereas the membership fee was kept as low as 10 rupees.

Analogously to the previous chapter, I first give a short introduction to the organizations and present an episode of contention for each. The episode serves more as an illustration of the nature of interventions made by both organizations. The following discussion on the political opportunities and action and discursive repertoire are based on the entire corpus of data-gathering done during my fieldwork. I then conclude this chapter with emergent insights about conditions for mobilizing for political society organizations.

Promoting our 'own' development

The SJKV was a young organization. Informants, who said that they were an enthusiastic lot of young adults that would be ready to talk and share their experiences, directed me towards them. They were indeed happy to share their struggle and to narrate those incidents to me that had shaped them and their work. The SJKV typically worked in a movement-mode that mobilized slum-wise, while creating the capacity for overarching solidarity. At the time of my fieldwork, they were on the verge of becoming brokers in certain instances from a typically challenger organization. Discursive questioning about the causes for their situation, during their first struggle to get clean drinking water into their slum-locality, triggered the birth of the SJKV itself in making two reflective connections. First, 'Even the cattle doesn't drink such water, but we do. Are we humans?' Second, 'We are humans, we are able to work and talk like anyone else. But why do we live like animals? [...] We live like pigs, do pigs want caste?' They had experienced discrimination since childhood, especially in government schools, inflicted by higher caste people. Once they met a man at an event who was a social work professor from a higher caste himself but who was an activist. They got into a conversation. The leader of what was then to become the SJKV said that all were talking about development in the name of the poor, but nothing was changing. The activist replied, 'That is exactly our mistake, the fact that we always wait for someone else to come and promote our development.' Upon this revelation a group of youth decided to do something about the water and they gained their first activist experience. It was a lesson which taught them perseverance, fearlessness in the face of repression, and loyalty from the community, especially from the women in slum communities.

The initial members were just a group of friends from nearby localities. Through the publicity of their good work, the association had grown to 4,000 members by the time I met them. The association was organized in working committees, a convenor committee, and a slum leader committee. The lowest level consulted with the community. Whatever was decided there would be communicated to the committees above and implementation had to follow, whether it was to hold a protest or other action plans. Within these slum communities, when one community was struggling, others would come and support by being present for the protest, to make the noise required or just to bring and organize the food.

Three people worked full-time for the organization; they received a fellowship from the elite society organization Action Aid Karnataka. Those three fellowships amounted to 3,000, 4,000, and 5,000 rupees a month. Otherwise, people contributed for their own struggles. As a token of gratitude, the communities had contributed to the office in the form of furniture or their skills and time. The Karnataka Slum Development Board (KSDB) surprisingly offered them an office space near their homes in later years.

The SJKV had done an array of activities with the slum communities. They claimed that they had been able to effectively challenge the state up to the chief secretary, the chief minister, and the governor and had got slums declared and land rights assured. Upon effective work, they got publicity and at the time of the interview they were involved in 30 slum communities. Their main aim was to build awareness through regular meetings and groom strength from within the community in challenging their belief about their societal position, but also in imparting knowledge on how things were supposed to run according to the Constitution and policies. They highlighted that none of the slum communities were the same. Different political dynamics and leaders with different interests were found in each. As the active members of the SJKV were slum-dwellers themselves, they observed that they 'never feel that this is the other'. They lived and spoke the same way, so the organization equated to 'us'. The strategy of the SJKV was to have a network and friends in all slums they were working in and make the community understand that the SJKV was not there to solve their problems, but that they could do it together. They would not only interact with leaders but also go to the people directly, especially women and youth.

Episode: 'The value of our lives'

Through their work in a slum on securing drinking water, they got introduced to a community of load carriers living near the wholesale agricultural market. They were living 'like pigs' near a drain, where the water would rise during the rains and flood their huts (Figure 5.1). When SJKV approached them, they were shoved away, as many elected representatives who promised to do something previously had deceived the community. As SJKV succeeded in taking the community's women into confidence and made them file a slum declaration request, they gained the community's trust and the number of interested families rose to fifty-six. At that time there was governor's rule in Bangalore and they found a sympathetic ear in the then housing minister who wrote to the deputy commissioner. But they could not do anything as they were living on the streets and land was not available, despite having voter identity cards and ration cards. One day fire broke out in the slum and the transformer situated above crashed down, killing a woman. Outraged with grief, they blocked the road displaying the burnt corpse. Immediately, important bureaucrats came and gave a compensation of 12,000 rupees on the spot and advised them to file a case in the court against the electricity company to avail proper compensation. The community along with SJKV did not give up. They stated that it was the government who was responsible for not providing better living conditions, and they were invited to the office of the deputy commissioner. There they had a big verbal fight about the value of their lives and their fundamental rights as citizens. When they were instructed to a lower officer and were treated in an undignified and discriminatory manner, they threatened that officer with a letter accusing him on grounds of the Scheduled

Caste and Scheduled Tribe (Prevention of Atrocities) Act. The official then excused himself. They did a lot of running around, writing letters and defending their cause in terms of citizenship rights and restating that government officers were supposed to be servants of the people. Finally, some land was allotted to them at the periphery of Bangalore to which the community agreed. As they were about to shift, villagers, *panchayat* members, and real estate sharks of that area gathered around them with weapons and started threatening them. In their view, the relocation of the slum-dwellers would decrease the land value. SJKV mentioned that real-estate agents were all in cahoots with ministers. As the arguments became heated and even the community felt intimidated, the deputy commissioner pulled back the allotment fearing a law and order situation. An alternative land was given further away, where water and other facilities were a problem. Even there, farmers and villagers opposed the urban dwellers. Having reached saturation point, the SJVK with the help of other communities pulled together 400 people and blocked the national highway. Bureaucrats hurried to the site and tried to mediate between the villagers and the urban dwellers, but the high-ranking commissioner was locked up and held hostage by the villagers. SJKV members rescued him and finally got a new land allotted near the wholesale agricultural market itself. It took them four years to get the site declared, and with one and a half years of struggle, the community had grown very strong. They were one of the very few communities who got ground-floor BSUP housing done on that allotted land (Figure 5.3).

Figure 5.1   SJKV Episode 'The value of our lives' – the state of the community's residence at the time of fieldwork

Source: Author.

Figure 5.2   SJKV Episode 'The value of our lives' – a community member vividly narrating how they faced government officials

Source: Author.

Figure 5.3   SJKV Episode 'The value of our lives' – future dwelling of the community under BSUP

Source: Author.

Access through noise, achievement by tactics

The narratives of SKJV depict that, in sum, they accessed political opportunities that became available to them as a function of how they were able to escalate the issue or make noise to demand a response. But they also learned that demanding access to the structure and to its provisions often had a repressive spillover effect.

Access to formal political opportunities was shaped by various factors. In their first experience in demanding safe drinking water, an evidence-based approach (lab-tested water) coming from modestly educated slum-dwellers triggered the series of interactions between the community and the authorities. As in other cases under scrutiny, it was crucial to establish an ally within the bureaucracy to get heard. The possibility of doing so was mainly dependent on the political context and on the electoral cycle in Karnataka which underwent some turbulence prior to 2010. Governor's rule was in force from 20 November 2007 to 27 May 2008 due to the breakdown of the ruling coalition. They stated that during this period, they did not know where to turn to and were being sent from one official to another. During their initial struggles, they remembered that they were highly impressed by the police force. But in due course and because of the self-confidence they had gained, the deputy commissioner in the post during their struggles became an important ally. He had learned that SJKV persevered with the community. After their first few successes, SJKV would bring the commissioner's attention to the aggrieved communities. The commissioner qualified SJKV's proceedings as a 'headache' but SJKV persevered in presenting the plight of the community. Over time, having gained credibility through their sustainable work and especially after gaining the status of declared slum, officials were in constant touch with SJKV to gather the needs of the slum-dwellers. Such an interaction, they claimed, also has its basis in their reputation that they truly worked with/for the people and that non-cooperation by the state had its consequence in terms of SJKV's response.

The highest mention of using available means of appeal was the Prevention of Atrocities Act. With this act in hand SJKV members, being slum-dwellers themselves and largely belonging to the Scheduled Caste (SC) and Scheduled Tribe (ST) categories of the population, threatened bureaucrats for their verbally or non-verbally expressed discriminatory behaviour. It was during their first struggle that they learned that when dealing with opposing agents of the same category of caste, the Act did not work anymore in their favour and they consciously discussed the limits of the Act. At the time of facing the authorities in the episode 'The metro is coming' as presented at the very outset of this book, they knew the power of gaining procedural knowledge of the guidelines.

During their first struggle to assert drinking water, they touched upon the electoral cycle and the logics of representation. The elected representative of their area was the only source of opposition and he deployed high measures of informal repression against them. Surprisingly, the councillor was from an SC/ST category himself and repressed his 'own' people in a way. SJKV pointed out that the assumption that an SC/ST person would not commit atrocities was engrained in the Act and thus was of no use. Given the political context, the leaders of SJKV further reflected that the reservation system of the minorities and the SC/ST population in the election quotas was not furthering the interests of the populations of those categories. Such representatives having come forward through those quotas were easily corrupted and were used as reserves for political coalitions or political recruitment through patronage networks. Neither were they given high ranks nor had they the power to initiate something new for the aggrieved communities, as the party that they were affiliated to would object. The patron–client dimension was highlighted during the narrative in connection with a particular slum (the same discussed in the context of DPI), observing that when agents of political parties as slum leaders infiltrated the community, they represented a 'headache' for SJKV. These agents would hinder the education of the dwellers and would function as brokers between the government and the community and not give power to the people. Even in such circumstances, SJKV claimed to have directly spoken to the youth and women about their rights. When the leaders lost followers, only then could the mobilization of the community begin. They did acknowledge that such an approach was extremely difficult and demanded lots of perseverance.

The most striking dimension of the political opportunities that emerged from the interviews was that of the informal repression they faced upon asserting their land or other rights. The imbrication of this form of repression with formal dimensions of political opportunities was multifaceted and diverse in its repressive force. The triggering source of informal repression in most cases stemmed from assertion over land or space for the urban poor to dwell in. Other instances involved a type of perpetuated repressive culture in dealing with the urban poor or the explicit demonstration of power through repressive means. In their first struggle it seemed that through an evidence-based mobilization on the bad quality of water, SJKV could assure cooperation from the bureaucracy through means of escalation. The only source of impediment in a life-threatening way was the local councillor. Members of SJKV narrated that counter (threats of) repression was almost invited and necessary to either resist or to claim respect. In another episode of 'Shifting targets', SJKV were advised to liaise with and to put up the board involving a more radical political civil society organization that was known for its violent tactics to keep the repression initiated by private landowners at bay. Another strand of narration that depicted some sort of counter-repression was the repeated harassment 'for no reason' by police forces of community members (including children) who were living near a police station. Upon seeking advice from the SKJV, the activists advised them to collectively beat up harassing policemen. After execution, the community indeed claimed having gained peace and respect. Informal repression involving land was observed to be fierce and was pushing the limits of SJKV's mobilization capacity. SJKV's narratives depict a nexus between land-sharks (real-estate agents), members of legislative assembly (MLAs), ministers, locals, and farmers in peripheral areas that influenced the allocation rationales of bureaucrats. The expression of such repression manifested itself in the form of armed and life-threatening violence against the urban slum-dwellers and the sympathetic bureaucrats. Such a nexus had been so strong that it overruled a formal government order under the paradoxical excuse of maintaining law and order. The tactics deployed by this nexus to drive away the slum-dwellers were as subtle as spreading rumours about the leader being corrupt and having accepted a very big amount to destabilize the mobilization and break the unity that culminated in the blocking of an important transit road. Subtle forms of discrimination, displayed through non-verbal body language and gestures of government officials 'receiving' slum-dwellers, were identified by SJKV. They compelled the authorities to recognize and render punishable such discrimination under the Prevention of Atrocities Act. In their opinion, such discrimination based on caste represented a closing of access to government services.

In SJKV's case, it seemed that the salient features of the perceived political opportunities were predominantly informal repression and access through noise or escalation. Despite the struggles and efforts, one can note that they did gain access and got things done, mainly through agents of the bureaucracy. Demanding the government's response through an experimental action repertoire genuine to their societal location of lower caste, modest education, and lower income class did show some effect and rendered the exercise sustainable to the slum-dwellers, as the discussion of the categories of 'action repertoire' and 'discursive repertoire' will show.

Mobilization from the location of caste

SJKV's action repertoire at the time of my fieldwork was the product of a delicately experimented array of tactics that they had incorporated into their activism. The targets were as diverse as private landowners, the police force, elected representatives, real-estate agents, farmers, and different officials from the various government agencies. Their lessons to establish such a repertoire were through the perception of their societal position. Depending on the kind of access they got, they used the available avenues of participation and appeal or else contentious tactics to get their way.

Within the formal realm, SJKV was able to use the official hierarchy for their own purposes in escalating issues to the higher responsible authority to implement what they had been promised. The strongest legal weapon in their hand, which was based on their specific societal position, was the Scheduled Castes and Tribes (Prevention of Atrocities) Act. They used it mainly as a threat against those who were obstacles to their quest for improved housing and who did not belong to SC/ST communities. The episode 'The value of our lives' depicts that this legal instrument for SC/ST communities was taken seriously, especially by government officials as it was as a threat of them being transferred. SJKV clearly also saw its limits: Within the framework of the Act one SC/ST person could not put a case on another SC/ST individual. The Act thus presumed that only other caste members would commit atrocities on these distinct communities. SJKV, however, narrated that in one of their instructive contentious episodes, in which an SC councillor threatened them informally through goons, formal legal action was not a possibility. On the other hand, they were conscious that they had to be sensitive beyond the Atrocities Act, as it did not consider verbal or symbolic attacks through gestures, especially when women were spoken to with wrong intentions. All of this they learned to understand in the 'context of the Constitution that the one who works for the government is a government servant' (interview with SJKV, Bangalore, 2010). They, thus, demanded the respect of being treated as a citizen. With time, SJKV understood how to navigate the formalities of slum declaration, to forward access to crucial municipal services. SJKV got to know all the different levels of administration and bureaucracy and learned to use the hierarchies for their purposes. When lower government officials were unresponsive they mobilized up to the highest ranks in order to put pressure on the lower ranks, whistle-blowing their inaction. If a responsive high-ranked officer was in place the consequences could get serious as he threatened the lower official with suspension. Administrative tactics included 'running around' getting documents signed, handing over requests to the highest ranked officers, making sure their orders were implemented, getting slums declared, and also claiming police protection and reminding them of their duties and guidelines when confronted with private landowners. The success of this skill was shown in the episode 'The metro is coming', which I narrated at the very beginning of the book, in which they got a declaration done within two weeks to halt the threat of eviction of a community to make way for the metro in Bangalore.

In the narrative only once did they consciously invite media attention, one that was facilitated through known members of the local press.

The way SJKV dealt with the communities, giving vital social skill resources, laid the foundation for more radical mobilization. Concretely, while encountering government officials, they were always made to speak out and present their plight and demand respect. The other level of building up the community was to build unity. Even in the face of existing ambiguous slum leaders, their approach was to first take the women and youth in confidence and make them all 'collective leaders', not believing in individual leadership. Having even faced guns pointed at them, they experienced that being committed to the struggle with life and having the sense of injustice engrained in them was the source of the strength and courage they had cultivated not only among themselves but also in the communities, as they struggled as equals. In comparison to other organizations, SJKV's achievement was to make their communities understand and resist undue favours through clientelistic practices at election time. Members of the organization told me that they could convince the communities in arguing the logics of re-election ambitions of the candidates without doing any work for the aggrieved.

When all the aforesaid measures failed to further their claim, they then employed contentious tactics to promote improved housing for the community. Their repertoire consisted of: sit-ins at government offices claiming that they will not leave the office until their work was done and in their slogans proclaiming that they were ready to give their lives; and gathering a substantial number of people to protest at specific venues, which could be government offices, construction sites, and homes of elected members. The numbers cited ranged from a team of 10 to go to an office to up to 500 women barging into offices with pots and buckets demanding access to water in slums. Numbers did matter to demand responsiveness. Evidence-based reports about water, declaration of slums, and acknowledgement of a non-registered community as well all mattered. The artefacts used during the protests were the available goods pertinent to the cause they were fighting for. The symbolic weight of an artefact could not go beyond using the dead body of a woman who had to live by a gutter and who was killed by a crumbling transformer to block a road to hold their protest (episode 'The worth of our lives'). Other forms of radical mobilizations were sit-ins where they settled to cook and sleep at the protest site until they were heard; undertaking hunger-strike, and threatening legal action against the opposite party. They narrated that they locked the slum board office and locked in the revenue administrative officer (*tahsildar*). Women were the main participants in the protest and the strongest shield in the event of repression. The SJKV mobilized them, consciously placing them in the front row, as opponents would not beat women and if it became necessary to lodge a case it could be stronger to take them along, they stated. In contrast, they said, 'Men could be purchased in the slums.' Either they would be given enough alcohol or a 500-rupee note and the opposite party would get the paper signed.

As described here, SJKV's action repertoire was diverse and adapted in response and according to the target. Members of SJKV were very committed to the cause, ready to use any means to reach their goal – even 'to give their lives'.

'Manusmriti is India's constitution'[1]

When I interviewed them, the organization was six years old and one of the leaders said, 'All resistance we do is from the location of caste.' The meaning of this statement articulates itself at multiple levels. First, the way Indian society functions in their view. Second, the discrimination they experience when they resist. Third, the type of discourses they have to deploy to the aggrieved communities to activate them. Fourth, how caste discrimination is reproduced in the cityscape.

The organizational discourse was informed by the biases in history that were produced by the dominant castes. The organizational leaders had developed a coherent knowledge base on Indian society's evolution. They believed the Aryans invaded India and deployed the *Manusmriti* (Hindu text on the organization of society) racially to their convenience and making it increasingly more rigid over time. The evolution of the caste system into our times had in their view been reified at many fronts. For one, by education: access to education was earlier privileged only to the higher castes and for them it continued the same way in the guise of access to primary education for all in India. They said that lower-caste people went to free government schools and the higher caste to private schools. The government schools were judged to be of substandard quality and did not equip children either with grounded knowledge or critical thinking to question their position. Even the higher-caste students who were able to enjoy a degree were not made to think critically as some equated the caste system to be a necessity for society to function and tended to see slum-dwellers in light of the legality of their habitation. Thus, the caste system, as they argued, was reified and did not groom them for empowerment, which could lead to transformation. The second front to reify caste was through religion, they stated. One of the leaders qualified religion as cheating of people, especially through idol worship. He deplored that religious scriptures were held above the Constitution of the country. He depicted how tribal people, who had no concept of caste or Hinduism, were brought under Hinduism and in the categories of sub-castes during census. The last front of caste reification was, in their view, electoral politics. They judged that Dalit representatives were of no use, as the lobby of higher castes with their nexus with religious institutions would be too strong to get anything through in favour of the Dalit population. History displayed this in their view at the very birth of the nation when Gandhi opposed Ambedkar's (Dalit who was the chief architect of the Indian Constitution) suggestion of a separate electorate for Dalits.

The second level of resistance from the location of caste was displayed and experienced during the deployment of their action repertoire. One such instance was when they had to publicly question the value of their lives while protesting about their living conditions armed with the corpse of a woman who had died because of the location of her habitation. They repeatedly said that during their struggles in the face of repression they were ready to fight until death. Other occasions were when they launched agitation or threatened legal action with the Atrocities Act in hand. They stated that they experienced caste discrimination when government officials expressed a sense of disgust through their body language or when they claimed that god was responsible for their plight.

The third level of caste-based resistance was the way they attempted to change the consciousness of the slum-dwellers in shaking the very foundations of their beliefs in terms of self-esteem and religious beliefs. The metaphor of equating the slum-dwellers to animals remained a very strong frame. Another strand of reasoning was to make the slum-dwellers understand the universality of being human against the notion of sub-caste even within their own communities in an attempt to unite the Dalits. Such unity was seen as the only means to real politics. Their argument and their action was hence based on the basis of a particular identity and their struggle was to assert equality and get proper and due treatment that redressed caste inequality. Making this leap from a caste location to a notion of equal substantial citizenship was to appeal to the community to recognize their discrimination in the first place.

The last level of caste-based resistance was mirrored in their understanding of the cityscape and the distribution of space. In rural India, lower-caste people live on the outskirts of the village; they observed the same geographies unfolding in the cities as well. Even when they knew that it was an achievement to house the slum-dwellers in 'pucca', or concrete, public housing complexes, one of the leaders equated it to a 'cement zoo' that was being built on the outskirts of the city in a ditch.

'Go with the flow' housing process

The DPI group I interviewed highlighted that not all groups working under the DPI banner were worth the name. They firmly distinguished themselves from the DPI wing that they said were highly corrupt and dangerous. To label them as a co-opted political society organization through their narration is grounded in the fact that they encouraged paying bribes in order to get things done to community members, on the one hand, meaning that they did indulge in informal tactics, and, on the other hand, they accepted vote-buying practices without challenging the community or the candidate who was involved in it. Even at the national level, Ghose (2003) noted that DPI members were found on governmental panels and committees. This tells us that DPI did not shy away from using the same means as the government did, even when expecting different outcomes (Najam 2000).

This group functioned through a network of active members spread across Karnataka who coached communities on the initial steps of the struggle and deploying whatever strategy was required with the means available in the community. Decision-making seemed to be triggered by the most experienced activists, who also maintained crucial links with officials.

The activists themselves all came from very modest background and had just primary education and were mainly in contract jobs. They all identified themselves with the attribution of Dalit. All financial needs to organize their struggles were pooled from the community, which also gave them a sense of ownership. They clearly distinguished themselves from the functioning of elite society organizations that, in their view, went and 'begged' for money. In terms of social skill resources, they possessed considerable levels as their action repertoire included dragging cases to court and filing right to information

(RTI) requests. Such tactics required tight follow-up and considerable amount of literacy to understand the complex system and to be able to respond to it. Their capacity to infuse incorporated resources into the community was valuable but had limits. While they encouraged slum-dwellers to go along with the main activists to learn the modalities of the struggle, they did not spread awareness about corruption, electoral cycle, and the collective power that slum-dwellers potentially had. On the relational front as well, they seemed well connected with 'useful' bureaucrats and could possibly count on other DPI sections in neighbouring states, but they did not mention any such instance where there was a need for it.

The description of the following episode presents the dynamics in a slum and demonstrates how efforts of mobilization can be taken hostage. The information about the slum was gathered cautiously by interviewing informants and dwellers, as the connections to the underground were very evident in this locality.

Episode: Blackmailing through housing

DPI was very active in a slum situated on a hill on a rocky ground that housed many families in a middle-class area and that was initially not declared. DPI was part of the struggle to get water and electricity into the slum. Nevertheless, when the slum-dwellers received a letter of eviction, because a middle-class man wanted the slum evicted, they organized a big protest in front of the state legislature and fought the eviction order legally. The slum community got a ruling in their favour and finally had the slum declared. Upon declaration, the in situ development under JNNURM BSUP was brought into the slum, a scheme from the Centre with huge funds and a complex toolkit to follow.

The first settlers in that slum always had a strong hold on the community. As the JNNURM BSUP was announced to be implemented in that locality, my informants narrated, the scattered leadership came together in view of the large amount of public funds flowing in, meaning that a lot of money could be made from it. Consequently, they pushed out all other actors (NGOs) in that slum, coercing the inhabitants to be on their side and not allowing them to collectively mobilize. Without any following and therefore any purpose left, DPI and other elite society organizations withdrew their activities from that slum.

Dynamics in the slum were steeped in patron–client networks, which even the KSDB, the agency implementing the JNNURM BSUP scheme, made use of in its operations. The slum board had only approached the slum leaders at the start of the implementation of the scheme – that was what they would have called public consultation. Even though there were four strong leaders in the slum who ordinarily competed with each other, they all came together 'for the greater good of lots of money'. This meant that they were managing the beneficiaries' list, keeping it non-transparent, and also managed all the information and the monitoring of the construction work. A women's non-governmental organization (NGO) tried to obtain information on behalf of the women, visiting the slum-board and also encouraging the women to form an independent committee and to engage as active actors in the process. But the women wanting to come forward were discouraged by their own husbands for fear of losing out on a house if they opposed the leaders. An internationally known NGO and CIVIC only came to inform the slum-dwellers, but upon suggestion to hold a protest with the women at the KSDB, they also backed out. The leaders did a meeting and asked the people to pay 1,500 rupees to enter their names in the list; when the women questioned why the money could not be paid directly to the slum-board, the leaders warned them that they could either leave or ride with them, but either way they should not complain. The women were too scared to question the leaders; it was the matter of getting a house, and with much corruption going on, any questions asked was repelled strongly through informal physical threats. They felt vulnerable worrying about their adolescent daughters or their husbands coming home late at night. At the time of fieldwork two killings had happened within the slum, when two gangs were fighting each other (*The Hindu*, 9 December 2010). The leaders were the very early inhabitants of the slum, who had started developing the land and managing the influx of people settling in. These first-comers got rich, as they would occupy more land, build a temple, sell or rent dwelling units in the informal market. As more people settled, they would get the slum declared and work it into their pockets. Many families were tenants within this informal housing market. My informants estimated that there were about 2,000 families living in the slum and that the housing scheme was planned for 1,500 and a transit site (empty land) for 500 families. The lists established were highly non-transparent and under the charge of the leaders. The transit arrangement was merely an open ground squeezed behind a maintained park and a private fenced site. The residents were given just some tin sheets and nothing else. There was insufficient sanitation and water, and no electricity. The displaced dwellers had to illegally tap those amenities or pay extra to get it from private sources, such as for water. Residents told me that during the monsoon, the site got flooded and that they were fighting rats and snakes within these tin shacks. Those who were supposed to get a unit in that slum did not even get a biometric card, but just a slip with their photo and a number on it. Apparently, the leaders silenced all opposing voices, oversaw the construction, and interacted with the officials and engineers. There were many rumours that the cement was mixed with loose elements and that the foundation was in soaked soil. Those who watched did not trust the quality of the construction at all. None of the slum inhabitants, of which many were construction workers, were appointed to building the blocks. Rumours went around that some multiple allottees (including leaders) had already sold flats. The notice letter about the scheme to be implemented came towards the end of March 2010. It was on 28 March of the same year that municipal elections were held. At that time, before the eviction, they started cutting all basic services and one month after the election, demolitions started (Figure 5.4). For the start of the work, even the chief minister himself had come. Five hundred people took the 2,000 rupees given for transit accommodation and the tin sheets and squeezed into the transit ground lying on the opposite side for over two and a half years (Figure 5.5). Other families scattered all around, having taken some rental housing. The informants agreed that the rationale behind getting the slum community scattered geographically was to breach any unity existing within the community that could confront the leadership. My informants continued to say that the leaders were close to the political parties and that 'they were like literally dogs of the political parties. They kept them there so that people didn't revolt, people voted for them during elections and there was a control over the people'. These party affiliations were all convenience based and depended on the political constellation, but the BJP was stronger than the Congress in this locality. In the 2010 municipal election, the BJP had won. DPI was closely involved in the slum prior to the JNNURM scheme, when the court case was still due and the struggle for the land was on. After the even stronger influence of the slum leaders along BJP alignments and after people getting scattered due to the demolitions, DPI's involvement receded as well and they left.

Figure 5.4   Episode 'Blackmailing through housing' – clearing the ground for construction

Source: Author.

This particular locality was making headlines. On 21 November 2012 one could read in the press in Bangalore (*Deccan Herald*, 21 November 2012) that an inauguration of the housing complex had finally happened. But in reality, out of the 1,500 units only 850 were standing and the interiors were not yet completed (Figure 5.6). The article also said that the residents alleged that 179 names were missing from the beneficiaries' list and that outsiders had been included.

Figure 5.5   Episode 'Blackmailing through housing' – arrangements for transit accommodation for one-third of the residents
Source: Author.

Figure 5.6   Episode 'Blackmailing through housing' – status of construction site
Source: *The Hindu*, from the article 'Living in the Danger Zone' (19 July 2013).

'The vicious circle of participation in corruption'

Expressions about the political opportunities in the DPI's narrative ranged from perceiving the system as highly corrupt to being hopeful at the same time that it will change for the better. They stated this against the background of the political turmoil that was ongoing during the time of fieldwork and that this was a temporary phase resulting from a loss of confidence, and would be a lesson to the chief minister. The striking feature was they did not display much reflexivity while talking about the corruption perceived and the hope for betterment. They perceived the political opportunities to be accessible to them, as they said that officers would receive them in the name of DPI. They knew the commissioners and they would address the concerned commissioner with letters and meet him, or they would follow it up with RTI queries. Closures and skewing the access happened in relation with land issues. At several instances in their narration, they brought up this issue. First, apparently even long-held and valid certification of land ownership from colonial times could be overruled by the financial interests of private actors, which they challenged in court. Second, favouritism demonstrated by the chief minister also extended to land allocation and conflicting agendas of diverse groups. The third instance was their narration of the row between government agencies over the ownership of a piece of land on which housing for the urban poor was to be facilitated but remained unutilized. The final instance where they described skewing access to housing, and thus land allocated to the urban poor, was in the episode of 'Blackmailing through housing'. The public housing delivery was rolled out upon an existing network of patronage that managed the beneficiaries' list.

Corruption is explicitly mentioned in connection with the electoral cycle. They described the process of candidates collecting voter identity cards from the slum-dwellers in exchange for some freebies or promises. After every election, DPI would be approached to do the running around to recollect the documents back for the slum-dwellers. Also, they expressed with some resignation that during election time slum-dwellers would go for canvassing for political parties and would forget DPI and their deeds. The slum-dwellers would excuse themselves and re(join) the DPI activities, engaging against the same government that they helped reinstate. But they did express some understanding for such behaviour, as political parties would shell out 500 rupees for a vote. If a (joint) family consisted of 10 members, they could avail in a short time 5,000 rupees of additional income.

'The fallacies of accepting the political context'

The action repertoire of DPI included an array of tactics ranging from administrative and legal to the radical. The first interaction would occur with a letter on a DPI letterhead; they did not fear addressing it at any level required. The next means towards increasing the levels of radicalness came through the use of the available means of appeal, being mainly the instruments of RTI and court cases. To do that they would have accumulated considerable amounts of incorporated resources and procedural knowledge to hand in their claims, but also to follow them up. Their knowledge was also highly pertinent for the required housing procedures, for which they were ready to run around from pillar to post. At the extreme end of radicalness, the tactics they deployed were sit-ins at police stations, locking in the police, blocking the station, and stopping a train or blocking a road.

In DPI's case, it seems relevant also to highlight what other means were encouraged to engage with the authorities. They openly declared that paying a bribe was part of getting documentation done in a timely manner and hence encouraged the aggrieved parties to pay a part of the bribe expected. With the acceptance of the corrupt political environment comes also the inaction in terms of resistance to vote-buying. They explicitly declared that during election time, they did not interfere and that all could vote for whom they wanted.

'We have our leader no?'

The discursive repertoire of the DPI members I interviewed was mainly borrowed from the larger DPI organization. Their engagement in the struggles was driven by the motivation that the Dalit people had to grow and they gave the example of the DPI leader. In their eyes, it was a tremendous achievement that the main leaders of DPI at the all-India level had achieved to become ministers as Dalits and were representing them in the circles of formal political power. They claimed that the fact that DPI had strong leaders was the main motivation to convert their earlier organization called Karnataka Janara Sangha (KJS) to a wing of DPI. Otherwise, Dalits lacked unity and they believed that a strong leader could bring some continuity to their struggle. They were justifying radical tactics against formal authorities by saying that the government had to notice that there was some resistance. It was a source of inspiration that the wings in Tamil Nadu and Maharashtra (neighbouring states) had more force and that they feared nothing. They felt that if they would fear, nothing would happen. In their understanding, only if the government got scared of them would they get justice, otherwise they would all get 'looted'. It was through the display of such fearlessness that the police got intimated by them. They stated that the police did not dare confront them 'from front, but from behind', meaning that they would 'only' dare to press a legal case against such groups.

In comparison to the other cases under scrutiny in my study, DPI had access to a 'ready-made' Dalit ideology from the all-India DPI organization. DPI in its mission statement declared,

> Dalit Panthers of India are committed to empowering the fortunates through education and through organizing themselves in a manner that at once liberates their inadequacies and insecurities and delivers self-respect. This means a complete demolition of orthodoxy and archaic practices of the caste system, which have led to unfortunate pseudo-apartheid in the Society.... And that mission would be guided by principles enshrined in the teachings of Lord Buddha. (Dalitpanther.com, accessed on 31 March 2013)

Ghose (2003) recognizes the success of the Dalit Panthers that emerged in the 1970s, which comprised mainly of poets and writers. He observed that while the movement had contributed in a meaningful way to revolutionary literature and had campaigned against discrimination of Dalits, it subsequently had splintered and was co-opted into various government committees and panels (ibid., 101). This ambivalence between the success and the strong ideological base the Dalit Panthers once had and the decline and co-option of the movement in recent times was, in my view, reflected in the action of these DPI groups. On the one hand, they strove towards the more radical examples of neighbouring states to proclaim their resistance against the discrimination of Dalits and, on the other hand, they did not have any qualms in stating that bribes had to be paid. It is also to be considered that Dalit Panthers, having a strong leadership rooted in a strong ideology, was the very reason that this particular group decided to come under the umbrella of DPI, expecting to be able to present a more united force. In this sense, the lack of reflexivity of their action can be explained that a discursive base was readily available to identify and build a collective identity. It can be noticed that they did not invest as much in identity work as did SJKV, neither in terms of challenging their self-perception nor in bringing awareness to the communities about the electoral cycles and the perpetuation of their dependency. Along the same lines, while in their action they seemed resigned in the face of vote-buying practices and had lost faith in democracy, they were still very appreciative of some of the DPI leaders who had officially reached the abode of formal representation at the Centre and were hopeful of improvement in Karnataka's political scenario after the significant turmoil that had occurred in 2010.

While DPI did not speak as much about informal repression as my other cases, it is nevertheless noteworthy that they thought that it was only through displaying fearlessness combined with radical action that they could prevent getting looted by the authorities and gain some respect.

Organizing urban learning communities

The enthusiasm with which members of SJKV narrated their stories and the passion with which they argued why they had developed certain strategies was contagious. The picture gathered from the interviews with key organizational members and the communities depict SJKV being confronted with an initially closed system, where they had to make considerable noise to get heard.

The narratives of SJKV showed that government officials were reluctant to give access to the slum-dwellers, but members mobilizing along with SJKV had to stay firm and if necessary make noise to escalate the issue. Such 'loud cracking up' of the political opportunities must be viewed from the fact that powerful government positions were generally not occupied by lower-caste people. Hence they could not count on known allies from the outset to further their claim. Once having got heard and having demanded mutual respect in the interaction, those high-ranking officers were kept as allies. It is also noteworthy that through such strong, varied, and genuine mobilization efforts, the state authorities did respond and SJKV got their claims addressed.

With time having cultured an argumentative repertoire, procedural knowledge, and self-esteem to approach agents of the bureaucracy they could maintain openings of the political opportunities. DPI, in contrast, seemed to be more deeply embedded in the socio-political context of Bangalore. They were able to maintain access to bureaucracy in getting documentation done on behalf of the slum-dweller and did not seem to have had any difficulty in approaching the judiciary or using available means of appeal. In this sense, they were able to maintain the political opportunities open within the formal realm. Accordingly, they deployed administrative and other formal tactics. Their repertoire of contentious tactics played out in situations where slum-dwellers were forcefully evicted and it was related to their status of being Dalits in a discriminatory way.

Social skill and discursive repertoire

In contrast to elite society organizations, both SJKV and DPI sourced their discursive repertoire from the particularistic identity of caste. DPI was a unique case, as it was the only one to be able to borrow from a 'ready-made' discursive repertoire of the DPI operating at a national level. The universalistic identity of citizenship was something to strive for and imbibe the notion of rights as citizens in the communities they worked with. The striving for citizenship rights and the learning process of deconstructing their own identity of belonging to low caste and to reconstruct it as worthy citizens by grasping resources, courage, and skill to engage in claim-making were the most powerful and sustainable tactic to assist communities to claim adequate housing. This was a particularly important effort in view of the fact that people at the margins of survival, at a cognitive level, are generally ill-equipped with strategic sophistication for claim-making (Thompson and Tapscott 2010, 14). The quality of claim-making differed drastically depending on the conception of the slum-dweller's identity and how the civil society organizations assisted in forging an identity in regard to their status in the city in three ways. First, when the dissonance between the legal and policy prescriptions and the lived experience was perceived as a matter of right to urban citizenship (as in the case of SJKV), then the community was likely to display high levels of social skill (Fligstein and McAdam 2012) and engage in committed claim-making performances. Second, when the dissonance was perceived as a matter of eligibility to a policy benefit (as in the case of the CIVIC, AVAS, or DPI communities), then though the community held lower levels of social skill it could fall back on some kind of network to engage in politics of proof-gathering. The episode 'Blackmailing through housing', where slum leaders were catering to their respective clients in the slums, is such an instance. While social skill resources infused into communities in terms of mobilizing skills were considerable, those were not sufficient to free them from political patronage.

Lastly, the (logical) consequence from perceiving the dissonance between legal and policy prescriptions and the lived experience in terms of a denizen, with very low social skills and no social network, could lead to total exclusion from the community and the geographical space. In my interactions with slum-dwellers who did not qualify for BSUP housing or were new migrants to the city but lived in the slum before the BSUP housing was being built in situ, they faced this third situation (Rao Dhananka 2016).

Even in the case of political society organizations, bureaucracy remained the main target and paradoxically also the only allies. In a way, it is not surprising as the delivery for urban services is concentrated in the hands of parastatals. The role then of the elected representative from slum localities would be to direct the attention of the parastatals to upgrade services for low-income settlements. Instead, narratives from both organizations reveal that they view elections as a money-making enterprise that was nurtured in everyday transactions. The episode of 'Blackmailing through housing' powerfully showed how systems of governmentality rolling out big public housing projects can strengthen networks of patronage in slum communities, especially during election season. Patron–client relationships in slums were dependency networks in which a patron from a political party collaborated closely with a slum leader affiliated to the same political party who gave favours to the clients – the slum-dweller – against some payment. A leader would reiterate that only he would be able to deliver such favours through his personal connections. For the slum-dweller, such an arrangement meant that he could bypass running around to the authorities for his needs for an extra charge, which he would anyway have spent on bribes along with losing his daily wage. So, going through patron networks could even represent a bargain. For the patron and the slum leader, on the other hand, such an arrangement meant that he could maintain an exclusive network of clients/followership to whom he could cater, guaranteeing also their votes to his affiliated party. Such networks then become self-sufficient and hinder efforts to mobilize collectively but represent to some extent a win–win situation for both. DPI was confronted with such a situation in the episode mentioned earlier and abandoned the community. Thus, such vertical, exclusive patron–client networks hinder horizontal, loose ties that are required for mobilizing.

When slum-dwellers out of rational calculus indulge in accepting freebies or money in exchange for votes and embroil themselves into logics of undue favour by politicians, then a viscous cycle of dependency and loyalty is triggered/continued throughout the electoral cycle which make the vote-buying option a safer bet for re-election of the candidate than proving himself by good work. DPI stated that they did not interfere during election time and that all were free to vote for the party of their choice, while SJKV educated the communities of their rights as citizens, but that they could accept the freebies and still vote for their party of choice. This latter option hints that vote-bank practices do not necessarily predict the outcome of an election. Björkman (2014a) reflects on this discrepancy and concludes that cash is a sign and instantiation of the networks of knowledge, authority, and resources that are necessary for navigating the opacities of the city's rapidly changing globalized economic logics and rationales for action. Exchange encounters and nurturing networks are not only performative but also speculative: The mediating power of cash allows money to be put to work in the hope of inducing reciprocity (ibid., 631). This is what I would like to call the economics of electoral politics.

Such performative and speculative networks were fuelled by informal political opportunities to engage in informal exchange circuits that in turn could trigger informal repression. One important takeaway from SJKV's case is that performative circuits of informal exchange could lead to grave informal repression and indeed influence demobilization to a considerable extent. The episode of 'The value of our lives' depicted that it was even possible that an informal nexus of actors having vested interest in public land could exert such power as to overrule a formal government order of land allocation. The commissioner in that instance had to strike a balance between maintaining law and order for the general public and having to commit to the duty of the welfare of the aggrieved citizen. Even though the state would be in possession of coercive means to guarantee law and order, it gave priority to the claim of the nexus.

Their learning curve to veer around the impediments they faced to mobilize was steep. Like the elite society organizations, both organizations discussed in this chapter faced considerable impediments to mobilizing, such as facing informal repression, and had to escalate claims in a noisy way to demand access and responsiveness from the state. The challenge of representation of the interest of the poor and facing the informal networks impeding mobilization efforts was similar to the challenges faced by elite society organizations.

Within the interventions of SJKV in particular in organizing communities, teaching to navigate the urban environment and the pedagogical effort was transformative and hence sustainable. Sustainability means that these 'transformed' communities are able to engage in claim-making on their own and can assist other communities or families that are facing similar challenges without the intervention of an external party. When the urban poor or the marginalized communities have the social skills and the procedural knowledge to engage in constructive claim-making with the state or other structuring targets, then the vision of an inclusive city becomes possible. The follow-up question then is, how to organize learning communities on a city-wide scale to endow them with tactical knowledge? What kind of pedagogy do urban areas require to equip citizens with such skill and knowledge to bring about a bottom-up culture of cooperative decision-making for the city and the co-creation of urban knowledges? Who are the pedagogues? How can learning communities then be organized? I attempt to give answers to this train of thought in the conclusion and offer an open-ended research agenda to find means to realize inclusive cities in practice.

Notes

1. From interview with SJKV leader.

Claiming housing despite Indian politics and governance

The overarching interest of this book was to investigate the 'actual' existing conditions for differently resourced civil society organizations to mobilize on the issue of adequate housing in the city of Bangalore in order to understand the impediments to social mobilization on the pressing issue of housing. I identified the concept of political opportunities stemming from social movement scholarship to be the pertinent conceptual tool to grasp this research question. The literature review on the concept revealed that there was a need to revisit it in view of post-colonial contexts. I put forward the argument that for the concept to be encompassing of a context like Bangalore (India), it needed to include informal dimensions and the fact that civil society was segmented (Chatterjee 2004). I argued that the development of a situated toolbox could serve the study of social movements in the Global South more widely, but also bring precision for Northern movements that are increasingly witnessing similar socio-political challenges as the South. In consequence, it was required to first look for differential openings of political opportunities in the democratic polity, policy, and law. I showed how everyday, informal practices of the investigated dimensions of political opportunities contrasted the formal prescriptions and argued for a provincialized understanding of democracy (Björkman 2014a). Second, I analysed the political opportunities offered by the housing policy under the Basic Services for the Urban Poor (BSUP) component of the Jawaharlal Nehru National Urban Renewal Mission (JNNURM) and argued for the requirement of a vernacular governance that takes into consideration cultural geographies. The general and the housing political opportunities were then related to the experience of the selected elite and political society organizations. In the case of the elite society organizations, I discerned how sourcing their discursive repertoire to justify their actions from the universal concept of citizenship made their interventions in the policy-affected communities independent of their intervention and that the interventions from political society organizations reflected their actions from the particular identity of caste. The organizational narratives revealed the differential political opportunities they faced and the different action and discursive repertoires that were developed in response.

In this final chapter I will first answer three lines of enquiry at the heart of this book: (*a*) To what extent are the political opportunities differential? (*b*) To what extent do informal exchange circuits skew conditions for mobilizing? (*c*) Are the action repertoires of diversely resourced civil society organizations different? In the second part, I will discuss four emergent themes: (*a*) Formal exclusions and informal inclusions: creating distrust and inequality. (*b*) Corruption mechanisms through formal illegality and repressive informality. (*c*) The making of the city and its citizens through skewed land allocation and housing opportunities. (*d*) Possible task division between elite and political society organizations. For each of these emergent themes, I formulate and discuss a thesis and I attempt to give recommendations for conceptual developments and socio-political inputs. In the third section, based on the reflections of these emergent themes, I will argue that an agenda for research and practice on an urban public pedagogy is required if the lessons from this enquiry are to be taken seriously. Such an agenda will entail the formulation and engagement with an urban pedagogy that equips the citizenry to co-envision and co-create inclusive cities.

Answering the research questions

The overarching question this book attempts to answer is: *What are the 'real' existing conditions for differently resourced organizations to mobilize on the issue of adequate housing in the city of Bangalore?* Based on my analysis, I concluded that they were not as favourable as the legal and policy framework suggest they were. The data compiled revealed that the conditions were favourable only when one considers the rhetoric of it. Still, going by formal prescriptions, when one studies the interrelations between the different legal and policy texts and the eligibility criteria to access the provisions the texts describe, one realizes that these remain largely closed for or out of reach of especially the less-resourced political society organizations. The instantiation of these legal and policy framework on the ground represent opportunities but also threats. There was almost a total lack of accountability to assure that the implementation of the prescribed legal and policy provision was accessible and reached the target population of the poor. Ambiguous formal prescription in combination with unfavourable institutional design, representing incentives for corruption, made access to political opportunities and entitlements a complex affair for the urban poor. It was all the more true for those who lacked social skills. Systems of governmentality (including delivery of public housing) kept the urban poor in dependency of the state and at the mercy of its actors. The access to governmental benefits was regulated through formal eligibility criteria that articulate around a colonial categorization of population. These systems of governmentality govern operations of inclusion or exclusion in the city. In the case of being excluded, the prevalence of informal exchange circuits represented a viable option to access formal political opportunities and entitlements. Concretely, exclusive networks of patron–client relationship involving bureaucratic corruption and legislative practices characterized these informal channels of access. While such informal relationships go against normative democratic theory, for the urban poor they may represent an efficient strategy for not having to run around to access the entitlement and not having to bribe officials. For the patrons, on the other hand, such an arrangement enables them to maintain an exclusive network of clients/followership to whom they could cater, guaranteeing also their votes to their affiliated parties. Such networks perpetuate themselves and hinder efforts to mobilize collectively as a community of policy target or as a community constituted by space, as patron–client networks mobilize on the basis of particular identities. Informal repression funded through and required by these informal circuits of exchange proved to be a major hindrance to mobilization especially regarding access to land and housing in the city.

Now let me turn to answering the empirical research question:

1. To which extent are the political opportunities differential?

Indeed, the political opportunities were found to be differential to the extent that they were more open to the elite society organizations. Accessing formal political opportunities requires substantial social skills. First of all, it is a task to understand these in their embeddedness in the legal framework. Second, to be eligible to them requires an education level that provided consistent literacy skill in order to read, write, and take notice of the opportunities present. Another form of exclusion was that information about political opportunities was published only in English. Due to the discrepancy between the eligibility requirement and the resource level of the slum-dwellers, policy frameworks like the JNNURM BSUP prescribed elite society organizations to represent the political society organizations. This type of mediated access also has its fallacy, as elite society organizations are not democratically accountable towards the citizens. My empirical base makes it seem that even favourable political opportunities have to be 'cracked' open through persistence, awareness, and contentious means for accountability regardless of the level of resources of the organizations. What are the real intentions of the government actors who are guardians of such openings? Toerell (2007) states that studies investigating democracies assume the benevolent intentions of government actors because normative democratic theories do not take into account the historical evolution and the cultural embeddedness of political practices (Sundaresan 2017). Benevolence in regard to democratic practice and governance is hence not linear; the complexity of underlying motivations for certain political practice and agency have to be acknowledged, and entrenched informal practices deserve to be paid equal attention as prescriptions for democratic Indian polity.

2. To which extent do everyday, informal exchange circuits skew conditions for mobilizing?

Informal exchange circuits skewed conditions considerably for the four organizations sampled. They made access to governmental agencies more expensive and made mobilizing more dangerous and hence discouraging. The intricate imbrications of formal and informal opportunities forged through institutional incentives for corruption roped the urban slum-dwellers into circuits and dependencies that for most have become a way of life. To resist such a probable involvement, some organizations invested considerable amount of effort in making communities aware of the operation of such circuits. This way of life consisted of keeping the urban poor in dependency of informal clientelistic networks that supply to the urban poor crucial services, identification documents, or entitlements through patrons that maintain exclusive connections to bureaucrats and politicians. While a direct citizen–state relationship would be possible through knowledge of rights, entitlement, and procedures, preventing the poor from gaining such awareness perpetuates such dependency. Hence the poor pay these patrons acting as agents, and actually pay more for the services and benefits entitled to them. Such circuits are strongly embroiled with the electoral cycle, which promotes patron–client structures and results in 'participation in corruption' that fulfils diverse ends, as Björkman (2014a) identifies in her treatise – that exchange is constitutive of enduring networks of trust, sociality, and accountability.

Informal repression that stems from these informal circuits of exchange is the greatest hindering factor to mobilization in Bangalore. As urban services, welfare entitlements, and agencies that allocate land are all crucial actors in the lives of the urban poor, the networks of these actors enmesh and extend to informal circuits of exchange. So, when urban poor communities mobilize and potentially imperil the balance of power that maintains these networks, then the backlash in form of informal repression is hard on the urban poor and weakens their mobilization efforts considerably.

3. Are action repertoires of diversely resourced organizations different?

Yes, indeed they are. Investigating the four sampled civil society organizations, we witnessed the development of different action repertoires in response to the political opportunities described above. My results confirm the hypothesis of Boudreau (1996) stating that less-resourced organizations engage more in radical (in his words 'direct') actions. Indeed, while elite society organizations did indulge in contentious action, their performances were cautious enough to be tolerated by the regime in place. Also, the backlash they experienced were hardly as fierce as experienced by the political society organizations. The contentious acts of elite society organizations were pursued to highlight the precarity of the poor or to contend the undemocratic state of affairs. The political society organizations engaged in radical contentious performances in order to get their human needs covered in the form of adequate housing. To further their claims, strategic bureaucratic allies were key to all four organizations. Once a relationship was established, all organizations tried to escalate their claim within the hierarchically organized bureaucracy. If the political society organizations did not get heard they took recourse to contentious tactics to force the government to pay attention. Those possessing the required social skills 'repressed' the government with its own tools in demanding the implementation of official prescriptions and guidelines.

The discourses deployed to frame their action were varied. The elite society organizations hardly recognized difference in terms of caste. Their vocabulary rather distinguished the poor and the well-to-do. Emphasizing the universal applicability of citizenship provisions and human treatment to all, both political society organizations argued their actions from the location of caste and that continuous caste discrimination had to be challenged. Those who succeeded to challenge the caste perception – and the low self-esteem that comes with it – in the slum-dwellers' community were the most successful in terms of the sustainability of their action. Especially in the case of SJKV, their aim was to bridge their historically marginalized position through a pursuit of citizenship in giving the communities vital social skill resources to challenge their perceived identity.

Emerging themes

Formal exclusions and informal inclusions: Creating distrust and inequality

Enquiring into the dynamics of citizens–state interaction around public housing delivery to the urban poor, there are particular informal exclusion mechanisms that arise. As many scholars studying India point out (Dudley-Jenkins 2003; Kaviraj and Khilani 2001 ; Randeria 2002; Lemke 2000, Corbridge et al. 2005), indeed systems of governmentality are at the heart of shaping citizens–states interactions, but they also shape possibilities of social cohesion and solidarity. Rationales of governmentality hinge on particular identities that serve to identify populations as targets of policy. On its basis, particularized trust networks develop. 'Particularized trust reflects social strains, where each group in a society looks out for its own interests and places little faith in the good intentions of others' (Uslaner et al. 2005) and nourishes certain perception of trust networks. Hence, *culturally justified perceptions of the urban poor foster exclusion mechanism that are translated into the operations of various policy domains in exploiting the existing stratification of society to maintain the status quo, creating distrust and inequality and further worsening conditions for mobilization.*

These cultural perception are fed by perpetuating ideas of how caste membership shapes communities' behaviour, their reliability, and the estimation to what extent they have the capacity to endure hardships and are reinforced by policy that ascribe certain identities (such as SC/ST or Other Backward Classes [OBC]) to populations (van Zomeren et al. 2008; Bhan 2017). I reflect on how the culturally justified perceptions exclude them from the banking system and how these justifications are perpetuated through the education system. The association between governmentality and the different policy domains is important to reflect on and to explain the continuing marginalization of the urban poor.

At several instances my interview-partners mentioned that there was a common belief that poor people would not be able to pay back if they availed loans. Not just because of their poor financial status but also because they were not considered reliable enough to be trusted to pay back the loan. AVAS was asked to avail the loan in its name – an elite society organization. Instead, AVAS pledged the loan to be in the name of the community and they guaranteed that the community would pay back. Through constant efforts of enhancing social skills in regard to saving and accountancy, the community had paid back the entire amount on schedule. The exclusion of the poor from the banking sector has serious consequences for the urban poor and their dependency on other sources of credit. Not being able to avail credit from banks due to their meagre financial situation prohibits attempts of establishing an independent livelihood that may sustain the family and better the resources for future generations. This exclusion makes them vulnerable, on the one hand, to loan sharks, often in the form of the slum leader, who keeps them in dire dependency and demands horrendous interest rates (deWit and Berner 2009). For the urban poor to get embroiled in patron–client networks is an easy path for financial purposes – and, on the other hand, to elite society organizations that are geared towards becoming some sort of an intermediary between the urban poor communities and financial institutions, which potentially disenfranchises them. Exclusion from the banking circuits also prevents them from entering formality, which gives them lesser recognition and leverage to deal with actors of the formal realm.

The dependency on sources of financial resources other than the banks makes systems of governmentality that deliver entitlements almost for all crucial requirements of life a central feature around which the lives of the poor revolve. The urban poor in such systems are treated as subjects to be receiving policy benefits that were designed for and on behalf of them by bureaucrats and politicians (mostly male), in general without their consultation nor involvement. In support of Chatterjee (2004), in Chapters 2 and 3 delineating the general and housing opportunities, I demonstrated why entitlements were inherently political. On the basis of the state of Karnataka, I showed that the welfare planning represented a substantial part of the budget. Hence this important welfare allocation and an institutional design that represents incentives for corruption make the coverage of basic human needs an unstable affair for the urban poor. This instability produced by the institutional environment makes prospects of inclusion into more stable predictable patron–client networks based on loyalty attractive. My sampled organizations suggest a strong reliance on bureaucrats more than politicians because of more stability of the former, as they do not get voted out, though they face the risk of transfers. Even though patrons are linked to political parties, their swaying towards higher bidders was common knowledge. So, systems of governmentality along with fragmented parastatals delivering urban services make the poor face a particular state in every locality (Gupta 2012, 34). The instantiation of governmentality at the local level being very particular, along with the fact that it operates on the basis of official lists of particular scheduled categories (SC/ST), exploits existing differences and perpetuates them. These two facets of governmentality together make conditions for city-wide mobilization on a particular issue very unfavourable. Unity cannot be enforced through a common identity (caste as segmenting) nor through a common idea of state (Gupta 1995), cancelling out the possibility of a sustained movement that displays the qualities of what Tilly (2004) called WUNC (worthiness, unity, numbers, and commitment). Non-mobilization is fostered through the fragmentation of the target (particular state) and the actualization of caste through governmentality.

Some of my interview-partners (SJKV) suggested that one of the main reasons for perpetuating and justifying derogative perceptions of the urban poor was the two-tracked education system, in which the poor attended Kannada-medium governmental schools and the well-off English-medium private schools. The association between mobilizing conditions and the education system reveal disturbing mechanisms to hinder claim-making. The experience of the slum-dwellers attending the former type of schools had not equipped them with the required fluency of writing and reading skills in Kannada and nothing at all in English. This is an alarming state of the education system that Vasavi (2003) calls elusive. The weak literacy skills of the poor seem to be exploited by the political system in a sophisticated way to keep their voice at bay. At the same time, the language cleavage (Kannada–English) is the enabling voice for the middle-higher classes. Let me illustrate this statement by concrete examples: All of my interview-partners of the four organizations said that for the poor lacking the required literacy skills kept them away from using formal instruments of appeal and they did not get invited for public consultations. Language is also politics. Citizen charters at governmental agencies were often displayed only in English, making the information inaccessible to those who have not had the privilege of attending English-medium private schools. In this regard it is important to mention that many governmental websites had their Kannada pages either not functional or 'under construction'. Important policy documents, such as the 'Special Component Plan' (requiring state budget to allocate a certain percentage to the benefit of SC/ST populations), were not available in Kannada for activists and the concerned to read and understand their content. Such examples give a glimpse into how preventing access to crucial information that could have enabled an articulate claim cancels out mobilization.

On the other hand, members of CIVIC clearly stated that publishing articles critical of the government in the English press was a form of protection from informal repression, as those actors did not read English newspapers. Hence, the colonial language was an opportunity for elite society organizations to voice their concerns without getting threatened. This two-tracked education system (public and private) that prevails in India perpetuates the cleavage between the poor from the lower castes and the well-off and continues to segment society through the lack of trust in each other and in each other's capacities.

With these instances described here that cancel out favourable conditions for mobilizing, what can be undertaken to reflect this state of affairs conceptually? Are there pertinent socio-political reflections to be attempted?

This study, like others (deWit and Berner 2009; Milbert 2008), depicts that exclusion from the formal realm is not the end of the road for the urban poor in India or elsewhere (Auyero 2000; Fernández-Kelly and Shefner 2006; Berner and Phillips 2005; Maiz and Requejo 2004). Theoretically, the interactions between the formal exclusion and the potential informal inclusion have to be taken seriously and, in my opinion, judged against two criteria: One, how do these interactions affect societal cohesion and democracy in the long term? Two, how do these interactions affect the urban poor community in the short term? It is wrong to think that informality is detrimental per se. Informal practices have developed because of unrealistic requirements of the formal. Balancing the short- and long-term effects on the urban poor need to be reflected in terms of how the informal way of life (Bayat 1997) can be transformed into a life of dignity where the urban poor are recognized as part of the city, not only as economic actors but also as substantial citizens (Holston 2008). Stretching informality to encompass dignity requires domain and scalar flexibility (Parthasarathy and Aoyama 2017) that prioritizes dignity over legality. Domain flexibility refers to the blurring of boundaries and responsibilities between the public, the private, and civil society and scalar flexibility refers to governance modalities to flexibly combine resources across spatial scales to work on local problems (ibid.).

In regard to the just stated, one question that deserves some reflection is: Does substantial citizenship mean being totally included into formality? One interesting lead to ponder on this was offered by AVAS, who encouraged one urban poor community to pay their taxes as a proactive step to enter formality and to have more leverage to claim basic services from the state. Proactively engaging with the 'formal state' would make them more 'worthy', instead of transgressing legality, in the view of an AVAS member. In their experience, registering their community-based organization and opening a bank account were often their first proactive inclusion in the formality of urban life, where otherwise it was constrained to the requirements of systems of governmentality. What is the slum-dwellers' collective capacity to enter the formal realm? What is at stake? How would it affect their lives, their interaction with the state? What are the incentives of the informal realm and the ones of the formal? How are they relevant for the urban poor? The crux of this reflection upon formality and informality leads to questioning the extent to which policy regimentation is required and the extent to which everyday, embedded practices could complement these. I am not suggesting that the urban poor should be left to their own devices as Berner and Phillips (2005) call it, nor highlighting de Soto's view of the poor as 'heroic entrepreneurs' (in Roy 2005); what I put forward is to give the tension between the formal and the informal more attention in the study of cities and the possibilities of the emergence of urban social movements.

On a methodological front, it was shown through my study that these exclusion–inclusion mechanisms are forged through a particular state that is found in every locality personalized through the local politicians or bureaucrat (Gupta 1995, 2012; Witsoe 2011, 2012). Hence, characterizing political opportunities through generic macro-indicators of features of the polity may lead to wrong conclusions about the favourability of conditions for movements. This insight has serious methodological consequences for the study of political opportunities, requiring more qualitative and anthropological methods of enquiry to make sense of how macro-level structures shape conditions for meso-level mobilizing.

On a socio-political level, it becomes clear that the state needs to expand its capacities in understanding the poor. The organizations I interviewed asserted that the state neither understood the needs of the poor nor their way of economics (Collins et al. 2009). Hence, institutional capacity that employs not only engineers but also personnel with skills to engage with the urban poor is crucial as also the capacity to produce data through participatory surveys that reflect the real policy requirements. One observation that emerged frequently was that indeed India had overdone with the number of its policy formulations (Gupta 2012), but policies addressing livelihood that would promote independence from state benefits were almost non-existent in the urban realm, highly corrupt, or not used at all.

Uslaner in his book (2008) *Corruption, Inequality and the Rule of Law* concludes, based on an empirical, quantitative enquiry, that those countries (including India) that implement particular social policies (with specific target populations) show higher levels of distrust within society and higher levels of corruption than countries (such as the Scandinavian nations) who have adopted the universal policies that transfer benefits to the entire population in the form of basic income. Led by Professor Standing, UNICEF in 2012 published the findings of their pilot project in basic income in India and came up with astounding results in regard to physical and social well-being of the community and increased social cohesion and trust. In view of the constitutional paradox discussed in Chapter 2, ongoing debates about a situated universal welfare policy are in my view a welcome contribution.

Formal illegality and repressive informality

One central thesis to this study was to investigate if the informal circuits of exchange that include forms of corruption and clientelism skewed formal conditions for mobilizing considerably. Analysing the formal opportunities and anticipating their interaction with informal circuits of exchange showed that the design of formal polity structures was prone to becoming entrenched with corrupt practices and that it was mainly their constitutional base and the rhetoric about them that was open. Such a formal design enabled government actors to engage in formal illegality, where the act was legal but the outcome contradicted the legal aim. Increasingly this is becoming a rationale to govern in a way that bypasses certain democratic safeguards (Polese, Russo, and Strazzari 2019). In the narratives of the organizations, the activists made it clear how such practices really affected their work by representing physical threats and prolonged administrative procedures. Entrenched corruption mechanisms reach out into various domains of socio-political life.

First, the imbrication of informal circuits of exchange with the electoral cycle cancels out opportunities for mobilization, because elections are fought on the basis of an economic calculus and network benefits rather than on the basis of a democratic logic.

Second, informal circuits of repression contribute in maintaining the status quo and inhibit movement organization.

I will begin by justifying the first thesis and present the mechanisms involved in what I would call the 'economics of Indian representational politics'. The important question remains: which goal do elected members pursue? The data suggests that the goal of electoral politics seems to be to recover the investments made into the electoral campaign, not only by attaining a position of power but also by collecting funds for the next campaign. An election ticket from a party or to launching oneself as an independent requires enormous investments; hence the elected term becomes the opportunity for return on investments and is driven by economic calculus.

When the electoral cycle can be divided into five stages, ranging from establishing and maintaining electoral rolls, the electoral campaign, the day of casting the vote, and the elected term to the re-election campaign, then there are at least four instances where opportunities to voice or mobilize are cancelled out.

As CIVIC's episode depicted, electoral rolls were kept faulty in order to mobilize unregistered voters on names of persons who were enrolled but not living in that constituency anymore. In consequence, this meant that the vote did not represent the interest of the person on whose name it was cast but rather the interest of the candidate for whom the vote had been bought. This means that the high prevalence of clientelism in Bangalore (Breeding 2008) and faulty rolls hindered mass mobilization of voters for a promising candidate who could really represent their interest.

During the election campaign, issue-based politics on formal terms and rational and deliberative debate should be the means to win over voters. But in Bangalore political parties invested such huge amounts of money to attain power that they were able to distribute freebies and bought a vote for as high as 500 rupees in 2010. In this sense, for the urban poor issue-politics and deliberative debate may take a back seat to the undue favours the politicians distribute. I call it 'undue favour' because they distribute items and money to recipients where actually such is not due. But in doing so, the politicians rope in urban poor communities into networks of loyalties on which the latter become dependent. The survey conducted by Breeding (2008) indeed showed that slum-dwellers felt obliged to some extent to be loyal to such patrons. In turn, for the politician who might have got elected this way, it was a means to control the community by keeping them in dependency, such that he could keep catering small favours to the community in view of re-election after five years. So, during campaign time this investment on the party ticket flows into buying votes and financing an army of canvassing personnel recruited from the poorer communities. Against such a deployment of resources, candidates from the poorer communities themselves face a very difficult challenge to win followership, as members of their own communities flock to those politicians.

The capital flow of campaign investment reaches further stages of the electoral cycle that will be described in the next points.

On election day, formally the citizens generally cast their votes and an election surveillance machinery that is well prescribed in legal documents is deployed. As the testimony of a woman candidate on booth capture included in Chapter 5 depicts, even the personnel of this machinery could be bought off in order to assure the victory of a certain candidate. The money invested in the campaign included bribes for the monitoring agency to exceed the spending limit and also bribes for the election officials who conduct the election and count the votes. In consequence, this means that when election officials can be bought off, they find themselves in the position of being able to choose the highest bidder. Even when honest candidates are able to mobilize a considerable amount of votes, the possibility of booth capture by more powerful parties makes their chances of victory indeed very slim.

Through the election term, the candidate who wins has two options to assure a re-election for the next term: either the incumbent works in favour of the constituency she/he represents and assures this to get potentially re-elected through recognized work, or she/he tries to assure re-election through bribes and engages again in clientelistic practices in view of the next elections. My data suggests that the incentive for the latter is stronger, as the incumbent sees the possibility to accumulate wealth through corruption and guarantee re-election through the same processes. Furthermore, in catering selectively to the urban poor communities, the vicious cycle of dependency can be maintained through patron–client networks that clearly overlap with the interests of political parties. Engaging in corruption allows the incumbent to have reserve funds to fund informal repression, for instance, against serious political competition or mobilizations against his interest, which was probably the strongest de-mobilizing factor.

Figure 6.1 summarizes the five points. I have shown in the figure that in the urban context of Bangalore, the imbrication of the electoral cycle and informal circuits of corruption demobilize very strongly. Informal repression, especially that is funded through bribe collection during the incumbent's term, is a source of demobilization that drives away activists, as my data reveals. Tarrow and McAdam's (2010) article entitled 'Ballots and Barricades: On the Reciprocal Relationship between Elections and Social Movements' thematizes the lacking dialogue between social movement scholarship and electoral studies. In their work, they identified six types of linkages between election and social movements on the basis of the political context in the US. These

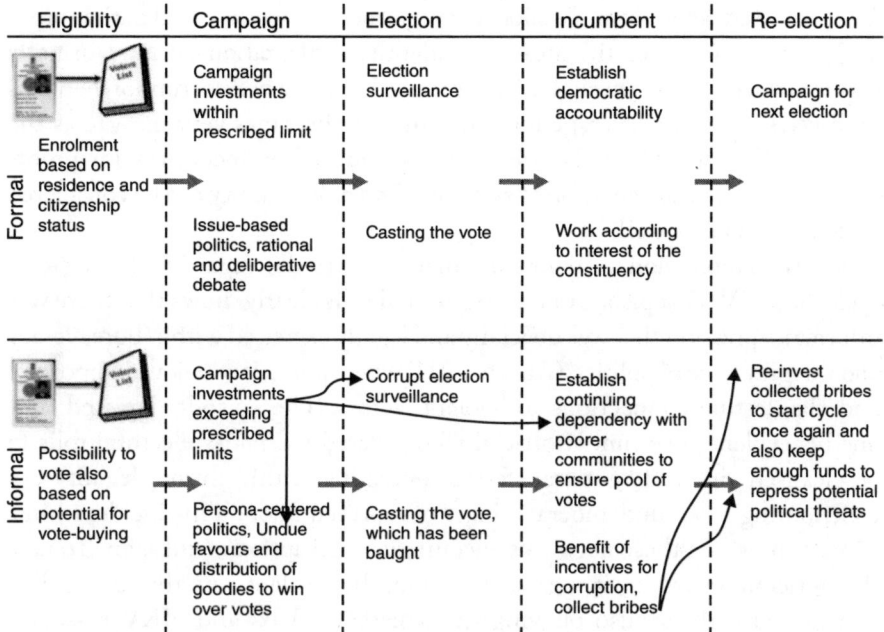

Figure 6.1 Electoral cycle and closure of opportunities

Source: Author.

linkages articulate the possible institutionalization of movements into political parties, pro- and re-active electoral mobilization or impact of movements on polarization of parties and their long-term impacts on de-/mobilization. My case situated in post-colonial India articulates linkages that go beyond these linkages and include the informal realm that has in my view a much stronger de-mobilizing impact on mobilization. But on the other hand, we should not forget that identity-based mobilization that may not always adhere to democratic principles is also a form of movement that must be taken seriously to make sense of the political landscape in India.

There were three mechanisms that sustain the status quo that could be identified within my data: Poorer communities were kept in dependency of the elected members for crucial services through patron–client networks by catering to their needs in fragments, where the contribution of the elected person was recognized, but where remaining work was left for the next election cycle.

Along with systems of governmentality and through electoral promises my data revealed that in some instances informal proof-gathering took place.

This occurred when slum-dwellers through their networks could gather proof of their status (caste certificates, voter identity cards, ration cards) – formally required documents – through illegal means. Hence, when corruption happens both ways, then the leverage for claim-making becomes very meagre as the slum-dwellers would be themselves be 'at fault'. The incentives for proof-gathering due to the operation of systems of governmentality can be considered as demobilizing as well.

Informal repression until now was mainly referred in regard to the electoral cycle, but CIVIC's episode of faulty electoral rolls clearly shows that there was informal repression that was officially and legally exercised within bureaucracy and the 'gray zone of politics' (Auyero 2011) where politicians enjoyed important and clandestine connections to 'violent' actors. The episode depicted how one benevolent government official who ordered the faulty electoral rolls to be cleansed city-wide got transferred, operating within formal legality but contributing to an undemocratic basis of representation. This incident hints towards how vast these networks encouraging corruption could span. To take this reflection further, it means that doing benevolent acts that go against corrupt networks as also blowing the whistle (CIVIC and SJKV episodes) against corrupt networks are reprimanded heavily, which again is demobilizing and inhibits change.

What emerges from this study is that there is a severe competition to represent the urban poor, not only through formal popular elections by the winning incumbent but also through other modalities: slum leaders who take forward the needs mainly to the bureaucracy and also elite and political society organizations. The slum leaders in many cases could have vested interests, but, as one member of AVAS stated, even genuine slum leaders could not be running around to assure services to their locality without having an income for the family. In this sense, she justified that they would take an extra commission from the community members. Elite society organizations especially were now almost 'invited' by policy regimes to represent the urban poor in interactions with the state, as they did possess the articulation and the social skills necessary to comprehend and adhere to policy requirements, as I demonstrated in the analysis of the housing policy. But now, one may ask: Which modality is the most legitimate, in view of the fact that formal election does not necessarily bear fruit as politicians in many cases are foremost concerned about making money rather than embodying the interest of the people? Organizational models of elite society organizations are in pursuit of tangible outcomes of their intervention in order to get funding. Slum leaders embroiled in patron–client networks and having vested interest would also be after that extra commission they would be able to make. So, who is the most legitimate? As argued earlier, the public education system does not back the possibility that slum-dwellers themselves could take forward their claims against such a governance system, except for some localities where strong organizations are present and adopt the people's cause.

Democratic theory and formal organization of democratic polities hold the separation of powers as one main pillar of the political system. My study shows that at the local level this strict separation is largely blurred through informal circuits of exchange. Even though electoral competition is very loud in urban India, there is still a void space between the slum-dwellers and the state apparatus that may come to be exploited by various actors. In view of this competition over representing the urban poor, at the theoretical level urban governance models have to embrace this political void that may be present at the local level. New conceptualizations of governance models have to come up with solutions to bring the needs and interests of the poor to the fore and to enhance participatory modes of governance and urban public pedagogy that feeds it, as I will argue in the final section of this chapter.

On a socio-political level, lessons from AVAS and SJKV showed that an efficient way to curb clientelism is indeed to bring awareness to slum-dwellers of their collective power and how to enjoy the electoral handouts, but without necessarily selling off their vote. Such awareness requires enormous time and effort, as both organizations showed, but are the most sustainable for the community and the democratic practice. This might seem very normative, as democracy is thought to be clear of clientelistic practices. Studies like Witsoe's (2011) show that corrupt politicians promoting identity-politics can be a very efficient way for urban poor communities to get their interests met, as they know that the candidate can deliver through corrupt means. Contexts like Bangalore's ought to be reflected within the benchmarks of what is worthwhile for all citizens and consider the means to integrate more substantially the marginalized of the city. This study does not have an answer to how to address this tension between normative ideals of a democracy and informal practices potentially beneficial for the urban poor. But, based on the insights from this research, I would encourage further conceptual reflection around these prevalent tensions.

The making of the city and its citizens: Skewed land allocation and housing opportunities

I argued in this book that focusing on the claim to adequate housing in the Indian urban context was a particularly useful claim for analysing civil society organization–state relations because of two reasons. First, urban land to enable housing is strongly regulated by the state. Second, there is hardly any third-sector delivery, as social housing requires specific expertise and substantial funds, which ordinary civil society organizations lack (Sen 1998). Hence, it was assumed that the principle target for claiming housing for the urban poor would remain to be the state. The empirical analysis based on fieldwork and policy analysis depicts a more nuanced picture involving issues of land as a primary exigency for explaining politics over housing for the urban poor. The content of this association articulates over two theses that can be formulated the following way:

First, claim-making is hindered due to the fragmented landownership, skewed land allocation, and urban land use as financial asset rather than means to facilitate dignified housing.

Second, the form of habitation itself shapes access to substantial citizenship. The value of the political currency of public housing and its implementation is played out in a way that demobilizes and tests the unity of the urban poor.

I will first discuss the first thesis regarding land in showing how different aspects of land allocation influence the claim of the urban poor. A conjuncture of different forces at the allocation level characterizes the competition for land and makes targets shift to the detriment of the urban poor.

As described in Chapter 3, the governance of land in urban India is very fragmented, as various government agencies own urban land. Governmental ownership of land means that it is for that particular agency to determine the use and to manage it according to the regulation and practices of that agency (Mahadevia 2009). I also argued that this particular disposition represented incentives for corruption as coordination between the different agencies regarding the governance of urban land had become difficult. Fragmentation of land ownership leads also to the fragmentation of target, when the claimants try to assert land. The process continues also to fragment the claimant base. To argue this last step of my reflection, I take recourse to Gupta (1995, 2012) who powerfully showcased that there was not one unified idea and experience of state, but rather that the state was particular to the locality, through particular government officials acting at the local level. In consequence, this means that when land ownership is fragmented between government agencies, then claimants meet 'that particular state' in that locality. When experience with one particular agency is not the same as the experience with another agency, which owns land in another part of the city, the claimants have less of a common base to mobilize collectively on the same issue. One member of SJKV went even further in saying that land fragmentation had the power to divide the community, when different agencies roped in some slum-dwellers into the clientelistic practices through extended networks within their communities. Increasingly, large chunks of land have been acquired by private developers and builders, who now constitute an additional set of actors that have either the muscle power or the money power to evict dwellers squatting on the land. Claims and stays of the court did not even enter the picture as money power could buy them off, as DPI narrated. But this financial input is often only of short relief. The fragmentation of targets explains furthermore why a city-wide social movement on housing was yet to be observed.

Another reason for the lack of movement involving land and housing emerges from the fact that within the urban realm the competition over land is heightened. With rapid and haphazard urbanization, land has become scarce and its value has rocketed. Urban land is a productive location, where businesses root themselves and thrive to cater to the masses or the demands of the economy. In other words, competitors are many, ranging from the urban poor, private middle/upper-class owners, businesses, and industries to land developers and also governmental agencies, which hold land as valuable assets. This competition takes place at the local, regional, and at the global level. At the local level, the competition takes place between urban communities themselves in attracting a scheme such as the BSUP into their locality through the relevant networks they maintain. Urban poor communities working with AVAS, for example, had a better chance of benefitting from the scheme than those not working with such an elite society organization, as they would have lacked the network to know about the upcoming scheme and play it out to their favour. It also takes place between slum-dwellers having encroached private land. In this case, the role of the state may change into one which brokers between the two parties, as shown in AVAS's experience. At a regional level, the competition of various industries for land allocation and the designation of Special Economic Zones are fought over as different studies have witnessed (Buschi 2013; Benjamin and Raman 2011a; Harriss-White and Heyer 2010). At the global level, the economic liberalization and the welcoming stance towards foreign direct investments in India make the competition for land open for multinational corporate entities. The actors of these global operations that have concrete repercussions at the local level (Keivani and Mattingly 2007; Shaw and Satish 2007; Baxi 2005; Sassen 2003) are the invisible targets for the urban poor claiming their share of land, as AVAS explained. Within such heightened competition, the state has a rather comfortable position of choosing the allottee according to the level of gains that can be made, which are increasingly being articulated through policy reforms, such as the Karnataka Industrial Policy. It is hence important to reflect on the incentives for land allocation by the state. One hypothesis is that the biggest incentives for land allocation, given the current scenario in Bangalore, is to give it to competitors whose investments are the largest and where local employment may be created, but also where yields from grand corruption could be expected (Jain 2001). Industrial policy is also increasingly allowing easy entry of capital, but also fast exit of capital, which is detrimental to area development. Press reviews about land scams, especially during the rule of Chief Minister B. S. Yeddyurappa (at the time of my fieldwork), are witness to this tendency. But what press reviews hardly reported was that land was not only a source of corruption but that it was linked to a source of informal repression, to assert the land for its value among many competitors, as episodes of SJKV and DPI depicted.

All in all, it seems that the rationale for land allocation has not occurred with a view to facilitating equitable urbanization, but as a financial asset making current mechanism.

Now, addressing the second thesis that I formulated regarding public housing delivery, there are three aspects that emerge worthy of discussion to take research on housing further. First, it is meaningful to recognize what adequate housing represents for the urban poor. It is not just a roof over their head, but impacts social and psychological features of life. Not only is it protection from the elements, but also a constituent to community, a source of self-esteem and safety, an opportunity for bankability, and a realm to safeguard health, education, and family ties (Bourke 2009; Gilbert 2007). Against the centrality of what housing represents, it is striking what assumptions are held by government agencies on the capacity of the poor to endure hardships. In none of the localities where the sampled organizations were working, transit housing arrangements were made for those projects that were realized in situ. It was assumed that they could put up their tents and tinsheets on the street, in the park, or wherever they found place without attracting complaints from the middle class. It can be imagined that the policy planners thought that the dwellers having lived in abysmal slum-condition could bear any arrangement. But in all cases of in situ realizations, the dwellers had far more stable and better habitation prior to the transit period. This worsening condition was also no trigger to speed up construction, nor change implementation guidelines. Even for those communities being rehabilitated under BSUP to the periphery, it was taken for granted that they could and would start building from scratch a livelihood, schooling, and other lacking amenities. This attitude of leaving the urban poor to 'their own devices' (Berner and Phillips 2005) so brutally almost reverses the welfare provisions meant for them. Gilbert (2007) problematizes this housing approach of delivering formal houses with the obligation of having to pay for all amenities without any subsidy, bringing these families to the brink of their financial capacity just on housing. On the other hand, the opportunity to avail a house in a city like Bangalore being such a rare occasion compels the community to comply with government orders for fear of losing out on it. Hence, SJKV's achievement of not compromising to get land and houses on the terms (ground-floor housing) of the slum-dwellers is noteworthy.

At the level of implementation, it seems that a model was adopted that made it possible to siphon off project money through three factors that emerged in my data. First, in not informing the urban poor communities about what exactly they were entitled to. Second, in encouraging tenders to use the lowest grade of building material, as tendering companies had to give a cut of their earnings to local politicians. Third, in none of the communities were the slum-dwellers, who often worked as construction workers, allowed to be employed to build their own houses. This enabled the contractors to hire the cheapest inexperienced labour force from rural areas beyond the borders of Karnataka, saving labour costs and also ensuring that those vulnerable workers could not mobilize.

Now what does such a state of affairs imply for the governance of land and housing especially in regard to the urban poor? Pierre (1999) outlines four types of urban governance models judging them against nine defining criteria. In his treatise, the 'corporatist model' is the most inclusive model for urban governance. Indeed aiming for participation as the key evaluative criteria promises that communities have a say. But in my view, what goes missing is the recognition of the fact that participation is indeed, as demonstrated, not equally open to all. Sassen (2003) identifies the dynamics of today's global cities that deepen the divide between segments as elite and political society (in her words, formal and informal workers). She depicts how citizenship is not merely the relation to the nation state, but how cities have become strategic sites for new types of citizenship practices. She argues that the embeddedness of citizenship is no more only 'in systems for owning and protecting property and to implement various immunities.... Today's citizenship practices have to do with the production of "presence" by those without power, and politics that claims rights to the city', in terms of Henri Le Febvre (Sassen 2003, 58).

She further states that the 'disadvantaged' in global cities can gain 'presence' in their engagement with power (Sassen 2003, 62). Claims to right to the city relate to different understandings of urban meaning (Castells 1983, 278). The conflicting object between the claimant and the institutionalized dominant interests is the meaning both parties assigned to the city's performance. For the claimant, namely members of political society, the meaning of the city was one that should maintain equality and welfare of its people, endorsing them with their citizenship rights. As a result, the practice of citizenship rights for members of the political society who are in the position to claim becomes a collective endeavour. For those representing the institutionalized dominant interests, the meaning of the city is one that provides them political power and the power to have control over resources.

Rajagopal (2011) argues that top-down engineered city master-plans, as implemented in Bangalore, become instruments asserting such a control. She therefore rather encourages understanding the eternal negotiations and politics within informal economies and activities. A reading and mapping of the city 'through endorsing the intertwined relationship of plural legalities, social history, economic, cultural and political geography to its built form, is imperative to devise place specific regulations' (ibid.).

At a conceptual level, the first takeaway is that housing cannot be studied without enquiring into the politics of land and its allocation and governance. Hence, land assertions in the urban realm and the modality of it are crucial to just starting to think about the possibilities of housing and the claims upon it. Benjamin's concepts (2008) of occupancy urbanism hints at this direction for future studies. He brings to notice that viewing terrains as being constituted by multiple political spaces inscribed by complex local histories gives the operations the poor maintain with the state embedded in lower bureaucracy the attention it deserves. Such a reading could project urban planning methods to be more inclusive and perhaps less normative.

At a socio-political level my case study showed that the best way for urban poor communities to gain ownership over the public housing delivery concerning them was to gain considerable social skills regarding the policy provisions and to participate in its design. This is true also regarding the informal entrenchments around land to resist informal repression arising from it. So, in parallel with the physical implementation of housing, asserting their voice over it would make it most sustainable. But when such projections go against the intentions of the implementing governmental agency, the means to tackle the problem do not only lie within the communities. However, they are the ones who could trigger it, as the examples of AVAS and SJKV showed.

Task division between elite and political society organizations

One very clear insight that the data brought was that political opportunities indeed presented themselves differently to elite and political society organizations. These two types of organizations also maintained very distinct networks and confirmed that civil society was deeply segmented. The evolved action repertoires and their respective achievements also showed that the types of organizations had different strengths and weaknesses. Building on these differentiators, I argue:

Given the segmented nature of civil society in India, a particular task division between elite society and political society to engage in collective claim-making could be beneficial for the city.

I will first elaborate on some core differences, discuss the tensions, and, building on their respective strength, suggest a collaborative model.

The most striking difference between most segments at the discursive level was the fact that elite society organizations never problematized the notion of caste in Indian society, whereas political society justified all their activities on the basis of caste. To me it seems that while elite society sees poverty as the syndrome for the condition of the slum-dweller, political society clearly delineates it as caste. In discarding caste from their vocabulary, elite society members do not recognize intra-/inter-community processes that determine the possibilities of mobilizing the community for a cause. Without overcoming this caste identification, as SJKV showed, it is very difficult to unite the community for a cause – especially in urban areas where a community living in one locality can be heterogeneous in terms of caste, religion, region, and language, as Haritas depicts in her research (Haritas 2013). Thematizing caste could be also fruitful to dissect, together with the community, the patronage circuits within not only the slum community but also the larger political realm. As Kanchan (2003) and Witsoe (2011) show, such circuits are primarily based on primordial identities. Such an exercise could reveal to the slum-dwellers the interconnectedness of their needs; the political response and the complex imbrication the actors of the governmentality system maintain help them to make more informed political choices that benefit them the most. Esman (1999, 364) hypothesizes

> that unless the community is not mobilised for political action – as Blacks have in the United States, and Dalit have not in India – the beneficiaries of affirmative action will not serve as effective representatives of their community and will not be under social and political pressure to perform on their behalf.

In other words, if target groups such as SC/ST in India do not get mobilized, they could remain in dependency of others to provide for them. Unfortunately, as found in my data, livelihood arrangements and the education system do not back such prospects. Gupta states that ignorance of the social world of the Indian bureaucracy, particularly the role of brokers in channelling bribes to officials, is the main cause of the failure to access (rural) land rights (Gupta 1995, 381).

This lack of 'self' mobilization creates this political void that is not only usurped by politicians but also elite society organizations. As visible in the case of CIVIC, their members spoke of multiple spaces where elite society organizations could connect to such a void. They termed these as the 'activist' space and distinguished these from the 'advocacy' space, which was focused on bringing awareness about issues. 'Competitors' to CIVIC stated that CIVIC had claimed their activist space by changing their organizational strategy from consultations with residents' welfare associations (RWAs) to working with the urban poor. 'Activist', in their understanding, was a term to describe the engagement with the state through on-the-ground interventions. But at the same time, they distinguished being involved in governance and not politics, governance being an administrative task in their understanding. Given the socio-political environment in Bangalore, was it possible to engage 'only' in governance and not politics but still be involved in claiming rights and services on behalf of the urban poor? I think at the core this was the experiment that CIVIC had embarked on. In my critical appraisal, I judged it was problematic, as it was not sustainable for the urban poor.

In my view, it is exactly this tension between the requirements of politics and governance that new modes of the thinking about urban spaces necessitate.

At a conceptual level, this investigation confirms the segmented nature of civil society in India. This segmentation was according to whether the community was treated as a target of governmentality or not. But it is certainly not the only attribute that segments civil society. In today's world, increasing inequality also fuelled by the global economy and the precarious conditions for citizens even in wealthy nations are only deepening and widening the gap. So, being sensitive to differential impacts of political opportunities and institutional arrangements in general is a lesson, in my view, for all type of empirical cases. This means that introducing the comparative axis at actor levels in a research design promises to be revealing.

At a socio-political level, in my view, one could foresee a task division between elite and political society organizations. The results of my investigation clearly showed that those organizations that were able to infuse a maximum of social skill resources into the community were the ones who had the most sustainable impact on them, equipping communities to independently engage in claim-making by understanding their socio-political environment and introspecting themselves. These were SJKV and AVAS, and SJKV was more efficient as they spoke from the same discursive repertoire as the communities they were assisting based on caste. On the other hand, CIVIC – with its aim of working within the system and demanding accountability – was highly successful in digging out important orders and prescriptions that could serve as formal/legal weapons to demand rights and services from the state. Formal tactics such as the Right to Information Act being less accessible to poorly literate slum-dwellers, elite society organizations such as CIVIC could bring valuable contribution in enabling access to prevalent political opportunities.

What I am concretely suggesting is that elite society organizations could focus on claiming accountability from the state in all public domains, make information about policies available, advocate with banks to open access to credit, guide communities to make a leap into formality, and, most importantly, raise funds to enable an income to promising activists from the community to carry out the necessary activities as un-coopted actors. This relates to the tasks that political society organizations could focus on, such as diffusing information in an accessible language, infusing social skill resources – from helping challenge self-perceptions to dissecting the socio-political environment with the slum communities – and mobilizing the communities in order to claim their place in the city as citizens, not just as city dwellers. While such a model suggests a division of tasks, it does not suggest isolation from each other.In my view, this proposition would enable more intense exchange through networks that would overlap due to the two-directional flow of information along with the transfers of incomes to select community activists, and by overcoming certain asymmetries of access to information and power.

A call for a critical urban public pedagogy

The question at the heart of the housing problem is: How can adequate and affordable housing be provided on a large scale, quickly (Monkkonen 2018, 17)? P.K. Das reminded us that claiming adequate housing is probably the only viable way to ensure dignified living for the urban poor in India. Monkkonen and other scholars argue that there is much thought on housing policy design, evaluation, and finance, but strategies of political organizing are the need of the hour. In this book, I discussed and depict the modality of asserting adequate housing in Bangalore. Today's housing question, rather, is: How can communities be organized to engage in claiming housing at scale? How can they be organized to collectively learn to claim, how can they learn to claim in a united voice, transcending identities, the very local state and the repression they face, and how can they learn to reconstruct a collective identity that is constituted by the urban space that they inhabit and enrich?

The lessons from this book have taught us the impediments that there are to such mobilizing, but the four civil society organizations have also shed light on community engagements and tactical strategies to bring about transformative change to claim adequate housing, resist co-opted forces, or to know how to navigate the socio-political landscape. Tactical knowledge and social skill based on particular resource base (often determined by socio-historical positions) are key to sustainable outcomes in community engagement and mobilizing.

Tactical knowledge deployed by these organizations had evolved over years of engagement in the public realm, developing a fine understanding of the working of the state represented in the urban, enmeshed with clandestine networks that included nodes of political patronage, repressive forces, and corporate power, as also the psychology of the larger public and vulnerable communities. In other words, they had learnt the meaning of the instantiation of the formal, normative democratic prescriptions in a provincialized embodiment on the ground. Within such a context, they had also learnt the relevant policies and how to redirect the consequences and arbitrariness of 'formal good governance' implementation for more equitable housing outcomes for the urban poor by understanding the vernacular demands of governance. They had learnt to assess threats and risks of violent backlashes to their actions and developed nuanced, adaptive strategies to protect themselves from informal repression. These learning outcomes of these organizations occurred for the larger part in experiential learning in everyday situations. Through this mode of learning they had negotiated meaning from competing frames and discourses and developed their tactics and justified them through a repertoire of stories. Developing tactical knowledge was at the core of the mobilizing effort.

The community meetings that AVAS held on accounting, saving schemes, and the importance of unity to hold one's ground, the series of interaction with slum-dwellers by the SJKV making them reflect on their worth and rights in an ever-expanding city, the awareness of government procedure imbibed by the DPI, the grievance redressal meeting that CIVIC held to open the eyes of government officials about guidelines prescriptions and their failing implementation: these are the milieus of learning – activists from such organizations are the pedagogues while the inhabitants, institutional and economic actors, and challengers emerge as urban learning communities.

Developing, transferring, teaching, and learning contextual tactical knowledge comprise the curriculum for what I would like to call a critical urban public pedagogy (CUPP) that is situated and much needed for social transformation to achieve inclusive cities. In the following, I dissect the approach in its components.

According to the *Encyclopedia Britannica*,[1] '*pedagogy* is the study of teaching methods, including the aims of education and the ways in which such goals may be achieved'. The act of teaching relates the teacher and learner, who work together to modify the learners' experience and understanding by enhancing his/her knowledge on a subject matter. *Public pedagogy*, as a concept, focuses on various forms, processes, and sites of education and learning that occur beyond formal schooling (Sandlin et al. 2011) and on the idea of outside curricula, both implicit and explicit, in many kinds of educational situations, in which learning occurs (Schubert 2010). These 'outside sites' are identified as institutionalized sites such as museums, public monuments, public artworks, cemeteries, and public parks (Sandlin et al. 2011). In their literature review spanning a sample of 420 publications, Sandlin et al. (2011) review the usage of 'public pedagogy' and identify that its theorizing and research have been largely influenced by the contributions of cultural studies as well as various arts-based approaches to examining learning in the public sphere (ibid., 339). Henry A. Giroux's work (1994, 1999, 2000, 2004a, 2004b in Sandlin et al. 2010) has been seminal to describing the intersections between historical context, theoretical traditions, and situations of practice. While his early work focused on public pedagogy as a means of engaging with the critical analysis of mass culture and media, his later work expanded to explore popular culture as a site for social justice, to critique counter-hegemonic possibilities, and to pave the way for a critical public pedagogy (Sandlin et al. 2010, 3).

Critical pedagogy has its roots in Marxist and neo-Marxist critical theory and frames a transformational educational response to institutional and ideological domination. Freire (1970/1998, in Gruenewald 2003) reiterated that all learners exist in a cultural context in his seminal work on 'pedagogy of the oppressed'. He asserted that acting upon temporal-spatial situationality is liberating. The spatial dimension of this situationality connects critical pedagogy with pedagogy of place that engages learners in what Freire called 'conscientizacao', meaning, 'learning to perceive social, political and economic contradictions and to take action against the oppressive elements of reality' (Freire, 1970 /1995 in Gruenewald 2003). Social movements hence also become spaces of learning (Darts 2004 ; Earl 2016). Gruenewald (2003) argues for a critical pedagogy of place, which educates citizens to have some direct bearing on the well-being of the social and ecological places people inhabit (ibid.). *Critical urban public pedagogy* (CUPP) relates to the urban as a space in which the substantialization of democracy happens in cities, according to Oldfield (2014), since the influence of cities is greater, as centres of economic, political, and cultural life (Wirth 1938 in Earl 2016), in which contradictions and tensions associated with historically and geographically accumulated strategies are expressed and played out (Merrifield 2013 and Brenner et al. 2012, both in Earl 2016). Earl (2016) claims that a new agenda-setting for cities must begin with the *reclaiming* of self and space through new forms of pedagogy.

By mapping the term CUPP, one could state that it involves acts of engagement that relate teaching and learning to enhance knowledge regarding a particular content (pedagogy) outside formal schooling (public) to reclaim the city (urban) through democratic means or forms of resistance (critical).

It is noteworthy that all the aforementioned references mainly discuss liberal democracies. To define such a situated approach begs an analogy to social movement concepts to situate the conceptual content for provincialized understandings of democracy and vernacular modes of governance.

A situated pedagogy connects the curriculum to the everyday lives and is interested not only in identity formation but also in forging collective identities and relationships by paying attention to environment and places. These places in turn need to be decoded politically, socially, historically, and aesthetically. In a situated pedagogy, spaces become performative for action, intervention, and perhaps transformation (Kitchens 2009). As such, learning moves beyond schools into learning communities and into public space.

In their review on public pedagogy, Sandlin et al. (2011, 359) conclude that there is a lack of studies that show how public pedagogy actually operates as pedagogy and 'how the intended educational meanings of public pedagogies are internalized, reconfigured, and mobilized by public citizens'. This may be due to the inattention to learning theories relating to public pedagogies. In this regard, McFarlane's book *Learning Cities* not only focuses on sites of urban learning (Mumbai's slums) but also articulates in an assemblage approach learning as 'an important political and practical domain through which the city is assembled, lived and contested' (McFarlane 2011, 1). In his sense, learning is a 'specific process, practice and interaction through which knowledge is created, contested and transformed, and how perception emerges and changes' (McFarlane 2011, 3).

I argue that viewing learning and co-production of situated tactical knowledge as urban practice is vital, as they must shape the curriculum for a CUPP that has to stand against a singular type of urban imagination that is promoted by inter-referencing strategies, transnational policy networks, and international finance institutions that were recommended by the same set of firms. This singular urban imagination of world-class and smart cities finds its physical way into the urban tapestry through policy mobilities and hoardings in Indian cities that display the projection of this assumed economically viable development model. The implementation of these urban fantasies demand speed and urgency as solutions to the urban crisis, as means of bypassing policy failures and democratic safeguards in order to leapfrog into envisioned urban futures (Datta and Shabhan 2017). Such tendencies stand in disjuncture with continuities of local developments (Ong and Roy 2010) and dull down possible radical imaginations of the urban future (Earl 2016). These circulated hegemonic visions of the city are then often perpetuated by the middle and upper classes and reinforced through the urban agenda setting mechanisms (Arabindoo 2010; Coelho 2009). A situated curriculum, hence, must serve to reclaim the city.

Engagement to reclaim the city requires scientific or technical expertise, but more importantly it requires a situated CUPP that imparts procedural and tactical knowledge of the regulatory decision-making environment and capacity to moderate collective envisioning of an inclusive city. Parnell and Watson (2009, 2014 in Patel et al. 2015) go further in adding that any knowledge formulation has to be worked from the bottom to identify, define, and find solutions to the problem.

A research agenda for a critical urban public pedagogy could follow these lines of enquiry:

- How to articulate and organize a situated CUPP?
- How does CUPP operate?
- Who are the pedagogues and how to support them?
- Which are the conducive learning sites for particular groups?
- How to organize learning communities?
- What are the situated knowledge requirements?
- What are the modalities to deliver tactical knowledge to engage in acts to reclaim the city?
- How can lessons from a particular place be compared with other cities?

What are the roles of different actors to support a CUPP approach to reclaim the city by imparting tactical knowledge? The Indian state and municipalities legally already have available capacities to implement CUPP and would 'only' need to activate resources. The 74th Constitutional amendment prescribes ward committees and the Street Vendors Act, for example, prescribes town vending committees; these are forums that if capacitated could be instrumental for bottom-up urban pedagogy. In a first instance, they would need to be constituted and the members of the committees trained; second, ward populations will need to be made aware of the existence and functioning of these committees that represent them. But most importantly, municipalities and parastatal state agencies will have to learn to let go of and devolve power to these Constitutional provisions for a bottom-up governance.

The roles of elite and political society organizations and their funders in this endeavour are crucial. As discussed in the last section on synergistic view of the capacities of both types of organizations and the possible complementary task division, they both have strengths and weaknesses. If collaborated with a view to imparting tactical knowledge (with the support of the state) they could assist ward and vending committees and most importantly could ignite communities in which they work. Such impact can be, of course, only achieved when funding mechanisms support such an approach and share such a view for societal change. Currently, increased corporate funding has become available because of the corporate social responsibility (CSR) legislation – Section 135 and Schedule 7 of the Companies Act, 2013 – and CSR Policy Rules that came into effect in 2014, requiring that minimum 2 per cent of average net profit be spent on CSR activities. Companies invest in the places they operate, concentrating CSR funding in metros and they in general shy away from funding long-term pedagogic projects that could challenge the status quo, as they demand immediate results. International and national donors often follow the same logic. Funding campaigns and funding particular activists within communities through the grant of fellowships that could cut the need for taking commissions as a means of livelihood could be a good way to support CUPP.

Of course, formal educational institutions such as schools, colleges, and vocational training centres could do their part in imbibing the Constitutional rights and duties and making civic education work for the city concretely by teaching actionable practice by imparting tactical knowledge. Establishing formal and informal circuits of knowledge exchange at all geographical scales could be modes of imbibing a culture for a critical urban public pedagogy, but also a means of protection against unpleasant backlashes.

The content for a CUPP imparting tactical knowledge indeed lies, on one hand, in the Indian Constitution and, on the other, it is to be sourced from the situated and co-produced knowledge in urban locales. But in a deeper sense, as Dunn (in Piliavsky 2014) puts it, it will also stem from the reality of societal organization that spans far 'lengthier than the epoch in which the normative order of the modern West took its present shape and established its queasy hegemony' and the creative alternatives to it.

A CUPP then must include conceptual leaps of social movement scholarship that presents a toolkit stemming this *normative order of the modern West* into disciplinary fields relevant for a situated urban practice. I argued all along this book that a provincialized understanding of democracy, a vernacular understanding of the mode of governance, situated policy learning, and learning to organize learning communities represent the hallmark to claim housing and a dignified way of life in a city – ultimately, to claim to belong to a space that nourishes one's dreams.

Notes

1. See https://www.britannica.com/science/pedagogy.

Epilogue

During the subsequent years after this research, I landed yearly in Bangalore. Hemming the road connecting the airport to the city, a tapestry of hoardings fuel dreams of fancy homes, jewellery, and cars. Of these, one hoarding caught my attention and never left me since. Against a crude cement multi-storeyed structure and featuring a luxurious villa, it displayed, 'The 1% Club, are you the ONE?' That question invited passengers to project themselves as part of an exclusive club that would be constituted through extreme urban inequality. What are the embodiments of a city that lures exclusiveness and caters to the ambitions of the higher economic class? The concept of 'worlding' (Roy and Ong 2011) not only invokes those practices that imagine alternative elite socio-economic configurations by co-referencing to 'modern' cities, but is also emblematic on a larger scale of the operations to enter into global networks of capital and exchange. Roy and Ong understand worlding practices as a process of dialectic urbanism between elite aspirations from above and aspirations and mobilization of local communities from below (Teo 2014). An illustrative example of this dialectic occurred on the 2 March 2017, the day on which the civil society in Bangalore was in a jubilant mood. In a sustained collective and creative effort, citizens had campaigned and achieved to deter the state government from building a 6.9 kilometre steel flyover connecting the city centre with the airport. The steel structure would have cost the city around 270 million dollars and 2,244 old trees of 71 species (Nagendra 2017). The proposal for the metallic giant stood in direct violation of numerous Acts and in contempt of several judicial orders. These texts of law required the state to conduct public consultations at large, engage in an environmental impact assessment, put the project financing under review, and follow rules to retain green, lakes, and heritage spaces. The state bypassed all of these requirements and pushed for the construction for the mere purpose of cutting travel time to the airport by 7–15 minutes by car for the 1 per cent club of the city's 11 million population. The steel lobby was strong and the political pressures to bag a massive infrastructure project that would cross-finance upcoming assembly elections were high.

The steel flyover is a useful metaphor for the state's attempt to flyover citizens' rights and accountability provisions firmly rooted in India's Constitution and to allocate public funds to the 1 per cent. The press reports on policy reforms, urban planning exercises, changes in zonal regulations and urban governance were illustrative of modes of bypass governance – a type of governance that literally bypasses democratic and environmental provisions for speed that has now become a persistent feature of new city-making strategies as a way out of the crisis in the Global South, as Datta and Shaban (2017) argue. They call the structural underpinnings of cities that operate by the imperative of speed 'fast cities'. The crisis in Bangalore remains an explosive cocktail consisting of infrastructure failures, environmental degradation, and municipal bankruptcy. In January 2014 the mayor declared Bangalore bankrupt and had to use vibrant public buildings and places as collaterals to underwrite loans to the municipality from public banks, by converting low-value public space into higher-value developments, unlocking land to be bid for in the real-estate markets (Goldman, Gidwani, and Upadhya 2017). Following such a financialization logic, the city's institutional and infrastructural architecture is undergoing major transformations (Idiculla 2017) to cater to private high-end investors that are rolled out through mushrooming para-statal agencies that undermine electoral accountability but cater to the 1 per cent club and this as fast as possible. Speed will be used as a guiding allegory to this epilogue to reveal undergirding mechanisms that shape current urban political opportunities and ultimately condition the 'right to city'.

The fundamental question raised in this book is: What are the 'real' existing conditions for differently resourced organizations to mobilize on the issue of adequate housing? I explored this question by investigating political opportunities, informal exchange circuits skewing conditions for mobilizing, and action repertoires of diversely resourced organizations. Here I seek to delineate major shifts in political opportunities since my fieldwork, as capital circuits are increasingly affecting policy and urban governance. I do this by contextualizing the results of this research in a larger political economy as the financial logic at global and local levels has heavily entered land and housing transactions and is reflected in the subsequent avatars of housing policy. With this rationale I discuss the structural underpinnings of financialized modes of governance and exemplify through the anachronic paces of state response in different policy domains. The four communities featuring in the book are revisited in view of the slower pace of state response keeping them in perpetual dependency. This book traced how money got infused into election cycles and had the capacity to demobilize communities holding housing claims. Here, by asking the question 'where the money comes from?' leads us to the city's hinterland where real estate and politics are hand-in-glove. Complex circuits of capital finally are increasingly shaping political opportunities for housing. Based on misconceptions regarding housing for the urban poor, I indicate modes to respond to today's housing question and put forward that it is the sense of belonging that has the potential to realize the right to the city.

Speed as an allegory to understand the 'urban'

Indeed the units of time has changed for different policy domains on the basis of modes of acceleration to deal with crisis and, second, due to the logic of competition. Datta and Shabhan (2017) articulate acceleration as the mode to deal with crisis and as the guiding trope of fast cities. These develop according to the authors along corporate-led visions, which are undergoing a global revival under the dominant rhetoric of 'crisis' (Datta and Shabhan 2017, 11). Such visions promote an accelerated process of innovation, entrepreneurialism, and economic growth and inscribe themselves within fast governance as governance by exception rather than experimentation with alternative imaginings to the dominant logics of capital (ibid.). The legitimacy for acceleration derives from the rhetoric of urgency, which calls for speeding processes of bureaucracy, planning, and democracy, which are perceived to be slowing down urbanization. Fast cities reorder urban temporality by actively engaging in innovation strategies designed to bypass ruptured infrastructure and unworkable regulatory regimes (ibid.).

Rosa (2013) argues that the logic of competition has pervaded every sphere of society and that the instigating metrics of performance has become the predominant principle of allocation of resources. He further argues that the only societal domain that until now has been spared the logic of competition is the regimes of welfare with their negotiated patterns of redistribution within a framework of rights and dignity that justify non-acceleration or even retardation. To illustrate the different pace of operation and state response, I will describe two events that occurred in Bangalore in 2016, which could not be more contrasting.

Anachronisms in contrasting policy domains

Early in 2016 two events occurred just a few days apart in Bangalore. First, a public hearing on evictions in Karnataka was organized by the state-wide slum dwellers' organization, Karnataka Slum Janara Sanghatanegala Okkoota. The second was the Global Investor's Meet organized by the Karnataka state government, which rolled out a red carpet for the corporates of the world.

On a sunny morning, I entered Gandhi Bhavan, where the public hearing on evictions were to take place. Life-size statues of Gandhi on the premises conveyed a sense of responsiveness to his legacy. The room was packed with slum dwellers, activists, and researchers who over two hours absorbed eviction narratives and stared at children's paintings depicting the bulldozer in the act of destruction.

It is a paradox that on the one hand the state is governed by the principle of welfare developmentalism supported by complex bureaucratic guarantees subsidizing food, free primary education, and citizenship and that on the other hand these accomplishments literally came under the bulldozer by the will of the same actor, the state. The plight by an evicted woman who exclaimed 'our stomach burns, the government has spoilt our children' and the jury member who picked the phrase and stated 'yes, our stomach burns and we need the fire to fight!' received resounding support from the public, in which representatives of state agencies were conveniently absent.

By contrast, an army of government officials stood ready at Bangalore's Palace grounds, where the state government, less than a week after the public hearing on evictions, welcomed representatives of corporations from across the world to the Global Investor's Meet, 'Karnataka Invest'. The event had to be worthy of Bangalore's high rank in the global cities investment monitor 2016 overseen by KPMG. A top-notch pop-up exhibition centre with air-conditioned meeting rooms and carpeted toilets, glossy documentation, and lavish food awaited the delegates and potential investors to be lured by the potentials of the land of Karnataka and the reliability of government support (Rao Dhananka 2017). I argue that both events are part of the same capital cycle of accumulation by dispossession (Harvey 2009), but that the state bureaucracy represents and paces itself very differently in respect to these diverse policy domains. The events are contrasted, first, by the speed with which the state actors respond and act; second, in the amount and diversity of the state agencies involved and the degree of coordination among themselves; and, third, in the way information is differently deployed (Rao Dhananka 2017).

At Bangalore's Palace grounds I could not help but notice the coordinated efforts of various government agencies, the impressive effort of information compilation and dissemination, and the persistent promotion of the 'ease of doing business' through higher procedural speed spurred by a single window clearance mechanism anchored in the nodal office called Udyog Mitra – a government of Karnataka undertaking. Single window implementation is an extremely complex and costly undertaking requiring a tremendous effort of coordination, information compilation, and political will.

The political will manifested itself most grandly in the amendments to the Karnataka Land Reforms Act, 1961, that allowed speeding up the approvals of land allocation for investors and made available a 'land bank' of 115,000 acres for industrial or real estate projects. Speed of sanctioning land and promising world-class infrastructure were the crux of the brand 'Karnataka'. Land is the material face of virtual global capital that is directed towards investments into property and real estate as an important route to access emerging markets (Halbert and Rouanet 2013). As several scholars have noted, real estate has become the frontier of wealth accumulation in India (Goldman 2011). Such investments require that transnational finance capital interface with state actors at a city-regional level. This interface intrinsically relates to the removal or bypassing of regulatory impediments.

Regarding the public hearing on eviction, across the urban cases speed of action was slow. Information about the eviction and the potential relief response was scarce and the multiplication of bureaucratic and governmental agencies high: 14 government agencies were directly involved in evicting the poor and 11 other agencies were indirectly involved or were sought after by the grieving community for support.

The low speed of action, the diversity and multiplication of bureaucratic and governmental agencies involvement, and the strategic deployment of information feed into and perpetuate what Akhil Gupta (2012) calls a structure of violence embedded in a state that is polycentric. He argues that violence becomes structural as it is impossible to identify a 'single actor' who commits violence. Violence becomes impersonal and enduring, contributing to the slow pace of uncoordinated response.

Why is slow pace constitutive of the situation of the poor? The pace itself represents a mechanism to perpetuate the dependency of the poor, as they remain a group to be catered to, as targets of policy in the sense of Chatterjee's political society, but dimming down the potential of resistance through a blurred and complex information base and the multiplication and anonymization of targets.

The four communities revisited

Following up with the fate of the four communities featured in this research confirmed the aforementioned mechanism, as I revisited the areas that had benefitted from the BSUP housing and spoke to some of the inhabitants whom I had interviewed previously. The areas had transformed. People did not refer to those as slum areas, but rather as the housing board quarters. These quarters were clearly identifiable as public low-income housing though.

In all four localities, cement blocks had replaced less permanent structures, but the buildings were of varying degrees of quality. Consistently, infrastructure for urban services and the services themselves such as water and electricity were implemented very weakly. 'Horatta' (running around) was still the motto of the day to get things done.

At this junction, I superimposed in my mind the memory of the locality in which CIVIC had worked and the current sight. The urban space had gotten a denser character through the ground-floor + 3 construction, despite the inhabitants probably having more space in their dwellings. While exploring these new spaces and recollecting the episode 'The quest for transit housing', I remembered the nightmarish transit arrangement that this community had endured and felt somewhat comforted that these dwellings offered them some peace and security. As I touched the walls of the corridors while trying to find my interlocutor, the brittleness of the walls made me remember the rumours that were going around stating that stone powder had been mixed to save on cement, as the builders who had received the tenders had to give cuts to local politicians. My interlocutor, indeed, stated that the last block that was built was the weakest, as funds had run out. The sanitary infrastructure especially was poor. Pipes were so narrow that they frequently got blocked, such that they had to run to the councillor and KSDB frequently. Proudly, he stated that the community according to him had stayed intact and that no external families had joined. Despite some infrastructure problems, my interlocutor was grateful to be dwelling in a better environment in an expensive city such as Bangalore. The better living conditions had inspired the community to display good behaviour, strive for higher ambitions than when having the incorporated identity of a slum dweller, and that they were determined to teach kids to strive for more in life. CIVIC was fondly remembered for having showed part of the way. No other civil society organization had approached the community after relocation.

I was very curious to discover the locality in which SJKV was active. My research had concluded that SJKV was the organization that had imparted considerable social skill to the community from the same socio-historical position of caste and promised to be the most sustainable approach for the community to assert a satisfactory housing situation. In fact, they had been the only BSUP target community that had secured themselves ground-floor housing, giving scope for incremental additions according to evolving needs. The rolling terrain in which the BSUP project was implemented was a landscape of generations of housing policies. I recognized immediately the housing structure of the community I had interviewed many years back. It had remained ground-floor housing. To my astonishment, it remained so, not because incremental housing was not of need, but rather because the houses built were not strong enough to bear more floors – as a resident told me. This community too complained that even though the buildings were up, there was no peace regarding the services. Water was intermittent, borewell water was not fit for consumption, and while electricity meters had been installed, there was no connection given but they would still get high bills. The biggest issue for them too was the sanitary installation. The toilet drainage would regularly overspill, especially during rains. The 'horatta' for them continued too. They stated that the MLA had promised to help after election. The leader of SJKV would still visit the community and when leaders called, the community would mobilize collectively to claim services from the KSDB. Despite suffering from inadequate services, their monthly expenses were higher than before. They would arrange the money every month by skipping one or the other bill.

The most noticeable housing outcome was in the locality in which AVAS was involved. The design of the BSUP in situ ground-floor + 3 redevelopment was dense, but still had allowed for small courtyards that were animated with children playing, small trees were giving shade to chatting residents, and there was an overall sense of calm. My interlocutors stated that buildings were by KSDB and that they had done all the 'horatta' required to get the services. With the support of the local MLA, all had Kaveri water connections with metering for water and electricity for every dwelling. For the construction of the last blocks, cement was taken from KSDB that let the residents build themselves, as construction workers were beneficiaries of this redevelopment. There was still support from the dedicated AVAS worker to maintain files, meetings were still held block-wise – in which the AVAS fieldworker (also resident) was still voluntarily involved – and accounting was maintained at the community level. Trustworthy documentation, in their view, was key to maintaining access with government agencies. Community saving schemes (some as old as 20 years) had matured to an extent that they were able to build a temple on their own. Women's groups were operating in this locality and safety was not an issue. The conclusion of my chat with the residents was that 'this generation doesn't have to struggle as hard'. They proudly narrated that through a good environment, good life was possible, that their youth were studying well and had good jobs. Feeling comforted that their youth were on a good path and that they were becoming increasingly self-sufficient, favours from politicians were decreasing. When a community can function beyond survival, then politics can be more issue-based, they went on to say. AVAS workers were still in touch in this community and had built ties of friendship. The organization had oriented itself away from housing and more towards youth encouragement programmes.

The episode 'Blackmailing through housing' remained problematic. As I stepped into the locality in which the Dalit Panthers of India was active, the circuits of patronage and corruption appeared still firmly rooted here. I was confused about the state of development. Was it not yet finished, or was it already dilapidated through use? As I learnt, it was both. The in situ development took 11 years to build and one building was still missing, hence some families were still living in sheds of transit arrangement. So, while some parts of the area were rather new, others were already wearing off, I was told. A group of women narrated the daily struggles they faced due to the very low quality of construction. The main concern was water. They had no connection for corporation water. There was a pump, but the motor was hardly ever working. So, they had to get water from ground-floor community taps and carry the heavy vessels to their respective floors. Women complained of health issues due to this situation. Water had the power to divide, as the first fetchers would fill in as many vessels as possible and lock the water up. Leaders were highly ineffective and external civil society organizations stayed away from the locality. Allocation had created lots of noise. Those who had the capacity to bribe had got ground-floors apartments and communities had got split through the allocation, they said. Newcomers had found dwellings either through networks or because some beneficiaries had rented out units. The women deplored this housing situation as nightmarish and nostalgically remembered the old slum with mainly pucca houses, the decorative rangoli they would put every morning and the healthy community that they were. Many women felt that youth were on a bad track and that the area had become unsafe for women. Financially, they found themselves in a more precarious situation than before, as ad hoc collection throughout the month to fix inconveniences of the buildings ate into their resources. 'How can we improve? We don't know', they deplored.

While all four communities experienced diverse housing outcomes, a common thread between all four was the lack of urban services. Before declaration of their localities by the KSDB, their position in regard to the state was one of constant informal contestation and negotiation with agents of the state because of their illegal status (denizen) in the city. As they now had entered the formal housing realm as beneficiaries of a public housing scheme, their position was one of a citizen that should enjoy urban services rightfully. Yet they were (in all four localities) excluded from adequate urban services. This exclusion from urban services seems to represent the lifeline that sustains political patronage networks. As residents of these formal quarters, they still had to run to them to access basic urban needs such as water, electricity, and sanitary installations and during election cycles, politicians could hold communities to ransom for votes in exchange of announced favours of election freebies.

Loyalty to patronage networks and cash become the currency for inclusion to access adequate urban services. As Björkman (2014b) elaborates, 'Cash, finally is a sign and instantiation of the networks of knowledge, authority and resources that are crucially necessary for navigating the opacities of the city's rapidly changing and increasingly enigmatic growing and globalising economies.' She notes furthermore, 'Exchange encounters are not only performative but also speculative' (ibid.). Now, what is the link between more or less petty cash transactions in a low-income locality and the city's larger political economy and how does that exchange get speculative character? To scope answers, one ought to ask the simple question of 'where does the money come from?' to pervade low-income communities with cash in view of elections.

The figure 6.1 in the book explained the imbrication of the electoral cycle and informal circuits of corruption that demobilized strongly. To trace elements of the answer to 'where does the money come from?' for this imbrication, we must expand the geographical focus to include the periphery and the city's hinterland and also rise in scale to include not only local networks but also those who operate outside particular localities.

Where the money comes from

My subsequent research led me to investigate Bangalore's peripheries where the city was fast approaching. The goal was to shift the gaze from technocratic understandings of green-field urban planning to everyday negotiations mediated through power structures that consolidate informal planning practice. I discovered that differential temporalities, particular knowledge networks, information exchange sites, and information asymmetry existed between parties requiring knowledge regarding the city yet to come in the peripheries of Bangalore. During fieldwork, I interacted with a diverse set of interlocutors and observed everyday business of the un-informed: at the local milk cooperative, schools, residential areas, farms; and the daily affairs of the informed: real-estate and planning actors and political representatives of the area. The latter group took part in the everyday information practices relating to territorial development and were skilled enough to navigate this knowledge networks and make opportunistic gains.

My long duration of waiting (sometimes with and other times without appointment) to interview local elected representatives at their offices in the southern fringe of Bangalore turned out to provide the most valuable insights. Even though it was a politician's office, it felt as if I was sitting in a real-estate office. Every time I enquired about the opportunity to talk to the electoral representatives, their entourage would say that the respective representatives were busy attending functions in and around of the city: weddings, house-warming ceremonies, even one-year birthday parties. They diligently postponed or cancelled the interviews, not to miss their attendance. They were not taking time off from their work to attend social functions; I came to understand that it was their work. These were the sites of information exchange to gain knowledge about how the urban built-up environment was coming up. People in the village knew which representative or contender owned how much land and where. They made it clear that only those who were involved in land transactions could raise the money required to finance a party ticket. As I was sitting in a local real-estate office conducting an interview of a real-estate agent, a group of men rushed in. It took a while to understand that it was in fact the local zilla panchayat representative with his team who had come to invite the real-estate agent to an inauguration of roadworks. On another day, again a party of young men entered and invited the real-estate broker to a *pooja* (Hindu ritual). The invitation letter in bright pink colour portrayed the goddess Durga displaying all her strength; on the reverse side there was a line-up of names who had sponsored the *pooja* – politicians and the real-estate agents. Our interviewee, who was also a political party member and was listed, confirmed that he had sponsored the *pooja* and stated attending such *pooja*s was very important to understand development projects.

Votes, real-estate opportunity, and finance went hand-in-hand. Real-estate unleashed the finance for political power and power made it possible to assert control over land. The real-estate agents accepted the final version of the masterplan and kept a copy in their offices. Two-dimensional masterplans indicating the different planning zones were accepted facts, but the emerging three-dimensional urban built environment, the timing, the look, and the deviation from the plan were all matters of networked and enmeshed relations of money and political power. While those involved in the planning exercise and the emergence of the built environment at the periphery gained knowledge in these networks and particular information exchange sites of social gatherings, the common people could understand the scope of the change in their environment only when the physical structures took shape.

Capital is not only circulating virtually, it has a very material face, as it flows into real estate and infrastructure (Halber and Rouanet 2014). Dramatic increases of land prices present the state actors with unique opportunities and challenges and lead them to tap into the real estate markets as a means to gain financial power and greater control over urban spatial change by monetizing land – by extracting revenue from land development or by distributing the profits to powerful corporate backers of the state (Shatkin 2014). At the periphery, greenfield development triggers land conversions from low-value agricultural land to high-value residential or industrial land, allowing for value capture. Once land has been opened up for development, recent amendments have made the industrial policy in Karnataka agile to protect and back easy entry and exit of domestic and international capital (Cook and Rao Dhananka 2017). It is real estate that embodies the 'gray zone of politics', which designates existing continuities between state action, routine politics, capital, and violence (Auyero 2011).

What I described here displays the same ingredients as anywhere in the world, as special UN rapporteurs Raquel Rolnik (2008–2014) (2019, in Forrest 2019) and Leilani Farah (current) have observed across the world. Rolnik (2019) published her observations in the book *Urban Warfare*, identifying real estate as the prime motor that extracts new profit from spaces communities occupy. The relentless process to convert land and housing into saleable assets, commodities for speculative investment, is reordering space and its dispossession (Forrest 2019). In 2019 Farah and Deva wrote a letter condemning business practices of big private equity and investment firms that have turned exploitative business models to industry standards. Undervalued properties and land – which remain affordable to local populations are purchased en masse, renovated, and offered at higher rental rate, hence driving out current tenants. This is disrupting communities, making landlords faceless and heartless, and promoting gentrification that restructures space city-wide. She reminded firms such as the Blackstone Group of ethical UN guiding principles on business and human rights and likewise the United States and other governments of their human rights obligations to regulate tax laws, towards tenant protection, and to support the right to adequate housing.

Realizing 'cities for people, not for profit'[1] through 'housing as a commons, not a commodity'[2]

The BSUP housing policy as part of the JNNURM was the first important post-neoliberal intervention in housing (Sengupta et al. 2018). As described in the respective chapter, policy had incorporated neoliberal premises by encouraging public–private partnership (PPP) and by making it conditional on state governments to carry out economic reforms that were more market friendly, which had been actively pursued by funding agencies. As Sengupta et al. (2018) illustrate, the World Bank, which had partly financed the Urban Reform and Management Project in Karnataka (as part of the JNNURM), threatened to pull out unless a number of enabling instruments including amendments to legislation were introduced (Baindur and Lalitha 2009 in Sengupta et al. 2018). The subsequent public housing policy was the Rajiv Awas Yojana (RAY), launched in 2013, ambitiously announcing slum-free cities. The aim was to include existing slums into the formal realm and to create institutional and market mechanisms to regulate land and housing shortage (Tiwari and Rao 2016, in Sengupta et al. 2018). This policy prescriptions did not take shape because of the failure to secure land for relocating slum dwellers. RAY was replaced with the Pradhanmantri Awas Yojana (PAY) that has the motto of 'housing for all by 2022'. Having PPPs at its core, it assists urban local bodies and other agencies for in situ rehabilitation of slum dwellers using land as a resource through the PPP model and interest rate subsides on loans for housing low-income households. Twenty million dwelling units until 2022 were pledged. The authors cautiously evaluate that with insufficient regulatory infrastructural reforms, ad hockery, inconsistencies, and deliveries being questionable due to supply-side and demand-side challenges, PAY will not be able to live up to its promises (Sengupta et al. 2018). Despite of welfare rhetoric the authors (ibid.) note that centrally designed housing programmes have enhanced neoliberal aspects by creating opportunities for the private sectors and introducing commercial and speculative elements into urban management and aimed at 'engineering investment-oriented markets in land, services and municipal debt'.

Key shifts in housing policies could be envisioned by juxtaposing a number of established misconceptions about housing for the poor with innovative approaches that are being documented across the globe. Sengupta et al. (2018) identify four misconceptions:

First, public housing schemes ought to deliver impoverished people complete homes, but incremental housing has now attracted considerable attention. The showcase housing intervention of AVAS had built on this premise: small plots and tenure that enabled incremental housing. Today that neighbourhood is denser, colourful, and has raised the residents from the status of formerly illegal poor slum dwellers to members of the emerging lower middle-class. The experiments of 'half-homes' of the celebrated architect Alejandro Aravena are witness to the triumph of incremental housing (ibid.). Indeed this rationale is inherent to making walls one's home – according to family size, needs, and wealth – in general. In particular, slum evolution has followed the same rationale – so, indeed with upgrading of infrastructure for safe and healthy living and the recognition that informal settlements and informal housing markets do contribute to the affordable housing stock, urban governance has scope to innovate and partner with actors that are not just in pursuit of profit.

Second, government promotes housing policy, but housing policies are formulated in the guise of economic policies. While India still faces a large affordable housing deficit coupled with municipal economic debts, the aim shifts to exploring multiple gains through housing policy, as they are inscribed within a larger economic framework that partners with the private sector (ibid.). What if housing for the urban poor quit the economic underpinning of a neoliberal framework and was viewed as a commons? Such experiments are increasingly gaining ground where land is taken off from the speculative real-estate market as shared-equity housing, community land trusts, and housing co-operatives. But for such experiments to scale up and to be enduring to preserve affordable housing stock, initial investment in the forms of subsidies and innovative and fair financial instruments need to be implemented (Schneider 2019).

Third, government has created conditions for effective private sector operation, but is the private sector able to internalize housing poverty into the market mechanism in a fair and sustainable manner? Sengupta et al. (2018) argue that the misconceptions elaborated earlier (complete homes, amalgamated policy goals) require relying on private capital and that governments have overestimated the pace of regulatory reforms regarding rents, land, master planning, and the capacity of urban local bodies to manage change. Creating conditions for private capital to enable social housing are thus far more complex (ibid.) and may require other complementary strategies. These could be having the poor and poor communities participate in the credit system through special instruments tailored to their capacities and needs that could keep them away from exploitative informal credit systems. Along with capacity building to navigate the credit systems and community saving practices, a new meaning could be given to private sector participation – a meaning of fair inclusion and the opportunity to lead a dignified life through proper housing.

Fourth, sufficient participation and enablement at the local level lead to satisfactory housing outcomes, but without the capacity to understand the policy regime and the implementation requirements, the top-down approach is destined to be reproduced (ibid.). As this research showed, the ambitious JNNURM had created empty shells, failing to devolve power to the local level without the time and budget to strengthen capacity. Even though the mission included elements of participation, it just remained a rhetoric, as implementing agencies did not have the capacity to carry out any participatory exercise with the concerned communities, not even with mediating NGOs. There are community practices across the world that are pioneering participatory housing through initiatives as diverse as participatory budgeting, participatory mapping, designing, transformative place-making through local economic development, and creating for themselves a space to co-decide at municipal levels. These lessons are internationally disseminated through transnational networks – see, for example, Community Architects Network (CAN), Habitat International Coalition (HIC), Slum Dwellers International (SDI) – to engrain sustainable practices elsewhere. Bottom-up initiatives have to partner with top-down political will that has the potential to shape up a common vision of inclusive cities, as the new global movement SHIFT initiated by the current UN special rapporteur on housing aims. It brings together civil society, multiple levels of government, multilateral institutions, national human rights institutions, academia, philanthropists, artists, private sector actors, and grassroots movements to understand and live the 'deep connections between housing and well-being' (unhousingrapp.org) and calls for participatory human rights based housing strategies. The former UN rapporteur Raquel Rolnik concludes her book (2016) with hope, noting that a global coalition of social movements is emerging, in which the right to the city is at the heart of the agenda. At the local level, P. K. Das (architect-activist cited in the Introduction) proclaimed, movements had to pave the way for 'right to adequate housing'. This right is not to only remain a means to prevent homelessness (Hohmann 2013), but to be able to assure that everyone can realize their potential, by having a safe home and the sense of belonging to a community and space.

In this book I attempted to find answers to why the issue of inadequate housing had not produced a sustained movement, one that had the potential to paralize the city, given the large number of slum d· ellers. One element to the answer was that every community faced particular issues and a particular state, which would be demobilizing and scattering the potential for movement emergence. I also noted that without imbibing social skills including the notion of citizenship in a city and the duties of the state, an overarching identity to claim adequate housing could not be forged.

As this book is going to print, India is witnessing a social movement of an unprecedented scale, fragmented in place, but united in the claim: It is the house – the home that evolved into a community – that holds the power to nourish a sense of belonging to a place which unleashes collective force, resilience, and imaginations of a bright future.

Notes

1. Borrowed from title Cities for People, *Not for Profit: Critical Urban Theory and the Right to the City*, by Neil Brenner, Peter Marcuse and Margit Mayer (2012).
2. Borrowed from CoHabitat Network's event 'Housing as a Commons, Not a Commodity'.

Bibliography

Abbas, H., R. Kumar, and M. A. Alam (2010). *Indian Government and Politics*. Delhi: Pearson.

Agarwala, R. (2008). 'Reshaping the Social Contract: Emerging Relations between the State and Informal Labor in India'. *Theory and Society* 37(4): 375–408.

Aiyar, S. (2013). 'Census Shockers: Imagine All of France in Slums and US sans Power'. *New Indian Express*, 24 March. Available at http://newindianexpress.com/opinion/article1514260.ece.

Alimi, E. (2009). 'Mobilizing Under the Gun: Theorizing Political Opportunity Structure in a Highly Repressive Setting'. *Mobilization: An International Quarterly* 14(2): 219–237.

Appadurai, A. (2002). 'Deep Democracy: Urban Governmentality and the Horizon of Politics'. *Public Culture* 14(1): 21–47.

Arabindoo, P. (2010). '"City of Sand": Stately Re-Imagination of Marina Beach in Chennai'. *International Journal of Urban and Regional Research* 35(March): 379–401.

Atitra Bhattacharya (2010). 'Land Titling Bill: Silent on Rights of Tribals and the Poor'. *Down To Earth*. Available at http://www.downtoearth.org.in/node/1633 (accessed on 21 February 2012).

Audenhove, L. Van. (2007). *Expert Interviews and Interview Techniques for Policy Analysis*. Brussel: Vrije Universitiet. Brussel.

Auyero, J. (2000). *Poor People's Politics: Peronist Survival Networks and the Legacy of Evita*. Durham, NC: Duke University Press

——— (2004). 'When Everyday Life, Routine Politics, and Protest Meet'. *Theory and Society* 33(3/4): 417–441.

——— (2006). 'Spaces and Places as Sites and Objects of Politics'. In *The Oxford Handbook of Contextual Political Analysis*, ed. Robert E. Goodin and Charles Tilly, 564–578. New York: Oxford University Press.

——— (2008). 'Patronage and Contention'. In *The Social Science Research Council, Contention, Change, and Explanation: A Conference in Honor of Charles Tilly*, 1–35. New York: Columbia University and the Social Science Research Council.

——— (2011). 'Spotlight: A Gray Area'. In *Contention and Trust in Cities and States*, ed. Michael Hanagan and Charles Tilly, 267–270. Dordrecht: Springer. Available at http://www.springerlink.com/content/978-94-007-0756-6#section=882413&page=4&locus=33 (accessed on 16 October 2012).

Baar, C. (1990). 'Social Action Litigation in India: The Operation and Limitations of the World's Most Active Judiciary'. *Policy Studies Journal* 19(1): 140–150.

Babu, Nikil M. (2016). 'Over 35 Years, Rs 2.8 Lakh Crore Government Funds for Dalit, Tribal Welfare Went Unspent'. *Scroll.in*, 21 September. Available at http://scroll.in/article/816914/over-35-years-rs-2-8-lakh-crore-government-funds-for-dalit-tribal-welfare-went-unspet (accessed on 22 September 2016).

Bakshi, P. M. (2010). *The Constitution of India*. Delhi: Universal Law Publishing.

Banarjee, B. (2002). 'Security of Tenure in Indian Cities'. In *Holding Their Ground: Secure Land Tenure for the Urban Poor in Developing Countries*, ed. A. Durand-Lasserve and L. Royston, 37–58. London: Earthscan Publications, 2002.

Barta, P. and K. Pokharel (2009). 'Megacities Threaten to Choke India'. *Wall Street Journal*. Available at https://www.wsj.com/articles/SB124216531392512435 (accessed on 22 August 2019).

Battilana, J. (2006). 'Agency and Institutions: The Enabling Role of Individuals' Social Position'. *Organization* 13(5): 653–676.

Baxi, U. (2005). 'Postcolonial Legality'. In *Postcolonial*, ed. H. Schwarz and S. Ray, 540–555. Cornwall: Blackwell Publishing.

Bayat, A. (1997). 'Un-civil Society: The Politics of the Informal People. *Third World Quarterly* 18(1): 53–72.

——— (2010). *Life as Politics: How Ordinary People Change the Middle East*. Amsterdam: Amsterdam University Press.

BDA. (2017). 'Revised Master Plan for Bengaluru 2031 (Draft)'. Bangalore.

Benford, R. D. and D. A. Snow (2000). 'Framing Processes and Social Movements: An Overview and Assessment'. *Annual Review of Sociology* 26(1): 611–639.

Benjamin, S. (2000). 'Governance, Economic Settings and Poverty in Bangalore'. *Environment and Urbanization* 12(1): 35–56. https://doi.org/10.1630/095624700101285262.

——— (2008). 'Occupancy Urbanism: Radicalizing Politics and Economy beyond Policy and Programs'. *International Journal of Urban and Regional Research* 32(3): 719–729.

Benjamin, S. and B. Raman (2001). 'Democracy, Inclusive Governance and Poverty in Bangalore'. In *Urban Governance, Partnership and Poverty*. University of Birmingham.

———. (2011a). 'The Worlding of Bangalore. Illegible Claims, Legal Titles'. *Revue Tiers Monde* 206: 37–54.

———. (2011b). 'Claiming Land: Rights, Contestation and the Urban Poor in Globalized Times. In *Urban Policies and the Right to the City in India. Rights, Responsibilities and Citizenship*, ed. M.-Hélène Zérah, V. Dupont, and S. T. Lama-Rewal, 63–75. New Delhi: UNESCO.

Bennett, A. (2003). *Typological Theory*. Available at www.gwu.edu/~gwipp/talks/BennettGWIPP.pdf.

Berner, E. and B. Phillips. (2005). 'Left to Their Own Devices? Community Self-help between Alternative Development and Neo-liberalism'. *Community Development Journal* 40(1): 17–29.

Bevan, Philippa (2009). 'Working with Cases in Development Contexts: Some Insights from an Outlier'. In *The Sage Handbook of Case-Based Methods*, ed. D. Byrne and C. C. Ragin, 467–493. Thousand Oaks: Sage Publications, 2009.

Beverley, E. L. (2011). 'Colonial Urbanism and South Asian Cities'. *Social History* 36(December): 37–41.

Bevington, D. and C. Dixon. (2005). 'Movement-relevant Theory: Rethinking Social Movement Scholarship and Activism. *Social Movement Studies* 4(3): 185–208.

Bhan, G. (2016). *In the Public's Interest: Evictions, Citizenship and Inequality in Contemporary Delhi*. New Delhi: Orient Blackswan.

——— (2017). 'From the Basti to the 'House' : Socio-spatial Readings to Housing Policy in India'. *Current Sociology* 65(4) : 587–602. https://doi.org/10.1177/0011392117697465.

Birkett, W. P. and E. Evans. (2005). 'Theorising Professionalisation: A Model for Organising and Understanding Histories of the Professionalising Activities of Occupational Associations of Accountants'. *Accounting History* 10(1): 99–127.

Björkman, L. (2014a). 'Becoming a Slum: From Municipal Colony to Illegal Settlement in Liberalization-era Mumbai'. *International Journal of Urban and Regional Research* 38(January: 36–59. http://doi.org/10.1111/1468-2427.12041

——— (2014b). '"You Can't Buy a Vote": Meanings of Money in a Mumbai Election'. *American Ethnologist* 41(4): 617–634. https://doi.org/10.1111/amet.12101.

Björkman, L. and W. Jeffrey (2018). 'Money and Votes'. In *Costs of Democracy: Political Finance in India*, ed. Devesh Kapur and Milan Vaishnav. New Delhi: Oxford University Press.

Block, F. (2004). 'Organizing versus Mobilizing: Poor People's Movements after 25 Years'. *Perspectives on Politics* 1(4): 733–735.

Blundo, G. and P.-Y Le Meur. (2009). *The Governance of Daily Life in Africa: Ethnographic Explorations of Public and Collective Services*. Leiden, NL: Brill Publishers.

Bogner, A., B. Littig, and W. Menz. (2009). *Interviewing Experts*. Hampshire: Palgrave Macmillan.

Boudreau, V. (1996). 'Northern Theory, Southern Protest: Opportunity Structure Analysis in Cross-National Perspective'. *Mobilization: An International Quarterly* 1(2): 175–189.

Bourke, A. G. (2009). *Encyclopedia of Urban Studies*, ed. R. Hutchison. Thousand Oaks: Sage Publications.

Breeding, M. (2008a). *Clientelism and Democratic Policy Representation: Evidence from Attitudes in Bangalore, India*. Available at https://sites.google.com/site/maryebreeding/current-research (accessed on 2 September 2009).

——— (2008b). 'The Influence of Clientelism on Policy Representation: Evidence from Attitudes in Bangalore, India'. *Annual Meeting of the Midwest Political Science Association*. Available at https://sites.google.com/site/maryebreeding/current-research (accessed on 2 September 2009).

——— (2009). 'Buying Turnout and Mobilizing the Poor: The Success of Mixed-Clientelist Strategies in Bangalore Elections'. Paper presented at the Annual Meeting of the Midwest Political Science Association.

——— (2012). 'Is the World Bank Responsive to Informal Institutions? A Research Note'. Paper presented at the Annual Meeting of the American Political Science Association.

Brenner, N. (2009). 'Restructuring, Rescaling, and the Urban Question'. *Critical Planning* 16(Summer): 60–79.

Brenner, N., P. Marcuse, and M. Mayer (2012). *Cities for People, Not for Profit: Critical Urban Theory and the Right to the City*. New York: Routledge.

Brockett, C. D. (1991). 'The Structure of Political Opportunities and Peasant Mobilization in Central America'. *Comparative Politics* 23(3): 253–274.

Bunge, M. (2004). 'How Does It Work? The Search for Explanatory Mechanisms'. *Philosophy of the Social Sciences* 34(2): 182–210.

Buschi, M. (2013). *Urbanisation, Law and SEZ (Special Economic Zones) in India, and the Policy Response in Gujarat*. Graduate Institute of International and Development Studies.

Byrne, D. (2009). 'Case-Based Methods: Why We Need Them; What They Are; How to Do Them'. In *The Sage Handbook of Case-Based Methods*, ed. D. Byrne and C. C. Ragin. Thousand Oaks: Sage Publications.

——— (2009). 'Complex Realist and Configurational Approaches to Cases: A Radical Synthesis'. In *The Sage Handbook of Case-Based Methods*, ed. D. Byrne and C. C. Ragin. Thousand Oaks: Sage Publications.

Carmin, J. A. and D. B. Balser (2002). 'Selecting Repertoires of Action in Environmental Movement Organizations: An Interpretive Approach'. *Organization and Environment* 15: 365–388.

CASSUM and Action Aid India (2007). *Institutionalizing Citizen's Participation. An Evaluation of the Community Participation Law and the Community Participation Fund*. Available at casumm.files.wordpress.com/2008/02/citizens-particpation-law.pdf (accessed on 18 October 2011).

Castells, M. (1983). *The City and the Grassroots: A Cross-Cultural Theory of Urban Social Movements*. London: Edward Arnold.

Castree, N., R. Kitchin, and A. Rogers (2013). *A Dictionary of Human Geography*. Oxford University Press.

Chakraborty, D., D. S. Babu, and M. Chakravorty (2006). 'Atrocities on Dalits: What the District Level Data Say on Society–State Complicity'. *Economic and Political Weekly* 41(24): 2478–2481.

Chandra, Uday (2015). 'Book Review: "Patronage as Politics in South Asia", Edited by Anastasia Piliavsky'. *Oxpol: The Oxford University Politics Blog*. Available at https://blog. politics.ox.ac.uk/book-review-patronage-politics-south-asia-edited-anastasia-piliavsky/ (accessed 20 July 2018).

Chandhoke, N. (2005). 'Revisiting the Crisis of Representation Thesis: The Indian Context'. *Democratization* 12(3): 308–330.

Chatterjee, P. (2004). *The Politics of the Governed: Reflections on Popular Politics in Most of the World*. New York: Columbia University Press.

Choudhry, S. (2010). 'After the Rights Revolution: Bills of Rights in the Postconflict State'. *Annual Review of Law and Social Science* 6(1): 301–322. doi:10.1146/annurev. lawsocsci.093008.131445.

Christensen, K. and D. Levinson (2007). *Encyclopedia of Community: From the Village to the Virtual World*. Thousand Oaks: Sage Publications.

CIVIC (2008). 'Pilot Slum and Urban Homelessness Study'. *Governance: An International Journal of Policy and Administration*: 1–225.

Clemens, E. S. (1993). 'Organizational Repertoires and Institutional Change: Women's Groups and the Transformation of US Politics, 1890–1920'. *American Journal of Sociology* 98(4): 755–798.

Coelho, K. (2009). 'The Politics of Civil Society: Neighbourhood Associationism in Chennai'. *Economic and Political Weekly* 44(26–27).

Collins, D., J. Morduch, S. Rutherford, and O. Ruthven (2009). *Portfolios of the Poor: How the World's Poor Live on 2$ a Day*. Princeton: Princeton University Press.

Connors, G. (2007). *Watering the Slums: How a Utility and Its Street-Level Bureaucrats Connected the Poor in Bangalore*. Massachusetts Institute of Technology.

Contursi, J. A. (1993). 'Political Theology: Text and Practice in Dalit Panther Community'. *The Journal of Asian* 52(2): 320–339.

Cook, I. and S. Rao Dhananka (2017). 'Urban Dreams in a Pamphlet: What's the Point of India's Global Investors Meets?' Available at https://medium.com/center-for-media-data-and-society/urban-dreams-in-a-pamphlet-whats-the-point-of-india-s-global-investors-meets-20894a888376 (accessed on 29 September 2017).

Corbridge, S., G. Williams, M. Srivatsava, and R. Véron (2005). *Seeing the State: Governance and Governmentality in India*. Cambridge: Cambridge University Press.

Coy, P. G. and T. Hedeen (2005). 'A Stage Model of Social Movement Co-optation: Community Mediation in the United States'. *The Sociological Quarterly* 46(3): 405–435.

Cruikshank, B. (1993). 'Revolutions Within: Self-government and Self-esteem'. *Economy and Society* 22(3): 37–41.

Dale-Bloomberg, L. and M. Volpe (2012). *Completing Your Qualitative Dissertation: A Road Map from Beginning to End* (2nd ed.). Thousand Oaks: Sage Publications.

Das, G. (2006). 'The India Model'. *Foreign Affairs* 85(4): 2–16.

Darts, D. (2004). 'Studies in Art Education Visual Culture Jam: Art, Pedagogy, and Creative Resistance'. *Studies in Art Education: A Journal of Issues and Research* 45(4): 313–327.

Datta, A. and A. Shaban (2017). *Mega-Urbanization in the Global South: Fast Cities and New Urban Utopias of the Postcolonial State*. Oxon: Routledge.

Davies, J. S. and J. L. Trounstine (2012). 'Urban Politics and the New Institutionalism'. In *Oxford Handbook of Urban Politics*, ed. Susan Clarke, Peter John, and Karen Mossberger, 51–70. Oxford: Oxford University Press.

Davis, M. (2006). *Planet of Slums*. London: Verso.

Denzin, K. N. and Y. Lincoln (2003). *The Landscape of Qualitative Research: Theories and Issues* (2nd ed.). London: Sage Publications.

Deva, S. (2009). 'Public Interest Litigation in India: A Critical Review Public'. *Civil Justice Quarterly* 28(1): 19–40.

Devas, N. (2001). 'The Connections between Urban Governance and Poverty'. *Journal of International Development* 13(7): 989–996.

Devasher, M. (2010). 'Transparency in Legislative Processes'. Accountability Initiative, Centre for Policy Research. Available at http://www.accountabilityindia.in/accountabilityblog/1908-transparency-legislative-processes (accessed on 9 June 2013)

Diani, M. (1992). 'The Concept of Social Movement'. *The Sociological Review* 40(1): 1–25.

DiMaggio, P. J. and W. W. Powell (1991). *The New Institutionalism in Organizational Analysis*. Chicago: University of Chicago Press.

Dittrich, C. (2007). 'Bangalore: Globalisation and Fragmentation in India's Hightech-Capital'. *ASIEN* 103(April): 45–58.

Doshi, S. and M. Ranganathan (2016). 'Contesting the Unethical City: Land Dispossession and Corruption Narratives in Urban India'. *Annals of American Association of Geographers* 107(1): 183–199.

——— (2018). 'Towards a Critical Geography of Corruption and Power in Late Capitalism'. *Progress in Human Geography*. https://doi.org/10.1177/0309132517753070.

Dreze, J. and A. Sen (2002). 'Democratic Practice and Social Inequality in India'. *Journal of Asian and African Studies* 37(2): 6–37.

Dudley-Jenkins, L. (2003). *Identity and Identification in India: Defining the Disadvantaged*. London: Routledge.

Dupont, V., D. Jordhus-Lier, C. Sutherland, and E. Braathen (2016). *The Politics of Slums in the Global South: Urban Informality in Brazil, India, South Africa and Peru*. Oxon: Routledge.

Durand-Lasserve, A. and L. Royston (2002). *Holding Their Ground: Secure Land Tenure for the Urban Poor in Developing Countries*. London: Earthscan Publications.

Earl, C. 2016. 'Doing Pedagogy Publicly: Asserting the Right to the City to Rethink the University'. *Open Library of Humanities* 2(October): 1–32.

Eisenhardt, K. M. (2002). 'Building Theories from Case Study Research'. In *The Qualitative Researcher's Companion*, ed. M. A. Huberman and M. B. Miles, 5–36. Thousand Oaks: Sage Publications.

Emigh, R. J. (1997). 'The Power of Negative Thinking: The Use of Negative Case Methodology in the Development of Sociological Theory'. *Theory and Society* 26(5): 649–684.

Engin, F. I. and B. S. Turner (2002). 'Citizenship Studies: An Introduction'. In *Handbook of Citizenship Studies*, ed. F. I. Engin and B. S. Turner, 1–10. London: Sage Publications.

Englebert, P. (2000). 'Pre-Colonial Institutions, Economic Development in Tropical Africa'. *Political Research Quarterly* 53(1): 7–36.

Esman, M. J. (1999). 'Public Administration and Conflict Management in Plural Societies: The Case for Representative Bureaucracy'. *Public Administration and Development* 366(April): 353–366.

Farah, L. and S. Deva (2019). 'States and Real Estate Private Equity Firms Questioned for Compliance with Human Rights'. Available at https://www.ohchr.org/EN/NewsEvents/Pages/DisplayNews.aspx?NewsID=24404&LangID=E (accessed on 28 February 2020).

Fernández-Kelly, P., and J. Shefner (2006). *Out of the Shadows: Political Action and the Informal Economy in Latin America*. University Park: Pennsylvania State University Press.

Fiss, P. C. (2009). 'Case Studies and the Configurational Analysis of Organizational Phenomena'. In *The Sage Handbook of Case-Based Methods*, ed. D. Byrne and C. C. Ragin, 415–431. Thousand Oaks: Sage Publications.

Fligstein, N. and D. McAdam (2011). 'Toward a General Theory of Strategic Action Fields'. *Sociological Theory* 29(1): 1–26.

———— (2012). *A Theory of Fields*. Oxford: Oxford University Press.

Forrest, R. (2019). 'A Review of *Urban Warfare: Housing under the Empire of Finance* by Raquel Rolnik'. *International Journal of Housing Policy* 19(4): 599–606.

Fox, J. (1994). 'The Difficult Transition from Clientelism to Citizenship: Lessons from Mexico'. *World Politics* 46(2): 151–184.

Galanter, M. (2009). 'Part I Courts, Institutions, and Access to Justice: "To the Listed Field ...": The Myth of Litigious India'. *Jindal Global Law Review* 1(1): 65–73.

Galanter, M. and J. K. Krishnan (2004). 'Bread for the Poor: Access to Justice and the Rights of the Needy in India'. *Hastings Law Journal* 55: 789. Available at http://ssrn.com/abstract=682324 (accessed on 18 September 2013).

Garcia, S. (1996). 'Cities and Citizenship'. *International Journal of Urban and Regional Research* 20(1): 7–21. doi:10.1111/j.1468-2427.1996.tb00298.x.

George, A. L. and A. Bennett (2005). *Case Studies and Theory Development in the Social Sciences*. Cambridge, MA: The MIT Press.

Gerring, J. (2007). *Case Study Research: Principles and Practices*. New York: Cambridge University Press.

Ghose, S. (2003). 'The Dalit in India'. *Social Research* 70(1): 83–109.

Ghosh, A. (2006). 'Banking on the Bangalore Dream'. *Economic and Political Weekly* 41(8): 689–692.

Gilbert, A. (2007). 'The Return of the Slum: Does Language Matter?' *International Journal of Urban and Regional Research* 31(4): 697–713.

Giugni, M. (2011). 'Political Opportunity: Still a Useful Concept?' In *Contention and Trust in Cities and States*, ed. Michael Hanagan and Chris Tilly, 271–284. Dordrecht: Springer.

Giugni, M. and F. Passy (2004). 'Migrant Mobilization between Political Institutions and Citizenship Regimes: A Comparison of France and Switzerland'. *European Journal of Political Research* 43(1): 51–82.

Goetz, A. M. and R. Jenkins (2001). 'Hybrid Forms of Accountability: Citizen Engagement in Institutions of Public-Sector Oversight in India'. *Public Management Review* 3(3): 363–383.

Goldman, M. (2011). 'Speculating on the Next World City'. In *Worlding Cities: Asian Experiments and the Art of Being Global*, ed. A. Roy and A. Ong, 229–258. West Sussex: Wiley-Blackwell. https://doi.org/10.1002/9781444346800.ch9.

———— (2017). 'The Problem'. *Seminar*, June, 12–16.

Goldman M., V. Gidwani, and C. Upadhya (2017). 'The Problem'. *Seminar*, June.

Goldstone, J. A. (2004). 'More Social Movements or Fewer? Beyond Political Opportunity Structures to Relational Fields'. *Theory and Society* 33(3–4): 333–365.

Goodwin, J. and J. M. Jasper (1999). 'Caught in a Winding, Snarling Vine: The Structural Bias of Political Process Theory'. *Sociological Forum* 14(1): 27–54.

Government of India (n.d.). 'Community Participation Fund'. Available at www.unh.edu/ democracy/.../PRIA-CommunityParticipationFund.pdf (accessed in November 2013).

——— (2007a). *Estimation of Urban Housing Shortage*. Delhi, 2007. Available at http:// mhupa.gov.in/ministry/housing/HOUSINGSHORTAGE-REPT.pdf (accessed on 3 November 2013).

——— (2007b). *The Constitution of India*. New Delhi: Ministry of Law and Justice.

——— (2011). *Census of India 2011*. Available at http://censusindia.gov.in/ (accessed on 10 October 2013).

Gowda, S. S. and G. P. Shivshankara (2007). 'Rural Migration to the Indian Metropolis: Caste Study Bangalore'. *ITPI Journal* 4(1): 67–69.

Grendstad, G. and P. Selle (1995). 'Cultural Theory and the New Institutionalism'. *Journal of Theoretical Politics* 7(1): 5–27.

Grinsell, S. (2010). 'Caste and the Problem of Social Reform in Indian Equality Law'. *The Yale Journal of International Law* 35(199): 2009–2010.

Gruenewald, D. A. 2003. 'The Best of Both Worlds: A Critical Pedagogy of Place'. *Educational Researcher* 32(4): 3–12.

Guériaux, C. (2012). 'The Normality of Informality: Shadow Economy out of Crisis'. *New Eastern Europe*. Available at http://www.neweasterneurope.eu/node/425 (accessed on 15 November 2013).

Guha Thakurta, P. and S. Raghuraman (2007). *Divided We Stand: India in a Time of Coalitions*. New Delhi: Sage Publications.

Günes-Ayata, A. (1994). 'Clientelism: Premodern, Modern, Postmodern'. In *Democracy, Clientelism and Civil Society*, ed. A. Günes-Ayata and R. Luis, 19–28. London: Lynne Rienner Publishers.

Gupta, A. (1995). 'Blurred Boundaries: The Discourse of Corruption, the Culture of Politics, and the Imagined State'. *American Ethnologist* 22(2): 375–402.

——— (2012). *Red Tape. Bureaucracy, Structural Violence, and Poverty in India*. Durham: Duke University Press.

Habitat International Coalition (2008). 'Acts of Commission, Acts of Omission. Habitat International Coalition. Co-ordintated by Housing and Land Rights Network'. Available at http://www.hic-sarp.org/documents/Housing%20and%20Land%20 Rights%20Network%20final%201%20may%2008.pdf (accessed on 16 August 2009).

Halbert, L. and H. Rouanet (2013). 'Filtering Risk Away: Global Finance Capital, Transcalar Territorial Networks and the (Un)Making of City-Regions: An Analysis of Business Property Development in Bangalore, India'. *Regional Studies* 48(3): 471–484. http://doi.org/10.1080/00343404.2013.779658.

Haritas, K. (2009). 'Citizenship, Law and Urban Poverty: An Analysis of the Legal and Political Status of the Urban Poor in India'. Master's thesis, Graduate Institute of International and Development Studies, Geneva.

——— (2010). 'Breaking Vote Banking Patterns: New Forms of Political Engagement by Slum Dwellers in Urban Bangalore, India'. Unpublished paper at Graduate Institute of International and Development Studies, Geneva.

——— (2013). 'Gender Identity in Urban Poor Mobilizations: Evidence from Bengaluru'. *Environment and Urbanization* 25(1): 125–138.

Harriss-White, B. and J. Heyer (2010). *The Comparative Political Economy of Development: Africa and South Asia Development*. Oxon: Routledge.

Harriss, John (2005). "'Politics Is a Dirty Rive'": But Is There a "New Politics" of Civil Society? Perspectives from Global Cities of India and Latin America'. Paper presented at the Conference on International Civil Society, Global Governance and the State, 1 April.

Harvey, D. (2009). 'Social Justice in the City'. *Interventions* 086. University of Georgia Press. https://doi.org/10.1111/j.1467-8330.1972.tb00486.x.

Harvey, D. L. (2009). 'Complexity and Case'. In *The Sage Handbook of Case-Based Methods*, ed. D. Byrne and C. C. Ragin, 15–38. Thousand Oaks: Sage Publications.

Helmke, G. and S. Levitsky (2004). 'Informal Institutions and Comparative Politics: A Research Agenda'. *Perspectives on Politics* 2(04): 725–740.

———. (2006). *Informal Institutions and Democracy: Lessons from Latin America*. Baltimore: Johns Hopkins University Press.

Hilgers, T. (2008). 'Recentering Informality on the Research Agenda: Grassroots Action, Political Parties, and Democratic Governance'. *Latin American Research Review* 43(2): 272–281.

Himanshu (2018). 'India's Politics and the Poor'. Available at http://www.ecfr.eu/what_does_india_think/analysis/indias_politics_and_the_poor (accessed on 7 July 2018).

Hohmann, J. (2013). 'The Right to Housing: Law, Concepts, Possibilies'. Portland: Hart Publishing.

Holston, J. (2008). *Insurgent Citizenship: Disjunctions of Democracy and Modernity in Brazil*. Princeton: Princeton University Press.

Holston, J. and A. Appadurai (1999). 'Cities and Citizenship'. In *Cities and Citizenship*, ed. J. Holston, 2–14. Durham: Duke University Press.

Holzner, C. A. (2003). 'The End of Clientelism? Strong and Weak Networks in a Mexican Squatter Movement'. *International Journal* 9(3): 223–40.

Huss, R., A. Green, H. Sudarshan, S. Karpagam, K. Ramani, G. Tomson, and N. Gerein (2011). 'Good Governance and Corruption in the Health Sector: Lessons from the Karnataka Experience'. *Health Policy and Planning* 26(6): 471–484.

Idiculla, M. (2017). 'The Transformation of Governance in "India's Silicon Valley"'. *Seminar*, June.

——— (n.d.). 'A Note on the Model Nagara Raj Bill'. Unpublished paper.

Inclan, M. (2018). 'Annual Review of Sociology a Continent in Movement but Where To? A Review of Social Movement Studies in the Region'. *Annual Review of Sociology* 441217(1): 1–12. http://doi.org/10.1146/annurev-soc-073117.

Jacob, Samuel (2012). 'Karnataka Political Parties Raise 1000s of Crores, Somehow'. *Citizen Matters*, 22 November. Available at http://bangalore.citizenmatters.in/articles/view/4673-karnataka-political-parties-raise-1000s-of-crores-somehow.

Jain, A. (2001). 'Corruption: A Review'. *Journal of Economic Surveys* 15(1): 71–121.

Jaiswal, J. V. (2007). *Housing Law in India*. Lucknow: Eastern Book Company.

Jamdaar, S. M. (2007). 'District Administration in Karnataka: Prospect and Retrospect'. In *Karnataka: Government and Politics*, ed. H. Ramaswamy, S. S. Patagudi, and S. H. Patil, 206–227. New Delhi: Concept Publishing Company.

Jasper, J. M. and J. Goodwin (2011). *Contention in Context: Political Opportunities and the Emergence of Protest*. Stanford California: Stanford University Press.

Javeed. S. A. (2007). 'Urban Government and Politics'. In *Karnataka: Government and Politics*, ed. H. Ramaswamy, S. S. Patagundi, and S. Patil. New Delhi: Concept Publishing Company.

Jayal, N. G. (2006). *Representing India: Ethnic Diversity and the Governance of Public Institution*. New York: Palgrave Macmillan & UNRISD. https://doi.org/10.1057/9780230626362.

Kadekodi, G. K., V. Rao, and K. Ravi (2007). 'Governance and the "Karnataka Model of Development"'. *Economic and Political Weekly* 42(4): 649–652.

Kamath, L. (2012). 'New Policy Paradigms and Actual Practices in Slum Housing'. *Economic and Political Weekly* 47(47–48), December.

Kanchan, C. (2003). 'Why Ethnic Parties Succeeded: Patronage and Ethnic Headcounts in India'. Los Angeles. Available at http://escholarship.org/uc/item/0vb620b2#page-6 (accessed on 26 March 2013).

Kapur, D. and P. B. Mehta (2005). *Public Institutions in India: Performance and Design*. New Delhi: Oxford India Paperbacks.

Karnataka Slum Development Board (KSDB) (2010). *Annual Report for the Year 2009–10*. Bangalore: KSDP.

Kaul, V. (2015). 'Why Are More than 10 million Homes Vacant in India?' Available at https://www.bbc.com/news/world-asia-india-32644293 (accessed on 7 July 2018).

Kaviraj, S. (2010). 'Religion and Identity in India'. *Ethnic and Racial Studies* 20(2): 325–344.

Kaviraj, S. and S. Khilani (2001). *Civil Society: History and Possibilities*. Cambridge: Cambridge University Press.

Keivani, R. and M. Mattingly (2007). 'The Interface of Globalization and Peripheral Land in the Cities of the South: Implications for Urban Governance and Local Economic Development'. *International Journal of Urban and Regional Research* 31(2): 459–474.

Khan, M. H. (1996). 'A Typology of Corrupt Transactions in Developing Countries'. *IDS Bulletin* 27(2): 12–21.

———— (1998). 'Patron–client Networks and the Economic Effects of Corruption in Asia'. *The European Journal of Development Research* 10(1): 15–39.

———— (2001). 'The New Political Economy of Corruption. In *Development Policy in the Twenty-First Century: Beyond the Post-Washington Consensus*, ed. B. Fine, C. Lapavitsas, and J. Pincus, 112–135. London: Routledge. Available at http://eprints.soas.ac.uk/2431/ (accessed on 24 August 2008).

Kitchens, J. (2009). 'Situated Pedagogy and the Situationist International: Countering a Pedagogy of Placelessness'. *Educational Studies* 45(3): 240–261. http://www.tandfonline.com/doi/abs/10.1080/00131940902910958.

Kitschelt, H. (2000). 'Linkages between Citizens and Politicians in Democratic Polities'. *Comparative Political Studies* 33(6–7): 845–879.

Kitschelt, H. and S. Wilkinson (2007). *Patrons, Clients, and Policies: Patterns of Democratic Accountability and Political Competition*. Cambridge: Cambridge University Press.

Klandermans, B. and D. Oegema (1987). 'Potentials, Networks, Motivations, and Barriers: Steps towards Participation in Social Movements'. *American Sociological Review* 52(4): 519–531.

Kohlbacher, F. (2006). 'The Use of Qualitative Content Analysis in Case Study Research'. *Forum: Qualitative Social Research* 7(1): 452–454. Available at http://www.qualitative-research.net/index.php/fqs/article/viewArticle/75/153 (accessed on 8 July 2013).

Kohler Riessman, C. (2002). 'Narrative Analysis'. In *The Qualitative Researcher's Companion*, ed. M. A. Huberman and M. B. Miles, 217–270. Thousand Oaks: Sage Publications.

Koopmans, R. (2005). 'The Missing Link between Structure and Agency: Outline of an Evolutionary Approach to Social Movements'. *Mobilization: An International Quarterly* 10(1): 19–33.

————— (2009). 'Political. Opportunity. Structure. Some Splitting to Balance the Lumping'. *Sociological Forum* 14(1): 93–105.

Koopmans, R., P. Statham, M. Giugni, and F. Passy (2005). *Contested Citizenship: Immigration and Cultural Diversity in Europe*. Minneapolis: University of Minnesota Press.

Kothari, R. (1994). 'Rise of the Dalits and the Renewed Debate on Caste'. *Economic and Political Weekly* 29(26): 1589–1594.

Kriesi, H. (1995). *New Social Movements in Western Europe: A Comparative Analysis*. University of Minnesota Press.

Kriesi, H., R. Koopmans, J. Wilhelm Duyvendak, and M. G. Giugni (1995). *New Social Movements in Western Europe: A Comparative Analysis*. London: University of Minnesota Press.

Kriesi, H., A. Tresch, and M. Jochum (2007). 'Going Public in the European Union: Action Repertoires of Western European Collective Political Actors'. *Comparative Political Studies* 40(1): 48–73.

Kumar, V. (2006). *India's Roaring Revolution. Dalit Assertion and New Horizons*. Delhi: Gagandeep Publication.

Kurzman, C. (1996). 'Structural Opportunity and Perceived Opportunity in Social-Movement Theory: The Iranian Revolution of 1979'. *American Sociological Review* 61(1): 153–170.

Laguerre, M. S. (1994). *The Informal City. New York*. New York: St. Martin's Press.

————— (n.d.). *The Informal City*. St. Martin's Press. New York.

Lama-Rewal, S. T. (2007). 'Les enjeux sociaux et politiques du renouvellement de la participation en Inde. Le conflit sur l'usage du sol à Dehli comme analyseur'. *La participation politique et ses défis: territoires, action collective et registres*. Lyon: Chaire UNESCO 'Politiques urbaines et citoyenneté'.

Laxman, N. (2011). *Patrons of the Poor: Caste Politics and Policymaking in India*. New Delhi: Oxford University Press. Available at http://www.oxfordscholarship.com/view/10.1093/acprof:oso/9780198069980.001.0001/acprof-9780198069980 (accessed on 4 May 2013).

Lecours, A. (2005). *New Institutionalism: Theory and Analysis*. Toronto: University Press of Toronto.

Lefebvre, H. (2003). *The Urban Revolution*. Minneapolis: University of Minnesota Press.

Lefkowitz, J. (2003). 'Success Empirical Tests People's the More Movements: Elaborate Model'. *Perspectives on Politics* 1(4): 721–726.

Legg, S. (2007). *Spaces of Colonialism*. Malden: Blackwell Publishing.

Leitner, H. and E. Sheppard (2015). 'Provincializing Critical Urban Theory: Extending the Ecosystem of Possibilities'. *International Journal of Urban and Regional Research*: 228–235. https://doi.org/10.1111/1468-2427.12277.

Lemke, T. (2000). 'Foucault, Governmentality, and Critique'. Paper presented at the Rethinking Marxism Conference, University of Amherst, 21–24 September.

Lijphart, A. (1996). 'The Puzzle of Indian Democracy: A Consociational Interpretation'. *American Political Science Review* 90(2): 258–268.

Lowndes, V. (2009). 'New Institutionalism and Urban Politics'. In *Theories of Urban Politics* (2nd ed.), ed. J. S. Davies and D. L. Imbroscio, 91–105. London: Sage Publications.

Madon, S. and S. Sahay (2001). 'Democracy and Information: A Case Study of New Local Governance Structures in Bangalore'. *Information, Communication and Society* 3(2): 173–191.

———— (2002). 'An information-based Model of NGO Mediation for the Empowerment of Slum Dwellers in Bangalore'. *The information society* 18(1): 13–19. doi:10.1080/01972240252818199

Mageli, E. (2004). 'Housing Mobilization in Calcutta: Empowerment for the Masses or Awareness for the Few?' *Environment and Urbanization* 16(1): 129–138.

Mahadeva, M. (2006). 'Reforms in Housing Sector in India: Impact on Housing Development and Housing Amenities'. *Habitat International* 30(3): 412–433. doi:10.1016/j.habitatint.2004.11.002.

Mahadevia, D. (2009). 'Urban Land Market and Access of Poor'. In *India: Urban Poverty Report*. New Delhi: UNDP and Ministry of Housing and Urban Poverty Alleviation, Government of India.

Maiz, R. and R. Requejo (2004). 'Clientelism as a Political Incentive Structure for Corruption' [Electronic Version]. University of Santiago de Compostela, 1. Available at http://www.essex.ac.uk/ecpr/events/jointsessions/paperarchive/grenoble/ws16/maiz_requejo.pdf (accessed on 14 March 2010).

Mathieu, L. (2007). 'L'espace des mouvements sociaux'. *Politix* 77: 131–151.

Mawdsley, E. and S. Roy Choudhury (2016). 'Civil Society Organisations and Indian Development Assistance: Emerging Roles for Commentators, Collaborators and Critics'. In *India's Approach to Development Cooperation*, ed. S. Chaturvedi and A. Mulakala. Oxon: Routledge.

McFarlane, Colin. 2011. *Learning the City: Knowledge and Translocal Assemblage*. West Sussex: Wiley-Blackwell.

McKinsey and Mumbai First. 2003. *Vision Mumbai*. Available at www.visionmumbai.org/aboutusdocs/McKinseyReport.pdf.

McKinsey Global Institute (2010). *India's Urban Awakening: Building Inclusive Cities, Sustaining Economic Growth.* New Delhi.

McAdam D. 1996. 'Conceptual Origins, Current Problems, Future Direction'. In *Comparative Perspectives on Social Movements: Political Opportunities, Mobilizing Structures, and Cultural*, ed. Doug McAdam, John McCarthy, and Mayer Zald, 23–40. Cambridge: Cambridge University Press.

McAdam, D. and H. Schaffer-Boudet (2012). *Putting Social Movements in Their Place: Explaining Opposition to Energy Projects in the United States, 2000–2005.* Cambridge: Cambridge University Press.

McAdam, D. and S. Tarrow (2010). 'Ballots and Barricades: On the Reciprocal Relationship between Elections and Social Movements'. *Perspectives on Politics* 8(2): 529–542. https://doi.org/10.1017/S1537592710001234.

McAdam, D., S. Tarrow, and C. Tilly (2007). 'Comparative Perspectives on Contentious Politics'. In *Comparative Politics: Rationality , Culture, and Structure: Advancing Theory in Comparative Politics*, ed. Mark Lichbach and Alan Zuckerman. Cambridge: Cambridge University Press. Available at http://socialsciences.cornell.edu/wp-content/uploads/2013/06/McAdamTarrowTilly07.pdf (accessed 22 August 2019).

——— (2008). 'Methods for Measuring Mechanisms of Contention'. *Qualitative Sociology* 31(4): 307–331.

McCarthy, J. D. and M. N. Zald (1977). 'Resource Mobilization and Social Movements: A Partial Theory'. *The American Journal of Sociology* 82(6): 1212–1241.

McKenna, C., M.-L. Djelic, and A. Ainamo (2003). 'Message and Medium: The Role of International Consulting Firms in Globalization and its Local Interpretation'. In *Globalization and Institutions*, ed. M.-L. Djelic and S. Quack, 83–107. Massachusetts: Edward Elgar Publishing Limited.

McMillan, A. (2008). 'Deviant Democratization in India'. *Democratization* 15(4): 733–749. https://doi.org/10.1080/13510340802191094.

Mehra, D. (2011). 'Caste and Class in Indian Cities: Habitation, Inequality and Segregation'. In *Urban Policies and the Right to the City in India: Rights, Responsibilities and Citizenship*, ed. M.-H. Zérah, V. Dupont, and S. T. Lama-Rewal. New Delhi: UNESCO.

Mehta, P. B. (2005). 'India's Judiciary. The Promise of Uncertainty'. In *Public Institutions in India. Performance and Design*, ed. D. Kapur and P. B. M. Mehta, 158–193. New Delhi: Oxford India Paperbacks.

Meyer, D. S. (2004). 'Protest and Political Opportunities'. *Annual Review of Sociology* 30(1): 125–145.

Milbert, I. (2008). 'Law, Urban Policies and the Role of Intermediaries in Delhi'. In *New Forms of Urban Governance in India: Shifts, Models, Networks and Contestations*, ed. J. de Wit. New Delhi: Sage Publications.

Ministry of Housing and Urban Poverty Alleviation and Ministry of Urban Development (n.d.). *JNNURM Overview.* New Delhi: Government of India. Available at jnnurm.nic.in/wp-content/uploads/2011/01/UIGOverview.pdf.

Ministry of Housing and Urban Poverty Alleviation (2009). *Modified Guidelines for BSUP.* New Delhi: Government of India. Available at urban.bih.nic.in/Docs/BSUP-Guidelines.pdf.

———— (2011). *Social Audit Methodology and Operational Manual for BSUP and IHDSP Projects.* New Delhi: Government of India. Available at http://mohua.gov.in/upload/uploadfiles/files/13Social%20Audit%20Toolkits%20(Methodology_OperationalGuidelines_SocialAudit).pdf (accessed in May 2013).

Ministry of Rural Development (2011). *Revised Draft Land Titling Bill.* New Delhi: Government of India. Available at http://dolr.nic.in/dolr/actandrule.asp (accessed on 10 May 2012).

Ministry of Urban Development (n.d.). *Model Municipality Disclosure Bill.* New Delhi: Government of India. Available at http://ccs.in/jnnurm.asp.

———— (n.d.). *Model Nagaraja Bill.* New Delhi: Government of India.

Minkoff, D. C. (1997). 'The Sequencing of Social Movements'. *American Sociological Review* 62(5): 779–799.

Mitra, K. S. (2006). *The Puzzle of India's Governance: Culture, Context and Comparative Theory.* New York: Routledge.

Mohr, J. W. and H. C. White (2008). 'How to Model an Institution'. *Theory and Society* 37(5): 485–512.

Monkkonen, P. (2018). 'Do We Need Innovation in Housing Policy? Mass Production, Community-based Upgrading, and the Politics of Urban Land in the Global South'. *International Journal of Housing Policy* 18(2): 167–176. https://doi.org/10.1080/1949 1247.2017.1417767.

Moore, M. (1980). 'Discussion Public Bureaucracy in the Post-Colonial State: Some Questions on "Autonomy" and "Dominance" in South Asia'. *Development and Change* 11(4): 137–148.

Nagendra, H. (2017). 'Bengaluru Will Lose Not 812, but 2,244 Trees from 71 Species'. *Bangalore Mirror.* Available at http://bangaloremirror.indiatimes.com/bangalore/cover-story/bengaluru-will-lose-not-812-but-2244-trees-from-71-species/articleshow/56989480.cms (accessed on 5 March 2020).

Nair, J. (2005). *The Promise of the Metropolis: Bangalore's Twentieth Century.* Oxford University Press.

Najam, A. (2000). 'The Four-C's of Third Sector–Government Relations'. *Erasmus* 10(4): 375–396.

Narayana, A., S. Krishnaswamy, and V. Kumar (2011). 'Lokpal Bill: Lessons from the Karnataka Lokayukta's Performance'. *Economic and Political Weekly* 47(1): 12–16.

Natraj, V. K. (2007). 'Backward Classes and Minorities in Karnataka Politics'. In *Karnataka: Government and Politics,* ed. H. Ramaswamy, S. S. Patagudi, and S. H. Patil, 397–413. New Delhi: Concept Publishing Company.

Neve, G. De and H. Donner (2006). *The Meaning of the Local: Politics of Place in Urban India.* London: Routledge.

Oommen, T. K. (ed.) (2010a). *Social Movements I: Issues of Identity*. New Delhi: Oxford University Press.

——— (ed.) (2010b). *Social Movements II: Concerns of Equity and Security*. New Delhi: Oxford University Press.

Ong, A. (2006). *Neoliberalism as Exception: Mutations in Citizenship and Sovereignty*. Durham: Duke University Press.

Osa, M. and H. Corduneanu. (2003). 'Running Uphill: Political Opportunity in Non-democracies'. *Comparative Sociology* 2(4): 605–629.

Pande, R. (2003). 'Can Mandated Political Representation Increase Policy Influence for Disadvantaged Minorities? Theory and Evidence from India'. *The American Economic Review* 93(4): 1132–1151.

Parnell, S. and S. Oldfield (2014). *The Routledge Handbook on Cities of the Global South*. Oxon: Routledge.

Parthasarathy, B. and Y. Aoyama (2017). 'Institutionalizing Frugal Innovation: "Domain Flexibility" and "Scalar Flexibility" for Sustainable Development'. Paper presented at the Conference on Frugal Innovation for Sustainable Development, Leiden, Netherlands, 11–15 February.

Patel, Z., Saskia Greyling, Susan Parnell, and Gordon Pirie (2015). 'Co-Producing Urban Knowledge: Experimenting with Alternatives to "Best Practice" for Cape Town, South Africa'. *International Development Planning Review* 37(2): 187–203.

Passy, F. (2003). 'Social Networks Matter. But How?' In *Social Movements and Networks*, ed. M. Diani, 21–48. Oxford: Oxford University Press.

Passy, Florence and Gian-Andrea Monsch (forthcoming). *Contentious Minds. How Talks and Ties Sustain Activism*. Oxford: Oxford University Press.

Peisakhin, L. and P. Pinto (2010). 'Is Transparency an Effective Anti-corruption Strategy? Evidence from a Field Experiment in India'. *Regulation & Governance* 4(3): 261–280.

Perry, A. (1998). 'Law and Urban Change in an Indian City'. In *Illegal Cities: Urban Change in Developing Countries*, ed. E. Fernandes and A. Varley. New York: Zed Books.

Pichardo, N. A. (1988). 'Resource Mobilization: An Analysis of Conflicting Theoretical Variations'. *Analysis* 29(1): 97–110.

Pick, D. and K. Dayaram (2006). 'Modernity and Tradition in a Global Era: The Re-invention of Caste in India'. *International Journal of Sociology and Social Policy* 26(7/8): 284–294.

Pierre, J. (1999). 'Models of Urban Governance: The Institutional Dimension of Urban Politics'. *Urban Affairs Review* 34(3): 17–20.

Piliavsky, A. 2014. *Patronage as Politics in South Asia*. Cambridge: Cambridge University Press.

Piven, F. F. and R. A. Cloward (1979). *Poor People's Movements: Why They Succeed, How They Fail*. New York: Random House Inc.

Plyushteva, A. (2009). 'The Right to the City and Struggles over Urban Citizenship: Exploring the Links'. *Amsterdam Social Science* 1(3): 81–97. Available at www.socialscience.nl (accessed on 29 July 2013).

Polese, A., A. Russo, and F. Strazzari (eds) (2019). *Governance beyond the Law: The Immoral, the Illegal, the Criminal*. London: Palgrave Macmillan.

Polletta, F. (2004). 'Culture Is Not Just in Your Head'. In *Rethinking Social Movements. Structure, Meaning, and Emotion*, ed. J. Goodwin and J. M. Jasper, 97–110. Oxford: Rowman & Littlefield Publishers.

Polletta, F. and J. M. Jasper (2001). 'Collective Identity and Social Movements'. *Annual Review of Sociology* 27(1): 283–305.

Porta, D. della and M. Diani (2006). *Social Movements: An Introduction* (2nd ed.). Oxford: Blackwell Publishing.

Prakash, A. (2011). 'Towards Understanding the Nature of Indian State and the Role of Middle Class'. Paper presented at EADI and DSA conference: Rethinking Development in an Age of Scarcity and Uncertainty: New Values, Voices and Alliances for Increased Resilience, York, UK, October.

Pylee, M. V. (1997). *India's Constitution*. New Dehli: S. Chand & Company Ltd.

Quinn Patton, M. (2002). *Qualitative Research and Evaluation Methods*. Thousand Oaks: Sage Publications.

Rajagopal, C. (2011). 'Place, Plural Legalities, Transformations and Continuity: The Informal Economy of the Historic Pete, Bangalore, India'. Paper presented at EADI and DSA conference: Rethinking Development in an Age of Scarcity and Uncertainty: New Values, Voices and Alliances for Increased Resilience, York, UK, October.

Raman, V. V. (2008). 'Examining the "e" in Government and Governance: A Case Study in Alternatives from Bangalore City, India'. *The Journal of Community Informatics* 4(2). Available at http://www.ci-journal.net/index.php/ciej/article/view/437/405.

Ramanathan, U. (2006). 'Illegality and the Urban Poor'. *Economic and Political Weekly* 41(29): 3193–3197.

Randeria, S. (2002). 'Entangled Histories of Uneven Modernities: Civil Society, Caste Solidarities and Legal Pluralism in Post-colonial India'. In *Civil Society: Berlin Perspective*, ed. J. Keane, 213–242. New York: Berghahn Books.

——— (2006). 'Civil Society and Legal Pluralism in the Shadow of Caste: Entangled Modernities In Post-Colonial India'. In *Hybridising East and West: Tales beyond Westernisation. Empirical Contributions to the Debates on Hybridity*, ed. D. Schirmer, G. Saalmann, and C. Kessler, 97–124. Münster: LIT.

Ranganathan, M. (2008). 'Beneficiary? Stakeholder? Consumer? Citizen–State Dynamics in Bangalore's Urban Reforms'. Paper submitted to conference: Cities and Citizenship, Graduate Student Symposium, UC Berkeley, 14–16 February.

Rangarajan, C. (2014). 'Report of the Expert Group to Review the Methodology for Measurement of Poverty'. Available at http://planningcommission.nic.in/reports/genrep/pov_rep0707.pdf (accessed on 21 August 2019).

Rao Dhananka, S. (2011). 'Exclusionary Conditions for Mobilising in Urban India: The Case of Bangalore'. Rethinking Paper presented at EADI and DSA conference: Development in an Age of Scarcity and Uncertainty: New Values, Voices and Alliances for Increased Resilience, York, UK, October.

——— (2016). 'The Production of Space and Governmentality in the Urban Poor's Claim over Land and Housing'. *South Asia Multidisciplinary Academic Journal* 14. Available at https://journals.openedition.org/samaj/4228 (accessed on 1 December 2019).

——— (2017). 'Eviction from and Invitation to the City: Competing Claims and Visions in Bengaluru'. *Seminar*, June.

Rao, U. (2011). 'Making the Global City: Urban Citizenship at the Margins of Delhi'. *Ethnos: Journal of Anthropology* 45(4): 402–424.

Rao, V. (2006). 'Slum as Theory: The South/Asian City and Globalization'. *International Journal of Urban and Regional Research* 30(1): 225–232.

Rastogi, A. S. (2011). 'Concept of Social Justice under Indian Constitution'. Lucknow. Available at http://www.lawyersclubindia.com/articles/Concept-Of-Social-Justice-Under-Indian-Constitution-3685.asp#.UaR0BIKSo2a.

Reichertz, J. (2004). 'Abduction, Deduction and Induction in Qualitative Research'. In *A Companion to Qualitative Research*, ed. U. Flick, E. von Kardoff, and I. Steinke. London: Sage Publications.

Reising, U. K. H. (1998). 'Domestic and Supranational Political Opportunities: European Protest in Selected Countries 1980–1995' [Electronic Version], 2. Available at http://eiop.or.at/eiop/texte/1998-005.htm (published on 17 July 1998).

Revi, A., A. Jana, and T. Malladi (2015). *Urban India 2015: Evidence*. Bangalore: Indian Institute for Human Settlements.

Ritchie, J. and J. Lewis, eds (2003). *Qualitative Research Practice: A Guide for Social Science Students and Researchers*. London: Sage Publications.

Robinson, J. (2011). 'Cities in a World of Cities: The Comparative Gesture'. *International Journal of Urban and Regional Research* 35(1): 1–23. http://doi.org/10.1111/j.1468-2427.2010.00982.x.

Rolnik, R. (2019). *Urban Warfare: Housing under the Empire of Finance*. London: Verso.

Roniger, L. and A. Günes-Ayata (1994). *Democracy, Clientelism, and Civil Society*. London: Lynne Rienner Publishers.

Rootes, C. A. (1999). 'Political Opportunity Structures: Promise, Problems and Prospects'. *La lettre de la maison Française d'Oxford* 10: 75–97.

Rosa, H. (2013). *Beschleunigung und Entfremdung. Entwurf einer Kritischen Theorie spätmoderner Zeitlichkeit*. Berlin: Suhrkamp Verlag.

Rose, N., P. O'Malley, and M. Valverde (2006). 'Governmentality'. *Annual Review of Law and Social Science* 2(1): 83–104. doi:10.1146/annurev.lawsocsci.2.081805.105900.

Roy, A. (2005). 'Urban Informality: Toward an Epistemology of Planning'. *Journal of the American Planning Association* 71(2): 147–158.

——— (2009). 'Why India Cannot Plan Its Cities: Informality, Insurgence and the Idiom of Urbanization'. *Planning Theory* 8(1): 76–87. http://doi.org/10.1177/1473095208099299.

——— (2010). *Mapping Citizenship in India*. New Delhi: Oxford University Press. doi:10.1093/acprof:oso/9780198066743.001.0001.

Roy, A. and A. Ong. (2011). *Worlding Cities: Asian Experiments and the Art of Being Global*. West Sussex: Wiley-Blackwell.

Roy Chowdhury, S. (2009). *Livelihood and Income: Informality and Poverty in Bangalore's Slum*. Bangalore: AISEC.

Rudolph, S. H. and L. Rudolph (1979). 'Authority and Power in Bureaucratic and Patrimonial Administration: A Revisionist Interpretation of Weber on Bureaucracy'. *World Politics* 31(2): 195–227.

——— (2000). 'Living with Difference in India'. *The Political Quarterly* (December): 20–38.

Sadanandan, A. (2009). 'The Parliamentary Election in India, April–May 2009'. *Electoral Studies* 28(4): 658–662.

Saldhana, J. (2009). *The Coding Manual for Qualitative Researchers*. London: Sage Publications Pvt. Ltd.

Sandlin, Jennifer A., Brian D. Schultz, and Jake Burdick (2010). *Handbook of Public Pedagogy: Education and Learning beyond Schooling*. New York: Routledge.

Sandlin, J. A., M. P. O. Malley, and J. Burdick (2011). 'Mapping the Complexity of Public Pedagogy Scholarship: 1894–2010'. *Review of Educational Research* 81(3): 338–375. https://doi.org/10.3102/0034654311413395.

Sankhe, S., I. Vittal, R. Dobbs, A. Mohan, A. Gulati, J. Ablett, S. Gupta, S., et al. (2010). *India's Urban Awakening*. Boston/Bangalore: McKinsey.

Sassen, S. (2003). 'The Repositioning of Citizenship'. *The New Centennial Review* 3: 41–66.

——— (2005). 'The Repositioning of Citizenship and Alienage: Emergent Subjects and Spaces for Politics'. *Globalizations*, 2(1): 79–94.

——— (2010). 'A Savage Sorting of Winners and Losers: Contemporary Versions of Primitive Accumulation'. *Globalizations* 7(1–2): 23–50.

Schenk, H. (2001). *Living in India's Slums: A Case Study of Bangalore*. New Delhi: Manohar Publishers & Distributors.

Schneider, B. (2019). 'CityLab University: Shared-Equity Homeownership'. Available at https://www.citylab.com/equity/2019/04/home-ownership-ideas-housing-co-ops-shared-equity-land-trust/585658/ (accessed 28 February 2020).

Schubert, W. H. (2010). 'Outside Curriculum and Public Pedagogy'. In *Handbook of Public Pedagogy: Education and Learning beyond Schooling*, 10–19. New York: Routledge.

Sheppard, E., H. Leitner, and A. Maringanti (2013). 'Provincializing Global Urbanism: A Manifesto'. *Urban Geography* 34(7): 893–900. http://doi.org/10.1080/02723638.2013.807977.

Schneider, A. and R. Zúniga-Hamlin (2005). 'A Strategic Approach to Rights: Lessons from Clientelism in Rural Peru'. *Development Policy Review* 23(5): 567–584.

Schock, K. (1999). 'People Power and Political Opportunities: Social Movement Mobilization and Outcomes in the Philippines and Burma'. *Social Problems* 46(3): 355–375.

Schram, S. F. (2004). 'The Praxis of Poor People's Movements: Strategy and Theory in Dissensus Politics'. *Perspectives on Politics* 1(4): 715–720.

Seidman, I. (2006). *Interviewing as Qualitative: A Guide for Researchers in Education and the Social Sciences* (3rd ed.). New York: Teachers College Press.

Sen, S. (1998). 'On the Origins and Reasons behind Nonprofit Involvement and Non-involvement in Low Income Housing in Urban India'. *Cities* 15(4): 257–268.

Sengupta, U., B. Murtagh, C. D'Ottaviano, and S. Pasternak (2018). 'Between Enabling and Provider Approach: Key Shifts in the National Housing Policy in India and Brazil'. *Environment and Planning C: Politics and Space* 36(5): 856–876. https://doi.org/10.1177/2399654417725754.

Sewell Jr, W. H. (1992). 'A Theory of Structure: Duality, Agency and Transformation'. *American Journal of Sociology* 98(1): 1–29.

Shah, G. (2004). *Social Movements in India: A Review of the Literature*. New Delhi: Sage Publications.

Shakit, M. (1974). 'Beyond the System'. *Economic and Political Weekly* 9(16): 629–631.

Sharan, S. (2011). *Reviewing the Right to Information through the Prism of Indian Policy Process*. The Hague, Netherlands: International Institute of Social Studies.

Sharp, J. (2009). *Geographies of Postcolonialism*. London: Sage Publications.

Shatkin, G. (2014). 'Contesting the Indian City: Global Visions and the Politics of the Local'. *International Journal of Urban and Regional Research* 38(1): 1–13. https://doi.org/10.1111/1468-2427.12039.

Shaw, A. and M. K. Satish (2007). 'Metropolitan Restructuring in Post-liberalized India: Separating the Global and the Local'. *Cities* 24(2): 148–163.

Sheppard, E., V. Gidwani, M. Goldman, H. Leitner, A. Roy, and A. Maringanti (2015). 'Introduction: Urban Revolutions in the Age of Global Urbanism'. *Urban Studies* 52(11): 1947–1961. https://doi.org/10.1177/0042098015590050.

Shigetomi, S. and K. Makino (2009). *Protest and Social Movements in the Developing World*. Cheltenham: Edward Elgar Publishing Limited.

Sivam, A. and S. Karuppannan (2002). 'Role of State and Market in Housing Delivery for Low-income Groups in India'. *Journal of Housing and the Built Environment* 17(1): 69–88.

Sivaramkrishnan, K. C. (2011). *Re-visioning Indian Cities: The Urban Renewal Mission*. New Delhi: Sage Publications.

Smitha, K. C. (2010). 'New Forms of Urban Localism: Service Delivery in Bangalore'. *Economic & Political Weekly* 45(8): 73–77.

Spencer, L., J. Ritchie, and W. O'Connor (2003). 'Analysis: Practices, Principles and Processes'. In *Qualitative Research Practice: A Guide for Social Science Students and Researchers*, ed. J. Ritchie and J. Lewis, 199–218. London: Sage Publications.

Standing, Guy (2012). 'Cash Transfers: A Review of the Issues in India'. Social Policy Working Paper Series 1, UNICEF India.

Stanford Encyclopedia of Philosophy (n.d.). Available at http://plato.stanford.edu/info.html (accessed on 27 July 2013).

Sudhira, H. S., T. V. Ramachandra, and M. H. B. Subrahmanya (2007). 'City Profile Bangalore'. *Cities* 24(5): 379–390.

Suh, D. (2001). 'How Do Political Opportunities Matter for Social Movements? Political Opportunity, Misframing, Pseudosuccess, and Pseudofailure'. *The Sociological Quarterly* 42(3): 437–460.

Sundaresan, J. (2017). 'Urban Planning in Vernacular Governance: Land Use Planning and Violations in Bangalore, India'. *Progress in Planning* (June). https://doi.org/10.1016/j. progress.2017.10.001.

Supriti and Barnhardt, S. M. (2002). *Urban Poverty Alleviation in India*. Bangalore: Ramanathan Foundation.

TAG Coordination Cell (2007). *REPORT: NGO Engagement with JNNURM*. New Delhi. Available at jnnurm.nic.in/wp-content/uploads/2011/01/Report_final1.pdf.

Tarrow, S. (1993). 'Cycles of Collective Action: Between Moments of Madness and the Repertoire of Contention'. *Social Science History* 17(2): 281–307.

Teo, S. (2014). 'Book Review: *Worlding Cities: Asian Experiments and the Art of Being Global*'. *International Journal of Urban and Regional* Research 35(1): 1–23.

Teorell, J. (2007). 'Corruption as an Institution: Rethinking the Nature and Origins of the Grabbing Hand'. QoG Working Paper Series 2007:5, The Quality of Government Institute, Department of Political Science, Göteborg University. Available at https://qog.pol.gu.se/digitalAssets/1350/1350653_2007_5_teorell.pdf (accessed on 22 August 2019).

Thakur, M. (2011). 'Review Article: Sociology of Social Movements'. *Sociological Bulletin* 60(2): 346–355.

Thompson, L. and C. Tapscott (2010). *Citizenship and Social Movement*. London: Zed Books.

Tilly, C. (2004). *Social Movements, 1768–2004*. London: Paradigm Publishers.

———— (2006). *Regimes and Repertoire*. Chicago: The University of Chicago Press.

Tilly, C. and S. Tarrow (2007). *Contentious Politics*. Boulder, Colorado: Paradigm Publishers.

Times of India (2012). '93% Dalit Families Still Live below Poverty Line, Says Survey', 28 October. Available at http://timesofindia.indiatimes.com/city/mangaluru/93-dalit-families-still-live-below-poverty-line-says-survey/articleshow/16987809.cms (accessed on 28 October 2012).

Turner, B. (1997). 'Citizenship Studies: A General Theory. *Citizenship Studies* 1(1): 5–18. doi:10.1080/13621029708420644

UN (2014). 2014 revision of the *World Urbanization Prospects*. Available at https://www.un.org/en/development/desa/publications/2014-revision-world-urbanization-prospects.html (accessed on 21 August 2019).

UNDP and Ministry of Housing and Urban Poverty Alleviation, Government of India (2009). *India Urban Poverty Report*. New Delhi: Oxford University Press.

Uslaner, E. M. (2008). *Corruption, Inequality and the Rule of Law*. *Political Science*. Cambridge: Cambridge University Press.

Vaid, N. (2006). 'A Critical Analysis of Impact on Housing'. Available at https://ccs.in/internship_papers/2006/Urban%20Land%20Ceiling%20Act%20-%20Nipun.pdf (accessed on 22 August 2019).

van Zomeren, M., T. Postmes, and R. Spears (2008). 'Toward an Integrative Social Identity Model of Collective Action: A Quantitative Research Synthesis of Three Socio-Psychological Perspectives'. *Psychological Bulletin* 134(4): 504–535.

Vasavi, A. R. (2003). 'Schooling for a New Society? The Social and Education Deprivation in India'. *IDS Bulletin* 34(1): 72–80.

Verma, A. (2001). 'Policing of Public Order in India'. *International Journal of Police Science and Management* 3(2).

——— (2009). 'Situational Prevention and Elections in India'. *International Journal of Criminal Justice* 4(2): 83–97.

Véron, R. (2010). 'Small Cities, Neoliberal Governance and Sustainable Development in the Global South: A Conceptual Framework and Research Agenda'. *Sustainability* 2(9): 2833–2848.

Vijayalakshmi, V. (2006). 'Corruption and Local Governance: Evidence from Karnataka'. Paper presented at the Conference on Development in Karnataka. Available at http://www.isec.ac.in/Karnataka_Vijayalakshmi-June_aligned.pdf (accessed on 22 August 2019).

Vora, R. and S. Palshikar (2004). *Indian Democracy: Meanings and Practices*. Delhi: Sage Publications Pvt. Ltd.

Wallace, P. and R. Roy (2011). *India's 2009 Elections: Coalition Politics, Party Competition and Congress Continuity*. *South Asia*. New Delhi: Sage Publications.

Wilkinson, S. I. (2004). *Votes and Violence: Electoral Competition and Ethnic Riots in India*. *Human Rights*. Cambridge: Cambridge University Press

Williams, G. and E. Mawdsley (2006). 'Postcolonial Environmental Justice: Government and Governance in India'. *Geoforum* 37(5): 660–670.

Wit, J. de. (2000). 'Towards Good Governance at the Local Level: The Role of Grassroots Institutions'. Working Paper, ISS.

Wit, J. de. and E. Berner (2009). 'Progressive Patronage? Municipalities, NGOs, Community-based Organisations, and the Limits to Slum Dwellers' Empowerment'. *Development and Change* 40(5): 927–947.

Witsoe, J. (2011). 'Corruption as Power: Caste and the Political Imagination of the Postcolonial State'. *American Ethnologist* 38(1): 73–85.

——— (2012). 'Everyday Corruption and the Political Mediation of the Indian State'. *Economic and Political Weekly* 47(6): 47–54.

Witzel, A. (2000). 'The Problem-Centered Interview'. *Forum: Qualitative Social Research* 1(1): Art. 22.

Wolcott, H. (2009). *Writing Up Qualitative Research* (3rd ed.). Los Angeles: Sage Publications.

Yin, R. K. (2009). *Case Study Research: Design and Methods*. London: Sage Publications.

Zérah, M.-H. (2009). 'Participatory Governance in Urban Management and the Shifting Geometry of Power in Mumbai'. *Development and Change* 40(5): 853–877.

Zérah, M.-H., V. Dupont, and S. T. Lama-Rewal (2011). *Urban Policies and the Right to the City in India. Rights, Responsibilities and Citizenship*. New Delhi: UNESCO and Centre de Sciences Humaines.

Zimmer, A. (2011). 'Everyday Governance of the Waste Waterscapes: A Foucauldian Analysis in Delhi's Informal Settlements'. Doctoral thesis, Rheinische Friedrich-Wilhelms-University of Bonn. Available at http://hss.ulb.uni-bonn.de/2012/2956/2956.pdf.

Index

acceleration, 73, 186
access, 3, 6–7, 11, 18, 26, 30, 32–33, 35–36,
    38–39, 41–43, 48, 53–54, 56, 58,
    62–64, 70, 73–74, 76, 78–80, 82, 86,
    89–94, 103, 106, 115, 126, 134–139,
    146, 148, 152, 155–157, 161,
    176–177, 188, 190, 192
accountability, 15, 19, 36, 44, 46, 70, 81, 87,
    88, 92, 102, 122, 155, 157, 185
accumulation by dispossession, 187
acrual-based double entry system, 73
Action Aid Karnataka, 130
action répertoire, 8, 11, 14–15, 18, 22–23, 28,
    59, 95, 98, 102, 107, 110, 116, 120,
    125–126, 129, 136–137, 140–141, 147,
    155, 158, 175, 185
    diversely resourced organizations,
        158–159, 185
administration, 8, 36–37, 40, 48–50, 56, 58,
    62, 67, 89, 93, 137
administrative arena, 35–36
affirmative action, 8, 32, 175
African-Americans
    Black Panther Party, 128–129
agenda, 7, 40, 43, 79, 89, 90, 93, 97, 107, 109,
    111, 146, 153, 155, 180–181, 197
Agenda for Bangalore Infrastructure
    Development (ABIDe), 97, 111, 114,
    116, 125
allocation, 9, 36, 46, 49–50, 81, 89, 103–104,
    119–120, 136, 146, 152, 155, 160,
    169–174, 186, 191
alternative imaginings, 183, 186
Ambedkar, Bhim Rao, Dr., 55, 140

anachronic, 186
analysis, 21, 23–24, 26, 29, 34–35, 61–62,
    70–71, 91, 93–94, 98, 168, 170, 179
Anglo-Indian community, 42
answerability, 19. *See also* accountability
anthropological studies, 8
anti-corruption bill, 26
anti-poor attitudes, 48
apparatus, 8, 31, 169
Aravena, Alejandro, 196
arbitrary, 9–10, 31, 49, 53, 85, 90–93
arbitration, 9
article 133, 55
article 243W, 38
article 32, 55
Aryans, 139
Association for Voluntary Action and Service
    (AVAS), 97, 110–126, 150, 162–163,
    168–169, 177, 190–191, 196
    brokering, 113
    citizenship, 125, 187, 198
    community meetings, 178
    corruption, 116, 191–192
    ground-floor + 1 houses, 113f
    patiently dealing with unresponsive state,
        115–120
    pay back loan, 160
    public private partnership, 113, 195
    social work, 115
    urban poor and, 171, 186, 196
Atrocities Act, 140

balance sheet, 64
ballot, 44, 166

Bangalore municipal corporation (BBMP), 70
banking system, 159
    exclusion of poor, 160
bargaining power, 118
Basic Services for the Urban Poor (BSUP), 23, 70, 73–74, 76, 78–80, 96, 99, 122, 154, 189–190, 195
    and Dalits, 128
    housing, 150, 185–186, 189–192, 194–198
    mobilization, 89, 184
beautification, 5
below poverty line (BPL), 104
beneficiaries, 78, 190–192
benevolent, 9, 36–37, 49, 124, 157, 168
Bharatiya Janata Party (BJP), 25, 39, 144
    donation, 46
bicameral model, 42
biometric card, 79
Black Panther Party, 128–129
Blackstone Group, 195
blackmailing
    construction site, 145f
    transit accommodation, 145f
booth capture, 47, 166
bottom-up, 38, 92, 133, 152, 182, 197
Brahmins, 42
    political elite, 43
bribes, 10, 53, 116, 147, 166
    judiciary, 57
British Raj, 48
brokerage, 61
Bruhat Bengaluru Mahanagara Palike (BBMP), 70
budget, 73, 103, 197
bulldozer, 100, 187
bureaucracy, 9, 32, 36, 48–54, 64, 93, 106, 115–116, 134–137, 149, 151, 158, 168, 174, 176, 186–187
    monumental, 53
    poverty and, 49
bureaucratic corruption, 19, 36, 103, 156
bureaucrats, 42, 71, 131, 136, 160
business, 30, 80, 103, 171, 188, 193–195
bypass governance, 185

campaign, 45–47, 124, 148, 165–166, 182, 184
campaign investment, 166
canvassing, 44, 46–47, 146, 165
capacity for repression, 15, 35–36, 54, 59–61
capital, 6, 12, 20–22, 61, 72, 81, 166, 172, 184–188, 194, 196–197
capital landing, 6, 22
carrot-and-stick principle, 76
cash, 7, 35, 40, 51, 101, 151–152, 192
    transfers, 7
caste, 2, 7–9, 12, 19–20, 25, 29, 31–34, 41, 43–46, 52–53, 55, 62, 79, 94, 105, 117, 120, 126, 130, 134, 136–141, 148, 150, 155, 158, 161–162, 168, 174–175, 177, 190
    and class, 29
    discrimination, 25, 32, 139, 158
    education to higher, 139
    identity, 33, 155, 175, 189, 198
    inequality, 141, 184
    mobilization from, 137–139
    and reservation, 33
casteism, 8, 46
caste identification, 175
census, 2, 9, 25, 140
Central funds, 90
Central government, 75
Central Sanctioning and Monitoring Committee (CSMC), 76
central–decentral tensions, 82
certification, 51–53, 78–79, 117, 146, 168
charters, 107
choice of tactics, 17
citizen charter, 107, 110, 161
Citizen's Ombudsman Bill, 26
Citizen's Voluntary Initiative for the City (CIVIC), 97–98, 103–104, 189
    and AVAS, 123
    democratic polity and policy literally, 109–110
    governance, 107, 185–186
    housing episode, 106
    political agenda, 109
    quest for transit housing, 101f, 189
    socio-political context, 110

citizens, 184–185, 187, 198
  elite society and, 157
  Skewed land allocation and housing
    opportunities, 169–174
citizenship, 10, 12, 15, 17, 20, 25–26, 30–32,
    41, 62, 120, 125–126, 129, 155, 158–
    159, 170, 173–174, 187, 198
  Association for Voluntary Action and
    Service (AVAS), 125, 190–191,
    196
  benefits, 20
  provisions, 158, 185
  rights, 34, 150, 186–187
  universal concept, 155
City Development Plans (CDP), 73, 76–77,
    81–82
City Volunteer Technical Committee
    (CVTC), 83, 86
City-level Technical Advisory Group
    (CTAG), 83, 86
civic documents, 45
civil rights, 30
civil society, 9–11, 15, 22, 25, 26, 29, 31, 34,
    53, 57, 59, 64, 70, 85, 96, 97, 184, 189,
    191, 197
  legal instruments, 56b–58b
  organizations, 6, 75, 154, 185, 191
claim-making, 150, 152, 170
claimant, 174
class and caste, 29
cleavages, 34, 43, 53, 162
clientelism, 14, 35, 48, 66, 95, 109, 164,
    166–165, 169
  prevalence of, 165
co-construct, 94
co-create, 155
co-opted, 39–44, 62, 91–92, 129, 141, 148, 178
collective action, 11, 18–19, 22, 34, 59, 109
collective leaders, 138
collective power, 142
collective violence, 59
colonialism, 20
communal, 32, 42, 120
communities, 1, 7, 17, 19, 23, 27, 31–33, 55,
    67, 85–86, 90–91, 94–99, 103–104,
    109–111, 113–116, 120–124, 126,
    128, 130–132, 135, 137–141, 148–153,
    155, 157–160, 165–167, 169, 171–174,
    177–182, 184, 186, 189, 191–192, 194,
    197
community-based organizations (CBOs), 85,
    88, 91, 95, 114–115, 122, 125
Community Architects Network, 197
Community Participation Fund (CPF), 83,
    85
Community Participation Law, 85
comparative urbanism, 21
compensation, 1
competition, 5, 9, 19, 45, 50, 89, 105, 117–
    118, 166, 168–171, 186
  urban poor, 168–169, 186, 196
completion, 101, 112, 123
concurrent list, 37, 39, 49, 53
Congress movement, 43
Congress Party, 40, 43, 46, 144
  donation, 46
conscientizacao, 179
constables, 60
Constitution of India, 12, 24, 30, 31, 40, 65,
    131
  Manusmriti, 139–141
Constitutional (amendment) article 243S, 85
constitutional list, 6, 36–37
Constitutional provision, 8, 37, 39, 80, 182
Constitutional tier, 55
Constitutional values, 54
consultants, 22, 80–82, 124
context, 23
convenor committee, 130
corporate consultancy firms, 7
Corporate Social Responsibility (CSR)
    legislation, 182
corporations, 1, 42, 70, 80, 84, 120, 187
corrupt political environment, 147
corruption, 4, 10, 14, 19, 26, 34–35, 36, 39, 40,
    47, 48, 50, 53, 59, 60, 62, 67, 76, 88,
    92, 106, 116, 123, 124, 125, 142, 157,
    164, 168, 170, 191–192
  bureaucratic, 36, 77, 103, 156, 187–188
  classification, 76

in courts, 57
and Dalit Panthers of India (DPI), 146,
    191
grand, 36, 43, 172
incentive structure, 92
informal circuits of, 166, 192
localization of, 64
petty, 36, 192
vicious circle of participation, 146
councillors, 86, 189
counter-repression, 136
courts
corruption in, 57
criminals, 44, 57, 59–60, 62, 64
crisis, 50, 54, 98, 181, 185–186
critical pedagogy, 179
critical urban public pedagogy (CUPP), 26,
    177–183
curriculum, 181
Indian Constitution, 183
lines of enquiry, 181
social movement, 183, 197–198
tactical knowledge, 182
curriculum, 179–181

Dalit Panthers of India (DPI), 128–129,
    141–142, 191
and corruption, 146, 191
Karnataka's political scenario, 149
leaders, 147, 191
mission statement, 148
political context, 147
ready-made Dalit ideology, 148
social skill and discursive repertoire,
    150–153
Dalits, 33, 74, 128–129, 140–141, 147–149
and Basic Services for the Urban Poor
    (BSUP), 128
and member of parliament (MP), 129
status, 149
welfare, 33
Das, P. K., 3, 177, 197
Data, 4, 23, 25, 27, 78, 98, 105, 129, 155,
    163–164, 166–167, 173, 175–176
de-mobilizing, 167

decentralization, 35, 39, 63–64, 73, 75, 80, 91
imperatives and entrenched centralization
    tendencies, 36–39
decentralized prescriptions
and centralized habits, 80–82
deliberative, 42, 103, 106, 165
delivery, 7, 9, 31, 50, 55, 64, 71, 74, 78, 87,
    102, 104–105, 119, 124, 146, 151, 156,
    159, 170, 172, 174
demobilization, 4, 152, 166–168, 170
democracy, 2, 4, 7, 8, 10–13, 26, 28–40,
    65–67, 89, 92, 94, 103–107, 149, 154,
    162, 169, 180, 183, 186
cracking open supposed to do, 103–107
democratic theory, 65, 169
demolition, 5, 100, 111, 120–121, 144, 148
demonstrations, 26
denizen, 103, 129, 150, 192
Department of Personnel and Administrative
    Reforms, 104
departmental inquiry, 60
deputy commissioner, 50, 134
deregulation, 6
Detailed Project Reports (DPRs), 73–74,
    76, 81
development department, 50
devolution of powers, 38–39
dignity, 162, 186
Directive Principles of State Policy, 31, 49, 53
discretion, 37, 39, 49, 60, 81, 89
discursive, 14–15, 17–19, 21, 23, 26, 29–30,
    32, 70, 95, 98, 109, 126, 129–130, 136,
    147–148, 150, 154–155, 175
discursive repertoire, 15, 136
and social skill, 150–153
dispossession, 25
district-level courts, 54
distrust, 54, 155, 159–164
domain flexibility, 162
drinking water, 130–131
droughts, 25

economic development, 38, 65, 197
economic growth, 5, 69, 186
economic liberalization, 171

economically weaker section, 3
economics of electoral politics, 152
economy, 2, 6, 12, 21, 67, 69, 171, 176, 185, 192
education system, 65, 159, 161–162, 169, 176
educational credentials, 98
election, 5, 19, 37–42, 44–48, 51, 60–61, 65–66, 84, 104, 106, 109–110, 114, 116, 118, 122, 124, 135, 138, 151, 165–168, 185–186, 190, 192
election booths, 60
election campaign, 124, 145, 165
Election Commission, 45
election surveillance, 166
electoral campaign, 165
electoral cycle, 142, 192
    stages, 165
electoral rolls, 103–106, 165, 168
eligibility, 44, 63–64, 79, 94, 150, 155–156
elite control, 11
elite society, 92, 96, 97, 109, 110, 117, 123, 124, 125, 127, 152, 158, 160. *See also* civil society
    Association for Voluntary Action and Service (AVAS), 110–114, 123
    citizens and, 157
    and urban poor, 168
elite society organizations, 109, 158, 160
    accountability, 177
    self mobilization, 176
    task division between political and, 175–177
elusive, 161
emergence, 3–5, 11–12, 15–16, 18, 21–22, 26, 122, 163, 194, 198
Emergency period in 1974, 43
empowerment, 31
enforceability, 19. *See also* accountability
enforceable, 31, 49, 53
entitlement, 5, 9, 19, 39, 64, 74, 79, 94, 106, 124, 156–158, 160
environmental degradation, 57, 185
equality, 32, 55
    legal rights of, 30
European democracies, 34

everyday practices, 4, 16, 26, 28–30, 93
evictions, 4–5, 111, 120, 138, 143, 144, 187–188
evidence-based mobilization, 135

fast cities, 185–186
favourable, 3, 11, 39, 45, 48, 62–65, 79–80, 82, 89–90, 125–126, 155–157, 161–162
favouritism, 146
federal system, 6, 36
fieldwork, 15, 24, 27–28, 39–40, 45–46, 50, 64, 70–71, 92, 94, 96–99, 121, 129, 137, 143, 146, 170, 172, 185, 193
finance, 48, 67, 74, 84, 87, 177, 181, 193, 195
financialization, 185
formal exclusions
    and informal inclusions, 159–163
formal illegality, 164
    and repressive informality, 164–169
formal institutions, 18
formal polity, 15
formal prescription, 156
formal realm, 163, 195
formal–informal interaction, 30
Foucauldian concept, 8
fundamental rights, 30–31, 55
funding, 25, 74, 81, 92, 96–99, 111, 168, 182, 195
funding campaigns, 182

Gandhi, Mahatma, 69, 140, 187
Giroux, Henry A., 179
global cities investment monitor 2016, 187
global capital flows, 22
global corporate entities, 126
global economy, 176
global financial circuits, 126
global operations, 171
Global South, 3, 20–21, 127, 154, 185
global urbanism, 4
globalized corporate entity, 119
globalizing capitalism, 20
governance, 4, 6–8, 21, 26–27, 31, 34, 42, 48–50, 53–54, 62, 64, 67, 69–75, 78, 80–81, 84, 86, 87, 89, 91–92, 96–99,

104, 107, 110, 113, 122, 124, 157,
    162–163, 165, 167, 169–171, 173–183,
    185–186
conceptualization of, 95
good, 93–94
and movement, 8
of municipalities, 38
and negotiations, 7–11
policy, 48
principles, 31
reforms, 72
Government of India, 38
Government of India Act, 31
government programmes, 66
government schools, 58
governmentality, 8–9, 19, 20, 50, 61–62, 64,
    71, 97, 156, 159, 168, 175. *See also*
    Foucauldian concept
parastatals and, 161
governor, 37, 38
governor's rule, 25, 134
gram sabha, 84
grand corruption, 36, 43, 172
grant-cum-loan, 74
gray zone, 59, 194
Greater Bangalore Municipal Corporation
    (BBMP), 118
green-field urban development, 192
grievance redressal, 104, 107–108, 178
grievances, 15, 22, 60, 103–104, 106
gross domestic product (GDP), 55
Gupta, A., 176

Habitat International Coalition, 197
habitation, 93
'Handbook of the Election Commission', 44
Haritas, K., 175
Helmke and Levitsky's theory, 16
High Court, 54–55
Hinduism, 140
home minister, 60
'horatta', 116, 189–190
horse-trading, 25–40
housing
    demolitions, 144

social movement, 171
urban land, 170
Housing Empowerment Resource
    Organization (HERO), 111
housing episode, 106
housing policy, 2–4, 6–7, 15, 23, 25–26, 96,
    154, 168, 177, 185, 195–196
    legal and policy prescriptions, 23
housing resources, 76
    and urban poor, 78–80
housing stock, 6, 196
housing subsidies, 3
human rights, 25, 108, 195, 197
Human Rights Commission, 1, 107

ideal-type, 41
identification, 33, 44, 66, 80, 157, 175
identity, 17, 19–20, 33, 39, 41, 51, 53, 61, 67,
    122, 140, 146, 148, 150, 155, 159, 161,
    167–169, 180, 189, 198
identity-politics, 169
idol worship, 140
illegal mining, 26
illiteracy, 32
implementation, 1, 17, 38, 63–64, 66, 70, 72,
    75, 79–85, 87–88, 91, 95–96, 99–100,
    102, 113–115, 119, 155, 158, 170–174,
    178–179, 181, 188, 197
incentives, 15, 18–19, 36, 39, 43, 55, 70, 73,
    76–78, 92, 94, 106, 116, 124, 156–157,
    160, 163, 168, 170, 172
inclusion, 39, 61, 63, 67, 81, 89, 94, 123,
    155–156, 159–160, 163, 192, 197
inclusive cities, 15, 153, 155, 179, 197
independent review and monitoring agency
    (IRMA), 75, 78
Indian anti-corruption movement, 26
Indian Constitution, 20, 22, 30, 32, 38, 140,
    183
    critical urban public pedagogy (CUPP),
    183
    as discursive foundation, 30–34
Indian land management, 26
Indian laws and penal code, 60
Indian Police Act of 1861, 59

Indian Supreme Court, 55
indigenous rights, 25
industrial policy, 172, 194
industrialization, 12
industries, 171
inequality, 29, 62, 141, 155, 159, 164, 176, 184
    caste, 140, 190
informal arrangements, 15.
informal exchange circuits, 30, 67, 152, 156,
        164, 185
    mobilization, 158
    mobilizing and, 157–158
informal inclusions
    and formal exclusions, 159–163
informal institutions, 18
informal realm, 163
informal repression, 10, 34, 119, 125, 135,
        136, 152, 156, 158, 162, 168
informality, 10, 18
information asymmetry, 193
information exchange, 193–194
infrastructure, 6, 17, 19, 36, 55, 64, 69, 71, 73–
        74, 80, 85, 89, 92, 97, 124, 185–186,
        188–189, 194, 196
infrastructure failure, 186
innovation, 3, 13, 21, 75, 127, 186
institutional interaction, 16
institutional set-up, 6, 8, 15, 18–19, 23, 26, 38,
        74, 76, 78, 81, 85, 92
institutionalization, 167
instrumentalization, 33
Integrated Housing and Slum Development
        Programme (IHSDP), 74, 87
Intelligence Bureau, 25
inter-referencing, 181
intermediary, 58, 160
International finance institutions, 181
Internet, 103
investment, 2, 45–46, 74, 117–118, 165–166,
        171–172, 187–188, 194–196

Jana Spandana, 104, 107
Janata Dal (JD), 40, 50
    donation, 46
Jawaharlal Nehru National Urban Renewal

Mission (JNNURM), 23, 26, 38,
        69–82, 87–93, 142, 144, 154, 156, 195,
        197
    ambivalent intentions, 70–73
    discourse, policy background, 71–73
    elite society organizations and, 154
    empty promises, 75–76
    favourable rhetorics, convenient loopholes,
            and arbitrary access, 90–93
    institutional set-up, 73–74
    intentions of inclusive planning, 82–89
    mechanics, 76–78
    mission statement, 71
    salience of political alliances, 89–90
    vernacular instead of good, 93–95
judges, 55
judicial activism, 54, 57
judicial review, 54
judiciary, 31, 35, 36, 41, 61, 121, 149
    bribes, 57
    Indian activist, 64
    world's most active, 54–59

Kannada, 57–58, 108, 161
Karnataka Budget 2010–2011, 50
Karnataka Housing Board, 26
Karnataka Human Rights Commission,
        57–58
Karnataka Industrial Policy, 172
Karnataka Janara Sangha (KJS), 129, 147
Karnataka Lokayukta (KLA), 58
Karnataka Municipalities Act 1964, 42, 44, 49
Karnataka Slum Development Board
        (KSDB), 2, 70, 79, 102, 112, 117–119,
        130, 143
Karnataka Slum Janara Sanghatanegala
        Okkoota, 187
Karnataka Urban Infrastructure Development
        Finance Corporation (KUIDFC), 80
Karnataka's political scenario
    Dalit Panthers of India (DPI), 149
knowledge networks, 193

land
    agricultural, 194

allocation, 117, 119, 120, 146, 152, 155,
    170–172, 186, 191
development, 6, 112, 171
industrial, 194
residential, 193–194
tenure, 45, 126, 128
land assertions, 174
land conversions, 81, 194
land economy, 6
land ownership, 170
land scams, 172
land tenure, 126
Law, 4, 10, 23, 30–32, 36–38, 40, 54, 57,
    59–60, 62, 73, 78, 83, 87–88, 91, 152,
    184, 195
learning communities, 149–153, 179–181,
    183
LeFebvre, Henri, 173
legal instruments, 59, 61
legal prescriptions, 4, 23, 150
legal profession, 56
legal rights, 30
legal system, 3, 61
legality, 62, 140, 155, 162–164, 168
liberal citizenship, 32
liberal democracies, 3–4, 180
liberalization, 35
Lingayats, 43
linkages, 14–16, 29, 71, 74, 124, 166, 167
literacy, 57–58, 142, 156
    skills, 161
local self-governments, 38
Loksatta, 110
low-income settlement, 74, 128, 151
low-intensity thermodynamics, 96
lower house (Lok Sabha), 41–42
lower-caste, 141
    free government schools, 139

Marxist and neo-Marxist critical theory, 179
master-plans, 174
material benefits, 33
mayor, 42, 86, 88, 185
McAdam, D., 11
McKinsey, 22, 72

means of repeal, 35, 44
member of parliament (MP)
    and Dalits, 129
members of legislative assembly (MLAs), 42,
    80, 136, 190
Members of Parliament Local Area
    Development (MPLAD), 75, 89–90
meso-level agency, 3, 16
Metro Corporation, 1–2
middle class, 46, 85, 91, 99–100, 108, 110, 172
    residents' welfare, 97
migrants, 39, 45, 150
mining mafia, 25
Ministry of Housing and Poverty Alleviation,
    5
Ministry of Housing and Urban Poverty
    Alleviation (MHUPA), 73, 76, 87
Ministry of Urban Development (MoUD),
    73–74, 76
minorities, 41, 66
    reservation system, 135
misconception, 186, 96
mobilization, 2, 10, 13, 14, 20, 26, 59, 63, 66,
    184
    identity-based, 167
    informal circuits of exchange, 158
    and politics, 22
mobilizing
    informal exchange circuits and, 157–158,
        185
monitor, 77–79, 85–86, 90, 98, 104, 123, 143,
    187
monopoly, 10
Morris-Jones, W. H., 8
movement, 3–4, 7–8, 10–17, 20–23, 26, 28–
    30, 43, 62, 65, 67, 121–122, 128–129,
    148, 154, 163–167, 171, 180, 183,
    197–198
municipal activities, 84
municipal bankruptcy, 185
municipal commissioner, 86
municipal corporation, 84
municipal elections, 45, 144
municipality, 37, 111, 182, 185
    governance of, 38

Nagara Raj Bill, 83
National Democratic Alliance (NDA), 40
National Election Commission, 45
National Election Watch report, 45
National Housing and Habitat Policy of
    2007, 74
National Slum Development Programme, 74
negotiations, 6, 9, 61, 80, 118, 178, 192
    and governance, 7–11
Nehru, Jawaharlal, 48
neoliberal development, 126
nested legislature, 39–43
non-governmental organizations (NGOs),
    86, 197
    women, 143
normative democratic theories, 157, 194

occupancy urbanism, 174
on behalf of, 14, 48, 58, 70, 96–99, 106, 112,
    114, 122–127, 143, 149, 160, 176
Other Backward Classes (OBCs), 33, 75, 159

parastatals, 39, 81–82, 87, 151, 161
Parliamentary arena, 35–36
parliamentary democracy model, 41
participation bill, 79, 83–84
participatory planning, 123
particularized trust, 159
partisan interests, 59
patron-client network, 80, 124, 135, 142, 151,
    156, 160, 166–168
patron–client relationships
    slum, 151
patronage, 7, 39, 61, 64, 66–67, 72, 90, 92–93,
    135, 146, 150–151, 175, 178, 191–192
pay back loan, 160
pedagogues, 153
pedagogy, 26, 67, 127, 152, 155, 169, 177,
    179–182
Peer Experience and Reflective Learning
    Programme (PEARL), 75, 90
Penal code, 57, 59–60
people's power, 114
periphery, 1, 5–6, 118–119, 126, 128, 132,
    172, 192, 194

personal liberty, 30
planning, 3–4, 6–7, 33, 37–38, 71, 77–78,
    81–90, 104, 123, 160, 174, 186,
    193–194, 196
pluralism, 30
police, 54, 56–57, 59–61, 64, 100, 117, 119,
    121, 134, 136–138, 147–148
    bribing, 119
    of duties, exigencies, co-optation, and
        capacity for repression, 59–61
    malfunctioning, 60
policy affected communities, 27, 155
policy prescriptions, 4, 15, 23, 93, 123, 150,
    195
policy-prescribed participation, 105
political agenda, 109
political alliances, 35–36, 40, 43, 63–64, 76,
    89–90
political corruption, 26
political cultures, 10, 89
political economy, 21, 185, 192
political elite, 36
political loyalty, 9, 10
political networks, 4, 124
political opportunities, 3–4, 7, 11–12, 14–17,
    23–24, 26, 34, 75, 80, 185–186
    differential, 155–157
    formal and informal dimensions, 34–36
    report card, 61–65, 63t
    six dimensions, 30
    theoretical framework, 16f
political parties, 105
political process model, 11
political reform, 12
political representation, 7, 35–36, 41, 105, 116
political reservation, 41, 66
political society, 9, 11, 188
political society organizations, 155
    task division between elite, 175–177
politics,
    and mobilization, 22
    of proof-gathering, 64, 150
polity, 7, 13–15, 17, 19, 23, 26, 28, 41, 48,
    61, 65–66, 105, 109–110, 154, 157,
    163–164

polling station, 44
pollution, 69
polycentric, 188
pooja, 193
poor monitoring, 78
poor, welfare of, 62
population, 2, 5–6, 8–9, 20–23, 25, 31, 42, 45,
    55, 69, 73, 79, 84, 125, 134–135, 140,
    156, 159, 161, 164, 182, 185, 194
    slum as, 21
post-colonial, 4, 10, 12, 62, 67, 154
    Constitutions, 49
poverty, 2, 5, 32, 33, 38, 69, 72, 175, 196
    alleviate, 49
    alleviation, 38
power, 2, 4, 8, 10–11, 13, 19, 25, 30–31, 33,
    35–39, 41–43, 46–48, 50, 54–55, 57,
    60–62, 64, 74, 80–84, 86, 89–90, 93,
    98, 103, 105, 174, 177–178, 191–193,
    197–198
preliminary slum declaration, 1
Pradhanmantri Awas Yojana (PAY), 195
Prevention of Atrocities Act, 55, 57, 58, 59,
    132, 134, 136–137
primary education, 141, 187
private, 33, 36, 72, 74, 117–118, 120, 126,
    136–139, 143, 146, 161, 162, 171, 185,
    194–197
private landowners, 138
pro-poor approaches, 6
procedural democracy, 8
procedural knowledge, 135, 147, 149, 152
project management, 85, 98, 123
proof, 39, 44–45, 50–51, 64, 100, 106, 117,
    124, 150, 167–168
proof of residence, 44
propensity, 15, 18
proportionality, 36, 40
protests, 26, 98, 128
provincialize, 13
provincialize democracy, 65
public consultation, 122, 142, 161, 184
public disclosure law, 87, 88
public distribution system, 104, 106
public education system, 169

public housing, 102, 118, 141, 151, 170, 174,
    192, 195–196
    policy, 7
    urban poor, 70, 159
public interest litigation (PIL), 57
public participation, 87
public pedagogy, 179–180
public realm, 178
public sphere, 10, 71, 92, 179
public-private partnership (PPP), 74, 112, 195

qualitative, 23, 24–26, 163

rapid urbanization, 4–7
Rajiv Awas Yojana (RAY), 195
ration card, 44–45, 79
re-election, 166
    campaign, 165
real estate, 2, 46, 84, 132, 136–137, 185,
    193–194
recognition, 30–34, 73, 75, 83, 97, 114, 160,
    173, 196
reflexivity, 148
reform, 12, 32, 38, 43, 55, 62, 69, 71–73, 75,
    77, 79–81, 83, 87, 89–91, 104, 172
regulatory department, 50
religious freedom, 25
religious rights, 30
remuneration, 43
representation, 40–41, 44–48, 61, 63–64, 67,
    72, 82, 89, 91, 105, 116, 123, 135, 149,
    152, 164, 168
Representation of People's Act (1951), 44
repression, 10, 178
repressive informality
    and formal illegality, 164–169
research design, 24f
research questions
    answering, 155–159
reservations, 8, 32, 43, 66
    and caste, 33
    categories of, 49
residence proof, 45
Residents' Welfare Associations (RWAs), 99,
    176

return on investments, 165
revenue, 37, 59, 139, 194
right to benefits, 125
Right to Information (RTI) Act, 107–109,
    141–142, 146–147, 177
    and CIVIC, 108
right to life, 30
right to the city, 26, 93, 174
right-based approach, 109
roadblocking, 128
Roy, Ananya, 6
rural–urban migration, 5

safe drinking water, 134
safeguard, 102, 105, 107–108, 134, 151, 172,
    181
saving schemes, 114, 190
scams, 26
scarce resource, 9
Scheduled Castes (SC), 8, 23, 31, 33, 41–42,
    50, 55, 75, 134, 161, 176
Scheduled Castes and Scheduled Tribes
    (Prevention of Atrocities) Act, 55,
    131–132, 137
Scheduled Tribes (STs), 8, 33, 41–42, 50, 55,
    75, 134, 161, 176
scheme, 3, 23, 26, 38–39, 51, 54, 62, 66, 70,
    72–77, 79–80, 82, 84–86, 89, 92, 100,
    103, 111–112, 114–115, 117, 119, 123,
    142–143, 171, 178
school, 52–53, 58, 80, 130, 139, 161, 173,
    179–180, 182, 193
secondary data, 4
security of tenure, 5, 74, 79–80
self-esteem, 158
self-perceptions, 177
self-sufficient, 151, 191
semi-structured interviews, 105
sense of belonging, 186, 198
sense-making, 17–18, 20
service organization, 110
SHIFT, 197
Shleifer-Vishny's model, 76
shortage, 2–3, 5–6, 195

situated, 4, 6, 13, 17, 67, 131, 142, 154, 164,
    167, 179–181, 183
situational knowledge, 13
Sivaramkrishnan, K. C., 70, 72, 77–78, 86,
    90, 92
slum, 1, 21, 97, 117, 187, 189, 191, 195–198
    declaration, 137–138
    patron–client relationships, 151
    as population, 21
    redevelopment programmes, 5
slum declaration, 1, 131, 137
Slum Dwellers International, 197
Slum Janara Kriya Vedike (SJKV), 128, 169,
    189–190
    access through noise, achievement by
        tactics, 134–136
    clean drinking water, 130–131
    community's residence, 132f
    formal political opportunities, 129
    future dwelling, 133f
    land fragmentation, 170–171
    slum declaration, 137
    slum dwellers and, 149, 173
    social skill and discursive repertoire,
        150–153
slum leader, 105, 116–117, 122, 124, 129–130,
    135, 138, 142, 150–151, 160, 168
slum redevelopment, 5, 79
slum upgradation, 6
slum-dwellers, 1–3, 14, 22, 23, 51, 61, 74,
    114, 118, 131, 134, 136, 140, 141, 142,
    151, 156
    DPI and, 146
    formal realm, 163
    governance system, 169
    Slum Janara Kriya Vedike (SJKV) and,
        149, 173, 176
    status proof, 168
    sustainability, 159
sociability
    and trust, 124
social cohesion, 7, 159, 164
social differences, 62
social equity, 8

social functions, 193
social hierarchies, 67
social housing, 128, 170, 197
    policy, 2
social identity, 13, 19, 33
social interactions, 17
social justice, 38, 54, 179
social locations, 13
social mobilization, 154
social movement, 3–4, 11, 26, 29, 67, 154,
        166, 180
    self-referential confines scholarship,
        20–22
social movement organizations (SMOs), 3,
        10, 12, 17, 65–67
social movement scholarship, 166
social movement theory, 13
social order, 31, 55
social qualifications, 62
social reforms, 32
social skills, 150, 156, 158, 159, 177, 198
    and discursive repertoire, 150–153
social welfare, 39, 48
social work, 97, 115
societal conflicts, 34
sociology of law, 4
Special Component Plan, 161
Special Economic Zones, 171
speed, 36, 48, 53, 56, 76, 82, 172, 181,
        185–188
State Election Commission, 44
State list, 37t
subsidies, 3, 173, 196
Supreme Court, 37, 54–55, 89, 107, 121
sustainability, 152
    slum dwellers, 159
system of discourses, 17

tactical knowledge, 152, 178, 181–183
tactics, 17–18
tahsildar, 139
task division, 36, 155, 175–176, 182
tax, 37, 120, 125, 162, 195
Technical Adivsory Group (TAG), 83, 86, 92
technocrats, 71

territory, 8, 41, 44
toolkit, 85–87, 90, 100, 102, 183
top-down, 38–39, 91–92, 174, 197
transit housing, 102, 189
transnational policy networks, 181
Transparency International (2005), 57
tribal welfare, 33
trust, 1, 31, 46, 54, 61, 110, 117, 124, 155,
        157, 159, 162, 164
    and sociability, 124

Udyog Mitra, 188
UN guiding principles on business and
        human rights, 195
UN special rapporteur on housing, 197
UN World Urbanization Prospects, 5
UNICEF, 164
Union list, 37t
Union, federal level, 30
universalism, 34
untouchability, 55
untouchables. See Scheduled Castes
upper house (Rajya Sabha), 41–42
upper-class bureaucrats, 87
urban development, 6
urban economy, 6
urban governance, 69, 72, 80, 81, 86, 91, 185,
        196
urban imagination, 181
Urban Infrastructure and Governance (UIG),
        74
urban land, 118
    housing, 170
    scams, 81
urban learning, 180
urban learning communities
    organizing, 149
urban local bodies (ULBs), 37–38, 71, 74, 76,
        80–82, 87–88, 90, 195–196
urban planning, 6, 76, 86, 185, 192
urban politics, 4
urban poor, 70, 74–75, 89, 91, 97, 103, 118,
        157, 162, 186, 196
    AVAS and, 171
    bureaucracy and, 53

CIVIC and, 102
governance of land and housing, 173
housing, 6, 110
housing approach, 173, 177
housing for, 3
and housing resources, 78–80
mobilization, 96
political opportunities, 156
public housing, 70, 159
severe competition, 168–169
taxes, 162
urban poverty, 72
urban public
pedagogy, 177–183
urban public pedagogy, 182
urban realm, 163
urban renewal programmes, 5
urban slum-dwellers, 157
urban vision, 86
urban-planning, 6
urbanization, 2, 65, 69, 186

value capture, 194
VAMBAY, 112
vernacular, 13, 58, 70, 93–94, 106, 154, 178, 180, 183
vested interest, 7, 37, 64, 82, 85, 152, 168
violence, 29, 59, 188, 194
against women, 25
structure of, 188
Vishny and Sheifler model, 92
Vokkaligas, 43

volatile political networks, 4
vote, 40, 61
vote banking, 35, 90, 106, 151
vote-bank politics, 7
vote-banking, 34
vote-buying, 147
voter identity card, 79, 131, 146, 168
voters' list, 44–45, 61
votes, 118, 124, 151, 165, 192–193
vulnerability, 69

wards committee, 85
Weberian ideal-typical model, 95
Weberian style bureaucracy, 49
welfare, 50, 186–187, 195
welfare benefits, 8–10, 24, 39, 49, 51, 53, 56, 103
whistle-blowers, 124–125
women, 191
empowerment, 106
non-governmental organization (NGO), 143
protest, 139
violence against, 25
World Bank, 93, 95, 124, 195
world class city, 69, 73, 93
worlding, 184
Worthiness, Unity, Numbers, and Commitment (WUNC), 161

Yeddyurappa, B. S., 172